Twickenhamshire:

A Riverside Realm of Gardens and Villas in the Age of Enlightenment

Twickenhamshire:

A Riverside Realm of Gardens and Villas in the Age of Enlightenment

Edited by Chris Sumner *and* Michael Symes

First published in 2021 by Redcliffe Press Ltd,
81g Pembroke Road, Bristol BS8 3EA

Reprinted April 2022

e: info@redcliffepress.co.uk
www.redcliffepress.co.uk
Follow us on Twitter @RedcliffePress

© the contributors

ISBN 978-1-911408-78-9

British Library Cataloguing-in-Publication Data
A catalogue record for this book is available from the British Library
All rights reserved. Except for the purpose of review, no part of this
book may be reproduced, stored in a retrieval system, or transmitted,
in any form or by any means, electronic, mechanical, photocopying,
recording or otherwise, without the prior permission of the publishers.

Design and typesetting by Stephen Morris www.stephen-morris.co.uk smc@freeuk.com

Printed and bound by Cambrian Printers, Aberystwyth

Redcliffe Press Ltd is committed to being an environmentally friendly publisher.
This book is made from Forest Stewardship Council® certified paper.

Front cover:
Extract from *The Prospect of the River Thames at Twickenham*. Painting by Peter Tillemans, *c*.1724-30; see also p.15, Fig. 1.6
The background map is an extract from John Rocque's *Exact Survey of the City of London* etc. of 1741-45; see also p.12, Fig. 1.4

Contents

Preface 7

Chapter One: Twickenhamshire: An Overview 9
Michael Symes

Chapter Two: The Arcadian Thames 35
Chris Sumner

Chapter Three: The Garden of David Garrick's Villa 46
Suzannah Fleming

Chapter Four: Strawberry Hill 57
Chris Sumner

Chapter Five: Radnor Gardens 74
Mike Cherry

Chapter Six: Pope's Garden and Grotto 86
Chris Sumner

Chapter Seven: Poulett Lodge 100
Mike Cherry

Chapter Eight: Orleans House Gallery 106
Chris Sumner

Chapter Nine: 'Fair Howard's Elegant Retreat':
The Garden and Landscape at Marble Hill 116
Emily Parker

Chapter Ten: Other Gardens 128
Michael Symes

Select Reading and Principal Sources 150
The Contributors 152
List of Illustrations 153
Index 158

Preface

This book stems from a symposium planned to take place at Strawberry Hill in September 2018 but which, in the event, did not materialise. Of the two present editors, Chris Sumner was the organiser of, and a contributor to, the symposium, and Michael Symes was a contributor. The aim of the symposium was to give an up-to-date account of the major properties of the eighteenth century still remaining in Twickenham and its immediate environs particularly in the light of recent or current restoration or refurbishment, and also to provide an overview linking them and presenting the area as a unified whole with its own distinctive character. It seemed to the editors that material based mainly on what had been planned by the speakers would constitute a worthwhile publication that would be of interest to residents and also appeal to those interested generally in cultural history.

The book is written with a garden history slant, since at the time gardens had particular status and propulsion as a means of owners expressing themselves culturally and philosophically. It has often been said that the eighteenth-century naturalistic garden was Britain's one original contribution to the fine arts, and Twickenham embodied this new approach. But what gave the locality its special quality was its appearance as a riverside scene of both gardens and villas.

The period celebrated happens to coincide with the Age of Enlightenment, which made its presence felt in virtually every aspect of life, even if not always explicitly acknowledged. In the case of gardens, the central focus on nature and natural appearance, the Agricultural Revolution and later the Industrial Revolution, combined with botanical enterprise, a spirit of enquiry, free-thinking and scientific advance, all indicate a climate in which the new gardening, and discussion of it, could flourish.

The book is structured so as to present two general chapters, one an overview and the other on the River Thames, so central to the whole subject. These are followed by individual studies of the most important sites running from south to north, with a final round-up of other gardens of mainly historical interest.

Twickenham has been exceptionally well served for many years by local historians, mostly from within the diligent and productive organisation that retains its former name of the Borough of Twickenham Local History Society. It is no exaggeration to say that without their work much of what follows would not have been possible.

We should particularly like to thank those who have contributed essays to this volume and who have kindly provided photographs and other illustrations from their own collections. Special mention must be made of The London Borough of Richmond upon Thames, which has been very generous in allowing us to publish a large number of images from the Borough art collection and from its local studies collection, and we wish to thank Chris Burton, Arts Officer (Exhibitions and Collections), at Orleans House Gallery, Janine Stanford, Archivist, and Lara Bond, Local Studies Assistant, at the Local Studies Library and Archive, Richmond Old Town Hall, for their support and patient assistance.

The Lewis Walpole Library, Yale University, Farmington, Connecticut, is an essential resource for the study of Horace Walpole and Strawberry Hill, and we are grateful to the library for their generous permission to use a number of contemporary images, and to Susan Walker, Head of Public Services, and her colleague Kirsten McDonald for their kind assistance.

The Sauthier map of the Manor of Isleworth-Sion is reproduced courtesy of the Archives of the Duke of Northumberland at Syon, and we thank Chris Hunwick, Archivist, and Lisa Little, Library and Documentation Officer, Northumberland Estates, for their help.

Angela Kidner kindly forwarded photographs of Pope's Grotto following the recent repair work, and we are grateful to her, the photographer Damian Griffiths, Pope's Grotto Preservation Trust and Donald Insall Associates for permission to publish them.

The drawing for the restoration of the Shrubbery at Strawberry Hill is reproduced courtesy of Mark Laird, and we are also grateful to him and to Peter Inskip and the Landscape Agency for permission to quote from the Strawberry Hill Landscape Management and Maintenance Plan.

Plans of the gardens of Marble Hill are held in the Norfolk Record Office, and we are grateful for permission to publish them. Similarly, we thank the National Records of Scotland for the extract from the letter by Mary Lisles concerning the decoration of grottoes. We also thank the Garrick Club, London, for permission to reproduce the Zoffany paintings of Mr and Mrs Garrick; Sally Jeffery for information on John James; Michael Snodin for advice on the Lewis Walpole Library; Michael Cousins for advice on Richard Owen Cambridge and also on the Hampton Court House grotto; Patrick Eyres on Strafford House (Mount Lebanon); and Karen Bridgman for commenting on the plant list sent to Garrick by 'GB'.

In addition, Chris Sumner records his thanks to Michael Symes for the invitation to join him in writing and editing this book and for his tactful advice and correction of errors. He also thanks his partner Victor Nettleton very much for his patience and invaluable technical advice and assistance.

The Editors
January 2021

CHAPTER ONE

Twickenhamshire: An Overview
Michael Symes

The world of 'Twickenhamshire' is expressed partly through its remarkable cultural community in the eighteenth century and partly through the physical environment that community created, in the form of its riverside gardens and villas. There are cultural threads and a unity that run through all the major properties, so that it is not possible to treat any single one in isolation: context is all. Moreover, it was a concept rather than a specific place with precise boundaries. The term was coined by Horace Walpole, who used it twice in his letters, although it appeared in the shortened form 'Twitnamshire', a common enough abbreviation of Twickenham at the time and earlier. Walpole in fact used it to refer to the local populace rather than as an area on a map, once describing how 'all Twitnamshire is passing through my meadows to the races [presumably boat races] at Hampton Court', and a year later commenting that the actor David Garrick was laid up by gout, 'which is of more consequence to the metropolis than to Twitnamshire'.

The form Twitnam is demonstrably an abbreviation since it was often recorded as Twit-'nam, indicating how it was pronounced. In the seventeenth century the name was sometimes written as Twicknam, which may have led to such usage. Poets in the eighteenth century would frequently use the shortened form (even Twick'nham, as Paul Whitehead did) simply because of scansion: it was easier to fit a two-syllable name into a line than a three-syllable dactyl, e.g. Thomas Twining (of the tea dynasty) commenting on Pope: 'Poetic *Twit'nam* and its grot, Where Pope caught cold when he was hot'. Walpole used the full form in the title of his poem 'The Parish Register of Twickenham' but Twit'nam in the poem itself.

The essence of Twickenhamshire is that it was a community linked by artistic and cultural networking. Not a tightly-knit community such as the Bloomsbury Group, but a nexus of neighbours who frequently visited each other's houses and exchanged ideas, often suggesting additions or changes to their houses and gardens. Some of these suggestions may have been recorded, but most would have been during the course of conversation so we shall never know the full extent of such networking. It was, however, the oil that enabled Twickenhamshire to function. The means by which the glitterati of Twickenham demonstrated their common goal was through their gardens and villas, which thereby became a tangible and visible expression of the character of the place.

Twickenhamshire lay solely on the Middlesex side of the river. That is not to deny the considerable richness of the cultural life of Richmond opposite but to indicate that each side had its own individual character. The vital unifying component was that the properties were riverside, and it is impossible to think of the area without the river being at its heart. The first of the detailed essays in this volume is accordingly concerned with the Thames Landscape Strategy, in which eighteenth-century appearance (where now possible) plays a

1.1. *The House of the late Celebrated Mr. A. Pope fronting the River Thames at Twickenham*. Engraving by James Mason after Augustin Heckel, 1749. (Orleans House Gallery, LDORL: 03207)

prominent part. There are, however, some properties that were located further inland, such as Hampton Court House in Bushy Park and Whitton Park and Whitton Place, which physically do not fit into a riverside category but nevertheless demonstrate significant networking and developments in planting and garden-making.

The perception of properties not existing in isolation can be demonstrated by Augustin Heckel's three views of 1749–50, none of them centred on their supposed subject. That of *The House of the late Celebrated Mr. A. Pope* (Fig. 1.1), engraved by James Mason, places the villa left of centre, with Countess Ferrers' Summer House standing out on the right. *A View of the Countess of Suffolk's House near Twickenham*, again engraved by Mason (Fig. 1.2), puts Marble Hill right of centre, with the end of the Montpelier Row terrace displayed on the left. Finally, the view of 'the Earl of Radnor's House at Twickenham', engraved by Anthony Walker (Fig. 1.3), pushes Radnor House over to the right, with Cross Deep House slightly more central.

Twickenham was, and remains, a special place, unlike any other. One point to bear in mind is that at the time it was regarded as being out in the country and well away from London, though not so far that it was impossible to commute, as Richard Owen Cambridge did frequently on horseback, and share in whatever ideas, pleasures and culture could be derived from the metropolis.

Location

Although the boundaries of Twickenhamshire are a matter of personal opinion, and are accordingly flexible, nonetheless the idea of a sort of Twickenham Plus or Greater Twickenham, with its own character and identity, has had lasting currency. Walpole had given it county status, even if light-heartedly, and when we come to examine it there are many unifying elements that suggest an area both discrete and broad. Books written about it frequently

AN OVERVIEW

1.2. *A View of the Countess of Suffolk's House near Twickenham* (Marble Hill). Engraving by James Mason after Augustin Heckel, 1749. (Orleans House Gallery, LDORL: 00040)

1.3. *A View of the Earl of Radnor's House at Twickenham*. Engraving by Anthony Walker after Augustin Heckel, 1750. (Orleans House Gallery, LDORL: 03206)

11

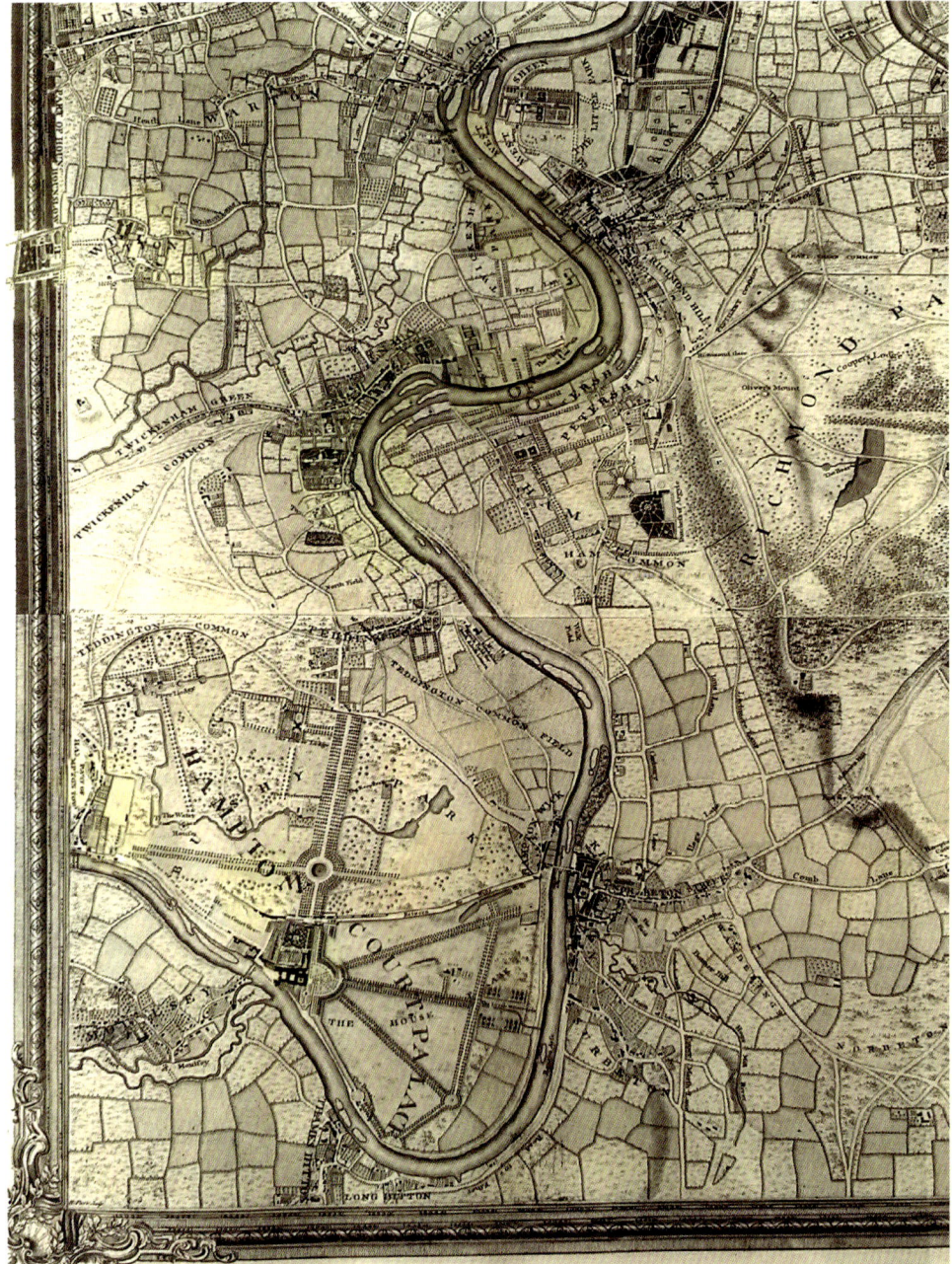

1.4. *An Exact Survey of the City of London, Westminster, the Borough of Southwark and the Country near ten miles round begun in 1741 and extended 1745 by John Rocque Land Surveyor & engraved by Richard Parr* (extract). (Chris Sumner Collection)

stray beyond the boundaries of the town itself, such as *The Fashioned Reed: The Poets of Twickenham from St Margarets to Hampton Court from 1500* (1992), while that fine and comprehensive book on prints, *Images of Twickenham* (1981), is often referred to without giving its full title, which continues *with Hampton and Teddington*. Even that is incomplete since its coverage starts in Isleworth.

A case can be made for Twickenhamshire stretching from Gordon House, Railshead, in the north to Garrick's Villa at Hampton in the south. Figs.1.4 and 1.5 indicate the possible extent

AN OVERVIEW

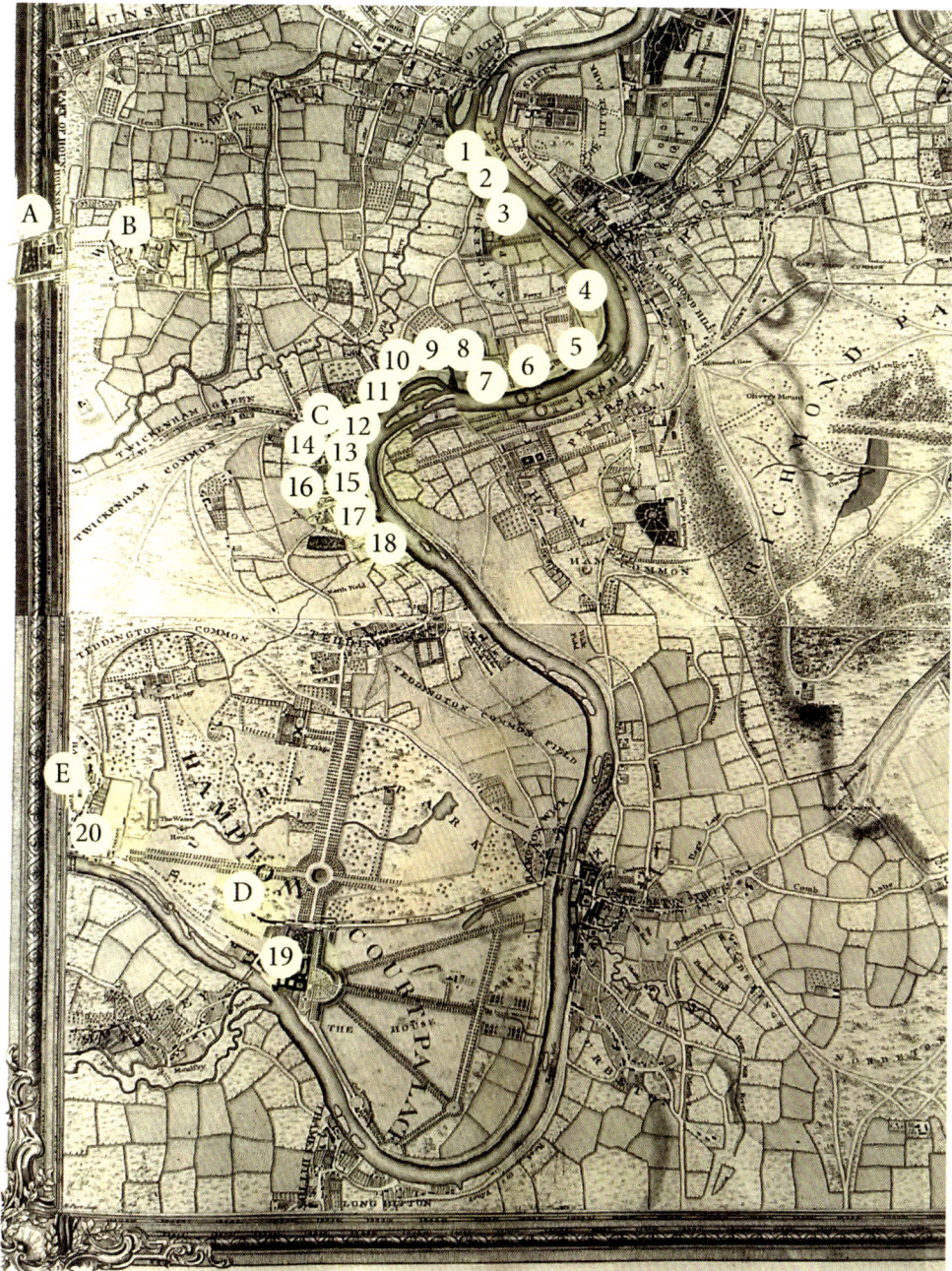

1.5 Location of sites discussed in the text.

Key to riverside sites:
1. Gordon House
2. Lacy House
3. Twickenham Park
4. Twickenham Meadows (Cambridge Park)
5. Little Marble Hill
6. Marble Hill
7. Ragman's Castle
8. Orleans House
9. Strafford House (Mount Lebanon)
10. York House
11. Poulett Lodge
12. Countess Ferrers' Summer House
13. Pope's Villa
14. Hudson's House
15. Radnor House
16. Cross Deep House
17. Strawberry Hill
18. Little Strawberry Hill
19. Hampton Court
20. Garrick's Villa

Key to inland sites:
A. Whitton Park and Place
B. Kneller Hall
C. Isaac Swainson's Botanic Garden
D. Hampton Court House
E. Charles Jervas's House

of our subject: it will be seen that Hampton Court occupies a significant space towards the south geographically although it played a limited part in the eighteenth-century cultural scene and cannot be said to be a meaningful element of the everyday community. Despite its obvious importance it is, accordingly, omitted from the survey in this book: a study of Hampton Court to a degree that did it justice would in any case have seriously unbalanced the coverage.

Boundaries in the eighteenth century were primarily by parish, which carried considerable weight. This explains how Henrietta Pye could describe Twickenham as 'a little *Kingdom* on the Banks of the Thames', which sounds as if it might apply to the whole of Twickenhamshire until she declares that Richard Owen Cambridge is the monarch of this kingdom, when it clearly should be Walpole. The boundary issue becomes apparent when she goes on to describe Walpole as the 'Abbot of Teddington', thus tying him to that parish. Further, she starts her descriptive tour at Twickenham Meadows not Twickenham Park, which is excluded because the parish boundary ran through the middle of the latter, with its northern half lying in the parish of Isleworth.

Each side of the Thames had a riverside path, a tow path for men (not horses) to haul barges along the water. The paths mostly survive, and were always more complete on the Surrey side: particularly along Cross Deep there was no room for one. A number of ferries operated from one bank to the other, as one or two still do.

The location is also significant in terms of its broader context, the neighbouring estates which by virtue of their associations or importance as designed gardens had some bearing on the Twickenhamshire properties. It is clear how much reliance there was on networking, as can be seen between those inside and outside the area. Some of the associations were royal: the former Richmond Palace stood opposite lower Twickenham Park, above what is now Twickenham Bridge; Hampton Court lay within Twickenhamshire; and the royal gardens of Richmond and Kew were just downstream. In themselves these properties conferred a dignity and status to the entire district. In the case of Kew and Richmond Gardens, as well as Syon House across the river from them, garden developments and transformations continued through the eighteenth century, from the time of Charles Bridgeman and William Kent in the first half of the century to Brown, William Chambers and others in the second. Chiswick, too, was not far away, that seminal exercise in the English Landscape Garden, while later developments, under Brown particularly, took place in and around Roehampton. Going further west along the river on the Surrey side there were the pioneering estates of Woburn Farm, Portmore Park and Oatlands, with Esher Place and Claremont, two of Kent's greatest works, slightly inland. The most up-to-date ideas about gardens were therefore circulating among many properties on the broader scene, and Twickenham was certainly a beneficiary.

Twickenham village (as it then was) could itself be sub-divided, the division formed where the Thames curves round Eel Pie Island. To the south and the west stretched Cross Deep, where the villas were tightly concentrated and jostled together without too much garden space down to the river. To the north and the east stood the larger properties such as Marble Hill and Twickenham Meadows, with more riverside frontage. Each sector constituted a panorama for artists working from the Surrey side: the most attractive of Cross Deep was painted by Peter Tillemans (Fig. 1.6). The name Cross Deep requires some clarification: first, it refers to the area both sides of the road from Twickenham leading south to Strawberry Vale, the road itself being called Cross Deep, as it is today. The fine house dating from *c.*1700 at the north end of the road is called simply Crossdeep, and the house adjacent to and south of Radnor House was called Cross Deep House, sometimes spelled Crossdeep House.

1.6. Panorama of Cross Deep from the Surrey bank, showing Radnor House, Pope's Villa, Countess Ferrers' Summer House, various dwellings, and St Mary's Church on the right. *The Prospect of the River Thames at Twickenham*. Painting by Peter Tillemans, *c.*1724-30. (Orleans House Gallery, LDORL: 00886)

1.7. View upstream from Richmond Hill, showing Orleans House, Marble Hill and Little Marble Hill. Painting by circle of Antonio Joli, *c.*1745. (Orleans House Gallery, LDORL: 00158)

The location determined the character of Twickenhamshire as a place, its essence being riverside gardens and villas, publicly viewed from the river or the opposite bank. So the Surrey side is of crucial importance, both in respect of views from it (the panoramas), which could be either from river level or from Richmond Hill (Figs. 1.7 and 1.8), and the views of it from the Middlesex side, whether these were of the flat lands of Ham or the prized backdrop of the Hill. George Mason, in his *Essay on Design in Gardening* (1768), pp.51-2, wrote that 'NATURE's favourite haunts are the *school* of gardening', ranging from the wildness of the Welsh mountains to the quieter scenery of Twickenham: 'her milder *train of graces* disperse themselves along the banks of THAMES…she assumes on RICHMOND-BROW a *gayer* and a *softer* dignity, making every sprightly work of art serve for her embellishment.'

1.8. View downstream from Richmond Hill, showing, on the Middlesex side, Twickenham Meadows, Twickenham Park, and the Railshead houses in the distance. Painting by Antonio Joli, c.1745. (Orleans House Gallery, LDORL: 00159)

The Period

Twickenham had been renowned for culture from at least as far back as Elizabethan times. Its epicentre was towards the north, focused on Twickenham Park as the local grand estate. There a series of notable owners including Francis Bacon and Lucy, Countess of Bedford, built up its reputation, encouraging John Donne to pen the poem *Twicknam Garden*.

For our purposes, however, Twickenhamshire with its own distinctive cultural flavour can be firmly anchored in the eighteenth century. It could be said that it lasted in effect during the life span of two key players, Horace Walpole (1717–97) or Richard Owen Cambridge (1717–1802). After 1800 it continued to be the home of artists, literati and others, but society and sensibilities had changed and the Victorian way of life and attitudes were very different. The eighteenth century saw it at its height, a Golden Age.

By 1714 John Macky could describe Twickenham as 'a village of curious Seats', thereby indicating that there were several, perhaps many, properties of individual interest, but what lit the fuse was Pope's arrival on the scene in 1719. Not only was he the greatest poet of the century but he promoted the concept of the villa and favoured Palladianism. He was also in the vanguard of the 'new gardening', which sought to free gardens from the shackles of regularity and symmetry and introduce, gradually at first, something more natural. Twickenhamshire could thenceforward be seen as a microcosm of developments in garden design, moving steadily from geometry through rococo eclecticism to more free and open landscape. The seeds of a riverside realm of gardens had been sown by the adjacent grounds of Orleans House and Strafford House back in the 1700s, but they were in the old manner of the baroque garden, certainly at first.

But Pope did not arrive directly in the midst of existing artistic or cultural residents. The crowded waterfront of Cross Deep, stretching north beyond St Mary's, was inhabited largely, and had been for some time, by tradesmen, merchants, builders, brewers, poulterers, tanners, wheelwrights, fishermen and watermen, often in dynasties, as Anthony Beckles Willson tells us. The expansion of Twickenham would have afforded many of them further opportunities.

As the Preface has suggested, the eighteenth century corresponds in large measure to the Age of Enlightenment, which encouraged freedom of thought, fostered the spirit of inquiry, and brought about advances in technology and agriculture among many other spheres of interest, which had a bearing on the ever more 'natural' approach to garden-making.

Twickenhamshire can be considered as two distinct entities, divided in mid-century. The first half is Pope's (d.1744) and the second half is Walpole's (arrived 1747, lived there for the next fifty years). Each half stands for very different sensibilities and tastes, and demonstrates shifts in culture that reflect changes in England generally. The area is both a microcosm of these changes and an instigator to some extent. Both stages, in their ambience and flavour, were ground-breaking.

Alexander Pope's Twickenham
Pope's culture was heavily classically-based, and he made his fortune translating the *Iliad* and *Odyssey*. Indeed, the amount he earned from the former enabled him to set up home in Cross Deep. His own poetry is full of classical references, even where the subject matter is topical and contemporary, as it so often was. The bible furnished many comparative references too, as when he referred to his own small plot of land as being but a plate of salad to Nebudchanezzar. He described his own villa and garden as 'my Tusculum', one of Pliny's country villas and as 'reconstructed' in an illustration in Robert Castell's book which covers Pliny's estates (1728). The classical world pervaded Twickenham in the first half of the century, and it became known as 'the classical village'. But there was an overlay of Italian Renaissance Palladianism – Macky had already opined that Orleans House was modelled on country seats in Lombardy. Palladio had of course based his own design work on classical precedent, and depicted many original classical buildings in his great *Four Books of Architecture* (1570). Visitors drew comparisons with Frascati (strongly Renaissance though a classical site), and the Thames was said to be the equivalent of the River Brenta in northern Italy (both Palladian and classical in its associations). By referring to the Thames as the Brenta there may even have been a half-pun on the local river Brent (as in Brentford). Some of this came from those who had actually seen such places on the Grand Tour, though Pope's poor health did not permit him to go abroad. Comparison was also made with the Vale of Tempe, the archetypal beautiful valley in classical Thessaly. Palladio had suggested that a villa should be near a river (as he himself effected), an idea Pope enthusiastically took up and as was embodied in his own villa and at Marble Hill, both of which were Palladian in style. In practice, therefore, Pope's classicism was filtered via Palladio, as was Lord Burlington's at Chiswick, where Pope had previously stayed under Burlington's wing.

Horace Walpole's Twickenham
Around mid-century there was a dramatic change in tastes and sensibilities generally. After Pope's death in 1744 no longer did the classical world wield such authority and influence, nor did classical precedents have to be followed. Native movements of culture were springing up – the novel, Gothic romance and horror (with architecture to match), English watercolour and the 'natural' look in gardens. The literary and intellectual approach of classicism

gave way to a sensibility founded more on feelings. This went hand-in-hand with a rise in the visual arts – paintings, prints, ways of seeing gardens. With regard to the last, the revolution meant moving from formal gardens that might well have to be 'read' (iconography) to those that could relax geometry and become either more open and natural or, where space ruled out grand landscaping (as mostly in Twickenham), a more decorative approach with shrubberies. Twickenhamshire encapsulates garden developments in the eighteenth century, moving from formal and artinatural through mid-century rococo and then opening up more freely, as at Twickenham Meadows.

When Walpole arrived on the scene, he responded to the aura of classicism and saw that he was faced with 'a situation where land is so scarce and villas so abundant as formerly at Tivoli and Baiae.' Both were classical Roman references, Tivoli being the Emperor Hadrian's vast villa complex and Baiae, on the bay of Naples, being the site of luxury villas owned by Lucullus, Pompey and Caesar, together with later emperors. Within a few years, however, Walpole exerted considerable influence in steering in a Gothic direction, and it was said by 1760 that Twickenham was no longer classical. One important element was theatricality, as embodied in Garrick's Villa and Lacy House, both of which Walpole visited regularly.

Orientation

The fact that many properties faced the river rather than the road (or were perceived to) posed a number of problems for the owners. First, a limited riverside frontage might mean that the substantive garden was behind the house, often across the road. This was particularly true in Cross Deep, Pope's Villa being the obvious example. But the price paid was that the main garden, even if of more interest, was less often depicted by artists, who by and large painted from the river or the Richmond bank.

Another problem was that a house would normally face the road. If it did, and that constituted the main entrance, the side of the house facing the river and thus more in an artist's view might be a secondary front unless it was designed as an architectural equal, as at Marble Hill. Houses set back from the river and across the road, however, could display a single principal front, as with Garrick's Villa.

A third issue was that the principal view of a garden was traditionally that which was obtainable from the house, which was also true of later gardens by Brown and Repton. But at Twickenham the garden was commonly best seen from the river, with the consequence that the view from the house was of lesser importance.

This unusual orientation both conferred on Twickenham its own character and facilitated a perspective and way of seeing that distinguished it from other groups of gardens. Visual records of the time are plentiful, and for an artist concerned with composition the garden would be given an ideal foreground in the form of the river, all the more so because of its resonances.

Politics

By and large, Twickenham, with its close royal connections, tended to represent the Court and the Establishment. So the leading figures were generally Whigs, although that presents the complication that from 1733 a Whig Opposition to the Whig government sprang up, based on Liberty (or what was perceived as such), reflected in the freedom of design and the naturalness of the new gardening. An exception was Pope, who was Catholic with Tory leanings: nonetheless political differences did not prevent him moving apparently freely between Whig and Tory circles. Where he saw extravagances and wasteful expenditure on gardens, however, he drew attention to them, and his ideal was to treat nature as 'a modest fair', neatly kempt but not ostentatiously so. An anti-Whig with a strong Jacobite streak appeared in the form of Thomas Wentworth, Earl of Strafford, but although he owned Strafford House (later Mount Lebanon) he was rarely there and is unlikely to have stirred up local subversive feeling.

Frederick, Prince of Wales, rebelled against his parents, George II and Queen Caroline, and became the beacon and talisman of the Whig Opposition camp, which gave a considerable boost to ideas of the pictorial circuit garden, as evinced at Kew, although because of his premature death in 1751 it was left to his widow, Princess Augusta, to bring them to full fruition with the help of William Chambers and the Earl of Bute.

Personalities and Networking

The sheer concentration of leading cultural figures of the day made Twickenham unique, quite apart from its riverside character. The area drew in these figures, many of whom wanted change, one main attraction being that they were like-minded in seeking to push new ideas forward. There was, in consequence, a great deal of networking, creating a culture of mutual help and advice when it came to developing villas and gardens. Most, if not all, significant gardens here came about as a result of conversations and discussions, the bulk of which were never recorded and did not necessarily result in drawings or plans – the evidence is the gardens themselves.

If it is impossible to know what was said or discussed, then it is equally impossible to deny the possibility, or in some cases the strong probability, that such conversations took place and had an impact in practice. What we do know for sure is that networking played a crucial role in determining what actually happened on the ground. Pope described how he discussed gardens all day with Lord Bathurst at Cirencester Park and how they fell asleep over a bottle of port in the evening, while Walpole claimed he persuaded Richard Bateman of Old Windsor to forsake all the *chinoiserie* in his garden and replace it with Walpole's preferred Gothic: 'I preached so effectually that his every pagoda took the veil'. In neither case do we have any record in the form of a plan, but it does indicate how things often got done.

The personalities involved were nearly all resident in Twickenham, but where they were visitors it was on a frequent enough basis to have made a mark. Above all there were writers: Pope, Walpole, Lady Mary Wortley Montagu, Henry Fielding, Paul Whitehead, Richard Owen Cambridge, Garrick (as playwright and occasional poet) and Edward Lovibond. Whitehead and Lovibond were lesser poets but nonetheless acclaimed in the community.

Henry Brooke, an Irishman, wrote in prose and in verse, and lived in Twickenham before moving to Dublin. Famous visiting authors included John Gay (*The Beggar's Opera*) and Jonathan Swift, who composed an amusing dialogue in verse on the rivalry between Richmond Gardens and Marble Hill.

With regard to developments specifically in gardening, there were the leading movers and shakers in terms of planting, the nursery trade and design. The list includes Batty Langley, Pope, Walpole, Thomas Vernon, the Duke of Argyll at Whitton (Fig. 1.9), Lord Bute prior to moving to Kenwood, Cambridge, Garrick, 'Capability' Brown's surveyor John Spyers and John Haverfield, gardener and surveyor. Others visited, including the great rococo designer Thomas Wright, Princess (later Queen) Caroline, who resided at Richmond Lodge, Brown himself and Lord Peterborough of Bevis Mount. Overall, it was a vibrant picture of garden-making, both aesthetically and in terms of progressive planting, with the Duke of Argyll leading the way in introducing new species into the country. Also noteworthy is the concentration on fruit generally but especially on exotics, including vines,

1.9 A *View of the Canal and of the Gothick Tower in the Garden of his Grace the Duke of Argyl at Whitton*. Drawn and engraved by William Woollett, 1757. (Orleans House Gallery, LDORL: 00012)

1.10. *The Seat of Mrs Garrick at Hampton in Middlesex*. Drawn and engraved by William Watts, 1784. *Seats of the Nobility and Gentry*, Plate 68. (Private Collection)

which is not perhaps what might have been expected.

A number of actors settled in Twickenhamshire – Garrick at Hampton (Fig. 1.10), Kitty Clive at Little Strawberry Hill, Hannah Pritchard at Little Marble Hill and Mrs Donaldson at Hampton Court House. Mistresses were provided with residences, as in the case of Henrietta Howard at Marble Hill and a couple of the actresses. There were several leading artists: Samuel Scott, Thomas Hudson, Sir Godfrey Kneller, Reynolds (on the Richmond side) and later Turner. All these together formed a community of a special kind. Many were identified with the place and the community, such as Pope, Gay and Swift, the most eminent satirists of the day, being described as 'the three Yahoos of Twickenham', the term drawn from Swift's *Gulliver's Travels*.

A significant number of the above were Freemasons – Pope, Walpole, Garrick, Langley, Haverfield and maybe others. This in itself facilitated networking. Also, because many of those who lived locally had their own network of contacts in London and elsewhere, they were open to a wide range of new thinking. One must remember, too, that from about 1710, when the 'new gardening' began (slowly) to be broached it was in the ever-growing medium of newspapers and periodicals, again centred in London.

One phenomenon of the area was the number of Scots who came south and left their mark on gardens and gardening. The Duke of Lauderdale had designed and planted at Ham House in the previous century, and Archibald Campbell, Duke of Argyll was born there. James Johnston, formerly Secretary of Scotland, retired to Orleans House in 1702 and created a substantial garden, with a special interest in fruit. John, 2nd Duke of Argyll, held the estate of Sudbrook Park, Petersham: Gibbs designed the house for him, and Campbell may have supplied some of the trees. James Lee, founder of the Vineyard nursery at Hammersmith in 1745, worked for a time for Campbell at Whitton as he developed the foremost private collection of trees in the country (Fig. 1.9). Campbell was uncle to John Stuart, 3rd Earl of Bute, who lived at Twickenham before becoming a great plantsman and botanist, leaving his mark at Kenwood and Kew among other places. Furthermore, it was said that Scottish gardeners were better educated than their English counterparts, which may have influenced Catherine the Great when she invited a significant number to work on her Russian estates.

Alexander Pope (1688–1744) was the most influential of the inhabitants in the early years, bringing with him to Cross Deep a high reputation as poet and, as was to be shown, instrumental in shaping the direction garden design was to take, particularly in shunning topiary and symmetry. Nature was espoused, but as yet still on the basis of a geometrical structure. He created his own villa and garden, with help from William Kent, Bridgeman and others, and was responsible for founding the taste for a riverside Palladian villa (Lord Burlington's villa at Chiswick stood some way back from the river). His ideas on gardening, often recorded by his friend Joseph Spence of Byfleet, spread widely and helped to raise the status of garden-making generally: he described it as closer to God's work than poetry and as kin to philosophy. He advised others in the locality, such as Henrietta Howard at Marble Hill and by tradition his great friend and art master Charles Jervas, who lived in London but moved to Hampton (see Other Gardens chapter).

Pope's relevant writings on gardens are to be found in Spence's *Anecdotes, Observations, and Characters of Books and Men*; his poem addressed to Lord Burlington (1731); and his essay in *The Guardian* in 1713. His letter to Martha Blount (1724) gives a full account of Lord Digby's gardens at Sherborne.

1.11. *Lacy House in Middlesex, the Seat of Richard Brindsley* [sic] *Sheridan Esqr.* Drawn and engraved by William Angus, 1795. *Seats of the Nobility and Gentry*, Plate XXXVI. (Orleans House Gallery, LDORL: 01060)

Horace Walpole (1717–97), antiquarian, scholar, gossip, commentator and voluminous letter-writer was the ultimate networker, and one who tried, sometimes forcefully, to persuade others of his taste and views. His personal contact list was vast, and he travelled far and wide, observing and recording his thoughts. In the Twickenham context he is of course famed for his promotion of Gothic, both in his extraordinary house at Strawberry Hill and in the ensuing creation (after a vision in a dream of a gigantic hand in armour on the staircase of an ancient castle) of the Gothic novel in the form of *The Castle of Otranto* (1765). He visited other parts of the neighbourhood frequently, and often left his mark on the development of house and gardens. The Gothic temple at Lacy House (Fig. 1.11) would be one example, contrasting with Garrick's classical model at Hampton. Walpole spent most 'garden time' on his own grounds but managed to advise others such as Henrietta Howard at Marble Hill and Garrick, whom he helped with planting. He may have advised his brother, Sir Edward Walpole, at Lacy House.

Even at Strawberry Hill itself, where one might have expected Walpole to take sole control, he established what has been called a committee of taste, though Walpole himself used the term 'Strawberry committee', including Richard Bentley, draughtsman and designer; John Chute, of The Vyne, Hampshire, designer and architectural adviser; Thomas Gray, the poet, as an arbiter of taste; and Thomas Pitt, amateur but widely employed architect. There was some rivalry between the members when it came to design, and they also came and went according to how they got on with Walpole.

Walpole was well aware of gardens nearby, and was not slow to comment on them. He dismissed the profusion of sculpture and, later, garden buildings at Radnor House, and regretted the decline of Pope's garden since the poet's death, complaining that the compartments that Pope had 'twisted and twirled and rhymed and harmonized' had become open and degraded so that 'if the Muses wanted to tie up their garters there is not a nook to do it in without being seen.'

One of Walpole's many achievements was the establishment of his own printing press in 1757. The first product was Thomas Gray's *Odes*, but later Walpole printed several of his own works, especially on antiquarian subjects. This was one of the first private presses and certainly the most famed in its time.

His garden writings are principally *The History of the Modern Taste in Gardening* (1770, but not published till a decade later), which, along with Thomas Whately's *Observations on Modern Gardening*, was the most well-known text of the day on the subject; his description of Park Place, Henley, in 'Mi Li: A Chinese Fairy Tale' (Tale V in *Hieroglyphic Tales*); and brief mention of individual gardens in his correspondence (see WS Lewis edition, 48 volumes with full index) and in his *Journal of Visits to Country Seats*. Some of his poems cover gardens.

Richard Owen Cambridge (1717–1802) was proclaimed by Henrietta Pye as the king of Twickenham. She described his realm in glowing terms: 'its Soil Gravelly, its Air balmy, clear, and healthful: The whole Place is one continued Garden. Plenty and Pleasure are the Ideas convey'd by its large Fields of Corn and its verdant Meadows; tis govern'd by a King, whose Arts (not Arms) recommend to the Dignity, the Government not being hereditary: He is proclaim'd by a Muse, and acknowledged by the People'. He lived at Twickenham Meadows from 1751 until his death in 1802, and achieved wonders in opening up and landscaping his extensive property. He was a wit and minor author, contributing to the periodical *The World* in the 1750s and penning a mock-heroic poem in the manner of Pope, *The Scribleriad*, but was no match for the earlier poet. During a sermon in church he seemed preoccupied, and his wife asked of what he was thinking. 'Of the next *World*, my dear' was his reply.

Cambridge was a devoted family man and a generous host. He would ride regularly into London and keep abreast of the latest news and developments, and regale his family by recounting them on his return. He was such a newsmonger that he was referred to as the Cambridge mail. He was very much in the swim as regards the new gardening and continued to keep in touch with owners and gardens. He had already gained experience of landscaping at Whitminster prior to his arrival at Twickenham.

Cambridge's garden writings are mainly to be found in *The World*, issues no. 76 (13 June 1754), no. 118 (3 April 1755) and no. 119 (10 April 1755). Other relevant works are mentioned in the entry on Twickenham Meadows in the final chapter.

Henrietta Howard (*c.*1688–1767), mistress of George II and Countess of Suffolk from 1731, had what amounted to a committee of taste in the manner of Walpole, although it was never described as such. She was established at Marble Hill from 1724 and lived there, on and off, till her death in 1767. Her numerous advisers were spread over a number of years and, consequently, over a number of changes in garden and architectural design. The early years were heavily influenced by Pope, who was said in *The History and Antiquities of Twickenham* (1797) to have been responsible for laying out the grounds; and those who also advised Henrietta were often close friends with Pope, who undoubtedly introduced them to her.

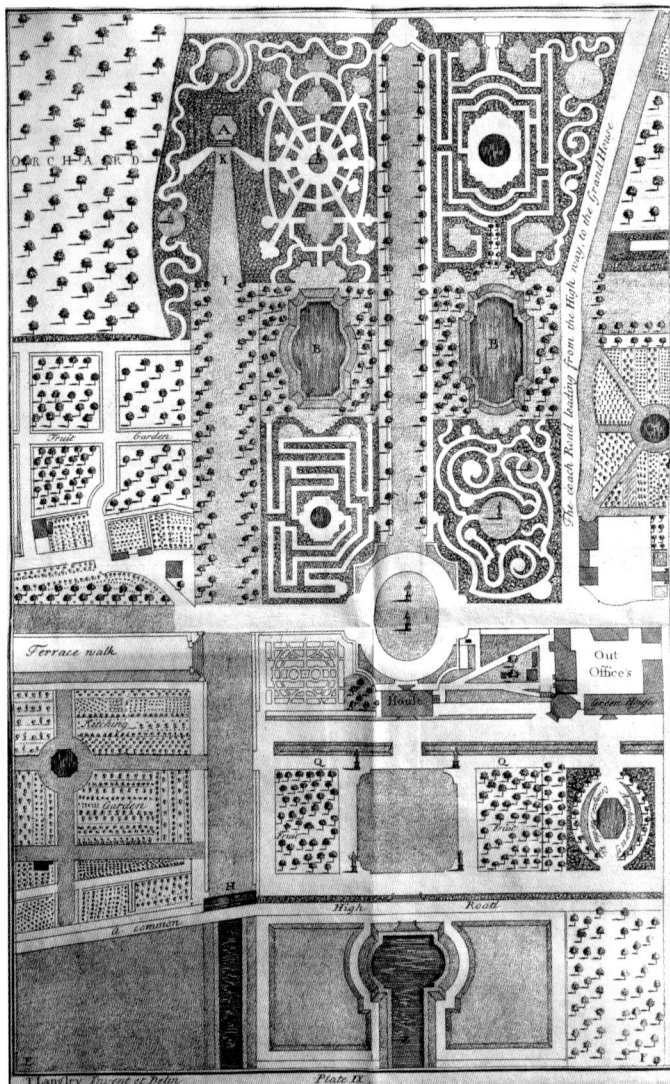

1.12. Plan of Secretary Johnston's house (Orleans House) by Batty Langley. *New Principles of Gardening*, 1728. Plate IX (printed in reverse).
(Private Collection)

She was at the centre of local society, and her circle was described as 'The Twickenham Club'. It included Lord Peterborough, whose main seat was at Bevis Mount, Southampton, where Pope had been involved; and Lord Bathurst of Riskings and Cirencester Park, where Pope had played a substantial part in creating an exemplar of the 'forest, extensive or rural' style of gardening as promoted by his contemporary Stephen Switzer. Other advisers included Archibald Campbell, to become 3rd Duke of Argyll, who was instrumental in obtaining the land and setting Henrietta up at Marble Hill. His role in advising her is likely to have been in the sphere of planting, his favourite pursuit. Then there was Charles Bridgeman, Royal Gardener, whose speciality was terracing, and who met Pope on site. Later came Walpole and Bentley, who assisted her in designing a Gothic farm building folly – but she designed part of it herself, showing that even in her older years she was actively engaged.

Batty Langley (1696–1751) was born in Twickenham, the son of a gardener. He showed impressive versatility, being at various times a gardener himself, a nurseryman, the designer of gardens, their buildings and plantings, an architect particularly in the neo-Gothic style, an author and, from 1729, involved in the manufacture of artificial stone. Little of his architectural work survives, but he is best known for his writings. Up to 1728, when he produced his most familiar work, *New Principles of Gardening*, his output mostly comprised plantings and garden layout, together with the promotion of a new asymmetrical (though still heavily geometrical) style, but then these activities ceased abruptly. He was involved particularly at Twickenham Park and Orleans House, a design for the latter appearing in *New Principles* (Fig. 1.12).

Otherwise his practical publications, with some reference to Twickenham, were *A Sure Method of Improving Estates by Plantations* (also 1728) and *Pomona, or the Fruit Garden Illustrated* (1729). He derived much material from the writings of Stephen Switzer.

Archibald Campbell (1682–1761), Lord Islay or Ilay and, from 1743, the 3rd Duke of Argyll, was born in Ham House but early on moved to Scotland, attaining high office there and becoming in effect ruler. A disagreeable man in character, he gardened in Scotland until coming south in the early 1720s. He employed Gibbs and Roger Morris as architects for his London home, and Morris in particular assisted him at various properties over a long period. The nucleus of his estate at Whitton, bought in 1722, was small but became steadily augmented. He created not so much a garden as an arboretum and nursery for his enormous collection of trees and shrubs. Horace Walpole called him a treemonger. The garden element, such as it was, was mostly confined to the canal and Gothic tower (Fig. 1.9). His surveyor was James Dorret, who aided him in Scotland as well as Whitton and Marble Hill; he shared his gardener Daniel Crafts (variously spelled) with Henrietta Howard as well. Having arranged the acquisition of land for Marble Hill for her he may well have advised on planting.

David Garrick (1717–79) was the foremost theatrical figure of the century, mainly as actor and manager but also as author, usually of prologues or epilogues but sometimes of entire plays. Given his popularity, there was no shortage of friends to give him advice about creating his garden on both sides of the main road, the villa being on the landward side. Brown was a particularly close friend, and doubtless gave him ideas, but both the Garricks were inveterate travellers to gardens (Mount Edgcumbe, Cornwall, was their favourite) and were independent enough to compose their own garden, especially when it came to planting. The front lawn resembles in some ways the style of Walpole, who helped them. Garrick would have advised James Lacy, his business partner, on the garden at Lacy House.

Charles Bridgeman (*c.*1680–1738) had significant input although not an inhabitant of Twickenham. Mainly a formalist in the baroque tradition, nonetheless he showed glimpses of new directions in his work: as Walpole commented, at Richmond he 'dared to introduce cultivated fields, and even morsels of a forest appearance, by the sides of those endless and tiresome walks, that stretched out of one into another without intermission'.

As Royal Gardener he was known to Princess, later Queen, Caroline and worked for her at both Kensington Gardens and Richmond Gardens, and would have been highly regarded in Twickenham. No payments have been recorded to him at Marble Hill, but the terracing is almost certainly his work, or at least his idea (Fig. 1.2). Terraces were his trademark, and there were prime examples not far away. At Oatlands, south of the river, he was responsible for the grand terrace, three-quarters of a mile long, in 1727, which was subsequently softened and naturalised; and at nearby Claremont there was his masterpiece, the huge amphitheatre, together with a separate terrace described as Vanbrugh's but presumably planned jointly by Bridgeman and Vanbrugh since one worked on the gardens while the other focused on buildings.

Thomas Vernon (c.1670–1726) was a substantial local land-holder in the earlier years of the century and, although not a designer himself, had a manifest impact on developments. He was a merchant trading with Turkey, which led to his introduction of possibly the first weeping willow (*Salix babylonica*) in England. Among his extensive properties (concentrated in Cross Deep) was the land leased to Pope for his villa and gardens, and he also stood in the way of Henrietta Howard expanding her territory at Marble Hill. His own home was the large and historic house of Twickenham Park, where he employed Batty Langley to design at least part of the garden.

Lady Mary Wortley Montagu (1689–1762) was one of the most remarkable women of her generation. In the words of Pope's biographer Maynard Mack, she was 'vivacious, ambitious, aggressive, self-educated far beyond the attainments of most women of her time, and beautiful'. Pope clearly worshipped her, and was instrumental in bringing the Montagus to reside in Twickenham on their return from a posting in Turkey, whence she introduced inoculation into this country. She was, however, sharp-tongued and could be vicious, even occasionally obscene, in writing, as Pope discovered when they subsequently fell out. Her satire was up to the quality of that of the three Yahoos, including the installing of the God of Dullness in a cave (Pope in his grotto). She is not to be confused with her daughter of the same name, who became the Countess of Bute on marriage to the 3rd Earl of Bute, the great plantsman. Having lived on Kew Green, after the Earl's death the Countess moved into (old) St Margarets House in Isleworth. Walpole was a regular visitor, and enjoyed her conversation, though she lacked the brilliance of her mother.

John Stuart (1713–92), 3rd Earl of Bute, botanist and horticulturalist, lived in Twickenham before moving to Kenwood and later Kew Green. He was friends with Frederick, Prince of Wales, after whose death in 1751 he advised Princess Augusta on developments at Kew, including the botanical side. He was Ranger of Richmond Park from 1761 to 1792. Nephew of the 3rd Duke of Argyll, he excelled in planting at his properties of Luton Hoo, Bedfordshire, and Highcliffe, Hampshire.

John Haverfield (c.1694–1784), a surveyor from Twickenham, became supervisor of the gardens at Kew in 1758 and then also of Richmond Gardens in 1762. There was a dynasty of Haverfields: the son, also John, had joint responsibility with his father at Richmond, then sole responsibility, and later branched into private practice. Thomas, another son, worked at Kew before assuming control at Hampton Court gardens in 1785. Haverfield House on Kew Green was the family home for generations. Haverfield supplied seeds and plants from Kew.

John Spyers (*fl.*1764–post 1790) was born in Isleworth, the son of a gardener. His uncle Joshua lived in a large property, to become known as Grosvenor House, in Twickenham and was the principal member of the family nursery business there. John may have learnt surveying within the business: at all events, by the early 1760s 'Capability' Brown was beginning to employ him as surveyor and draughtsman, a function he fulfilled for many years, becoming indispensable in drawing up Brown's plans. He inherited Grosvenor House when Joshua died in 1768, together with other property close by, but later moved to Hampton Court. He became a topographical artist, concentrating on Hampton Court (150 views) and depicted Marble Hill (see Fig. 9.6) and Twickenham Park.

AN OVERVIEW

James Lacy was the business partner of Garrick and ran Drury Lane theatre with him. He arrived in Railshead c.1750 and is said to have rebuilt the house there, which would become known as Lacy House. The Gothic temple in the grounds (Fig. 1.11) is likely to have dated from his twenty-five year tenure of the property, particularly as it paid homage to Garrick and Shakespeare. Lacy was succeeded by his son Willoughby, who spent his inheritance and took up acting to make money, but ego predominated over talent.

Richard Brinsley Sheridan (1751–1816) found fame as a playwright from the success of *The Rivals* (though initially a flop) and his comic opera *The Duenna* in 1775 at the age of twenty-four. Later he abandoned writing for the theatre in favour of a political career. He leased Lacy House in the late 1780s from Mrs Keppel, Sir Edward Walpole's daughter, but his extravagance prohibited a lengthy residence.

James Gibbs (1682–1754), leading architect in Twickenham in the early period along with Roger Morris, was responsible for Orleans House Octagon, Pope's Villa, the Green House at Whitton and possibly Countess Ferrers' Summer House. He designed Sudbrook House at Petersham. He did not, however, settle locally.

Roger Morris (1695–1749), 'Master Carpenter of the Board of Ordinance' and architect, lived in Cross Deep from 1743 until his death in 1749. He had earlier been involved with the houses of Whitton Park, White Lodge in Richmond and Marble Hill, making him, along with Gibbs, the principal designer of villas and residences in the district. Hudson's Villa is attributed to him. He had a hand in the garden works at Marble Hill and possibly other properties.

John James (c.1673–1746) was an architect and author, famed among garden historians for his translation of a classic text on formal French gardens by Dezallier D'Argenville in 1712. He lived at Hampton Court or Hampton while he was apprenticed to Matthew Banckes, and was married at St Mary's Teddington, but was later based at Greenwich. His Twickenham commissions included Orleans House and the rebuilding of St Mary's Twickenham (leaving the mediaeval tower). The surviving Gordon House, Railshead, which was extended by Robert Adam, has been tentatively attributed to him, but there is no evidence.

James 'Secretary' Johnston (1643–1737), owner of Orleans House and patron of John James, Gibbs and Batty Langley, was keenly interested in gardens and represented the first of the wave of prominent Scottish garden and plant pioneers who came south into the area, including Lord Bute and the Duke of Argyll. He could be said to have initiated the concept of Twickenhamshire as a *Gartenreich* along with Thomas Wentworth.

Thomas Wentworth (1672–1739), Lord Raby and then 1st Earl of Strafford (second creation) from 1711, bought a property later to be known as Strafford House in 1701. It adjoined Orleans House and the gardens were created at more or less the same period, possibly with some degree of rivalry (see Fig. 10.8). Strafford was, however, absent for much of the time, and it was his mother, Lady Isabella Wentworth, who resided there. Nonetheless it is thought that he designed the gardens, as he did at his principal seat of Wentworth Castle in Yorkshire. A subsequent house became known as Mount Lebanon from the cedars in the grounds.

1.13. *Mr Hudson's gothic house opposite his own*. Watercolour by Johann Henry Müntz, 1757. (Richmond Local Studies Collection, LCP 3051)

Lord Herbert (*c*.1689–1750), 9th Earl of Pembroke, was the co-designer of Marble Hill House with Roger Morris. His seat was Wilton House, where the original Palladian Bridge was built, to be followed elsewhere by at least three copies. He was in the forefront of those championing Palladianism.

Thomas Hudson (1701–1779), prominent portrait artist, took a lease on a house in Cross Deep, occupied previously by Roger Morris, from 1753 to 1779, and was thus firmly established in the Walpole era. At the start of his tenure the Palladian villa appeared, to the design probably of the deceased Morris. Across the road inland the strange Gothic concoction of 'Hudson's Gothic House' (Fig. 1.13) showed Walpole's influence, just as the tunnel under the road linking the two halves of the property showed Pope's.

Samuel Scott (*c*.1702–72), also an artist, who specialised in marine paintings, resided at the Manor House, near St Mary's Church, in 1763–4 and bought property in Cross Deep in 1755 but let it out. His main residence and studio were in London. He depicted a large number of riverside scenes in Twickenham (see Fig. 5.2).

Thomas Wright (1711–86) was not a resident but was reportedly brought in by the Earl of Halifax, Ranger of Bushy Park, to ornament the gardens of Hampton Court House in the 1750s. He was something of a polymath, astronomer (with a new theory about the Milky

Way), mathematician, rococo architect and garden designer. It is for his garden buildings that he is chiefly renowned. He worked at the great estate of Badminton and contributed individual garden features, whether built or planted, at numerous locations. He published designs for arbours and grottoes in, respectively, 1755 and 1758.

Lancelot 'Capability' Brown (1716–83) was of course the most well-known name in garden and park design in the century. But although he lived at Hammersmith and looked after Hampton Court in his capacity as, in effect, Royal Gardener (he refused to landscape it), and had acquaintances within Twickenhamshire, his input appears to be negligible. He visited Cambridge at Twickenham Meadows and complimented him on what he had achieved but gave no known advice. He is sometimes regarded as having had a substantial say in the layout of his close friend Garrick's grounds, but an account of 1780 makes it clear that his sole contribution was the planting of a single tree.

Humphry Repton (1752–1818) followed Brown but could not quite achieve his status. He worked on White Lodge in Richmond Park but not in Twickenham itself, although he was involved at Whitton.

Lady Diana Beauclerk, née Spencer, occupied Little Marble Hill right through the 1780s, when it was assuming its most decorative form (see Fig. 10.6). She was a hostess equivalent to the Countess of Suffolk, and, apart from Garrick in the vicinity, could number many of the 'greats' of the day among her circle, including Dr Johnson and Boswell, Oliver Goldsmith, Edmund Burke, Reynolds and Edward Gibbon. She was a not inconsiderable artist, and Walpole assembled a collection of her works at Strawberry Hill.

Charles Jervas (*c.*1675–1739), who had a property in Hampton for a while, was chiefly a portrait painter, whom Pope cultivated from about 1713, possibly earlier. Pope frequently visited his studio in London and was instructed by him (see Other Gardens section for Pope's likely part in forming his garden).

John Robartes (1686–1757), 4th Earl of Radnor, was a bachelor reputed variously to be dull or simple, but was a connoisseur and collector of paintings in addition to introducing Gothic to Twickenham ahead of Walpole. He erected a Chinese summerhouse, which irritated Walpole, by then firmly in the Gothic saddle.

Catherine 'Kitty' Clive (1711–85), popular on the London stage for forty years, lived at Twickenham from at least 1747, first at Little Marble Hill and then Little Strawberry Hill. Walpole described her as 'the laughter-loving dame' and 'A matchless actress'. It is possible that she may have had a garden connection with West Wycombe, where Kitty's Lodge could have been named after her (there are other candidates). She is recorded as planting jointly with Walpole.

Paul Whitehead (1710–74), who lived at Colne Lodge at the north of Twickenham Common, was a friend of both Pope and Walpole and thus connected their respective circles. He was an occasional poet and debtor, and achieved notoriety as the secretary of the Hell-Fire Club (so named later) at Medmenham Abbey. His poems included some local descriptions, e.g. of the cedar grove at Whitton.

Henry Fielding (1707–54), the author who established (not invented) the novel as a literary genre, his masterpiece being *Tom Jones*, resided in a cottage beyond the top of Pope's garden in 1747–8. He had known Pope and was related to Lady Mary Wortley Montagu, but did not stay long enough to make a significant impact.

Thomas Pitt (1737–93), 1st Baron Camelford, was related to the great William Pitt the Elder, who was himself a considerable garden-maker. Thomas's principal seat was Bocconoc, Cornwall, but he gave architectural advice widely including designing the Doric and Corinthian Arches at Stowe in addition to supervising the remodelling of the south front of the house, together with the orangery at Mount Edgcumbe. He took a house near Strawberry Hill for a while and became, temporarily, a member of Walpole's committee.

Daniel Craft (variously Crafts, Craftes or Crofts) was gardener to Lord Islay (Duke of Argyll) at Whitton but was lent out to the Countess of Suffolk at Marble Hill.

Thomas Ashe, nurseryman, lived immediately to the south of Strawberry Hill, adjoining the road. His chief claim to fame seems to have been his celebrated response to Walpole describing how he wanted his trees to appear: 'Yes, Sir, I understand: you would have them hang down somewhat poetical.'

Lord Burlington (1695–1753) was the 'invisible man' in the locality – not directly involved but his influence and inspiration are manifest in Pope's Twickenham. Pope was a friend of Burlington, impresario, patron, designer and passionate sponsor of Palladianism. This was everywhere apparent at Chiswick, where the villa and gardens embodied both Palladian and classical qualities, the same mixture as at Marble Hill.

The Garden Conference of 1719
The tradition of bringing in a number of people to help design a garden was established in the form of a conference or symposium convened by Princess Caroline in September 1719. She had just moved into Richmond Lodge and was anxious to develop a garden according to the most up-to-date principles, so she sought advice. It is not known precisely who attended this meeting of 'gardening lords' as they were referred to, but they included Pope, who described the conference in a somewhat scathing letter to Lord Bathurst that nonetheless indicated a range of views expressed by those present. From Pope's summary of those views we can deduce that formalists like Henry Wise, the Royal Gardener, and Bridgeman, that active pioneer, were present. Although the immediate outcome was unclear, we do know that in practice Caroline brought in first Bridgeman and then Kent to lay out Richmond Gardens as a much admired and visited site, and that the input from both was avant-garde for its time.

Garden Styles
From the time of Pope to the end of the century, residents included in their number some of the leaders in the sphere of garden-making. In the 1720s the key players were Pope, Bridgeman (though not a resident) and Batty Langley (Fig. 1.12), all of whom had grown up in a world dominated by formal, geometrical gardens but sought to find something more natural. The results, at this stage, do not look particularly natural to us today, but in essence consisted of strong axial lines and water in the regular shapes of a canal or round pond.

1.14. *A Map of the Manor of Isleworth-Sion in the County of Middlesex belonging to his Grace the Duke of Northumberland* drawn by CJ Sauthier, 1786-87. (Extract showing southern portion).
(Courtesy of the Archives of the Duke of Northumberland at Syon House, Sy:B.XIII.1e)

However, to the side of formal avenues, paths wound around in woodland in mazy serpentines, and even the most formal of patterns were often rendered asymmetrical. This combination was summed up in Langley's useful word, artinatural. In addition trees were allowed to grow without rigorous pruning and topiary. Such images as Tillemans' panorama (Fig. 1.6) and Rocque's map of 1744–6 (Fig. 1.4) indicate the still largely regular layouts, as at Orleans House and Twickenham Park. Pope's own villa had a simple lawn in front of the house, but a famous and varied garden at the back, with intricacy and many features packed into a small space.

1.15. *The Prospect of Richmond in Surry*. Anonymous engraving, 1726, showing both sides of the river, Richmond to the left. (Richmond Local Studies Collection, LCP 2674)

It is known that Pope and Bridgeman met at Marble Hill to discuss the garden and that Batty Langley was left out, although he was in the best place to win a commission. In the event, the plans of Marble Hill *c.*1749 (see Figs. 9.3 and 9.4) show a layout representing some characteristics of Langley, Pope and Bridgeman. Langley vented his disappointment by criticising the layout in 1728, but since he could hardly disparage work that had been carried out in his style he confined his comments to the terracing, which was a Bridgeman trademark rather than his. He claimed that the slope being cut into stepped terraces was ugly.

During the 1730s and 40s momentum was growing for a radically different approach to garden design, spearheaded by William Kent, who helped Pope with his garden. Even Kent could never free himself completely from straight lines, but an unstoppable force had been unleashed, and the English Landscape Garden was on its way. Large gardens outside, but close to, Twickenham showed the possibilities, revealed as circuits linking set scenes or tableaux (often centred on a building) in a naturalistic setting.

As regards Twickenham, scope was lacking for landscaping on a vast scale, but, following Walpole's arrival on the scene, the spirit of freedom (political and artistic) was definitely in the air, and in the case of gardens it was expressed through small rococo layouts stemming from Pope, though not so axial, or a larger naturalism. The term rococo has been applied to both the artinatural designs of the early period and some small gardens of mid-century, but there is a definite difference. Rococo in the artinatural garden refers to wiggling paths and asymmetry while in the later gardens it is primarily a matter of architecture and colourful shrubberies (the word shrubbery is not known before 1748).

Some gardens were new (Garrick's, Walpole's, Lacy House, Hampton Court House), some were modified from earlier regularity but others remained largely as they were, if well-established prior to 1750, admired and loved. The great precedent was Hampton Court itself, where 'Capability' Brown realised it would be sacrilege to destroy the magnificent design and in consequence made no move to landscape it, though the clipped trees in the fountain parterre were allowed to grow and spread. This is why the Sauthier map of 1786–7 (Fig. 1.14) indicates some layouts that were still mainly regular, as at Orleans House, Pope's Villa and Marble Hill. It may also have been a tribute to the deceased Pope and his contemporaries that they were left little altered. Pope's garden in particular was iconic and something of a shrine, and remained, though in a state of steady decline, until Baroness Howe tired of so many visitors and dismantled the house in 1807.

Overall, however, the development on the Twickenham side had been dramatic, as can be seen from a panorama from sixty years earlier than Sauthier, a view, looking south, of the two sides of the river in 1726 (Fig. 1.15). This shows a large number of dwellings on the Richmond side contrasted with the as yet undeveloped area of Twickenham Meadows and beyond. The very caption of the anonymous print, *The Prospect of Richmond*, indicates the significance and scale of Richmond at that time in comparison with the nucleus of Cross Deep and Twickenham village that was yet to blossom into Twickenhamshire.

Walpole's Gothicising of Strawberry Hill was not brand new: the neighbouring Radnor House was already crenellated and may have served as an inspiration (and as a spur to outdo it). For Walpole the essence of Gothic, as in cathedrals, was what he termed 'gloomth' but he rejected the idea that gardens should display that quality. On the contrary, they were to be 'riant'. Nevertheless, he had a small Prior's Garden next to a wall of his house, and the Chapel in the Wood was suitably shaded. As a whole his garden might be described as rococo, with its Shell Seat and other features within a confined area, but it depended on a circuit path taking Walpole or his visitors around an ever-changing scene, which was central to the larger pictorial landscape coming into fashion. It represents a smaller version of the circuit path at Kew, where the interior was flat pasture.

Small and intricate gardens, yet with the spirit of their landscaped contemporaries, proliferated in Walpole's time. Garrick's front lawn would be the perfect example (Fig. 1.10) – undulating lawn and paths, a mixed shrubbery, varied plantings and a grottified tunnel under the road to link up with the rear garden. Dominating the lawn was the Shakespeare temple – and buildings were at the heart of the pictorial landscape garden. This was most apparent in Thomas Wright's quirky assemblage at Hampton Court House, including a superb grotto. Buildings also appeared in, or were added to, several gardens: Radnor House, Poulett Lodge, Cross Deep House, Lacy House, Hudson House, the Ferrers estate, and as shown in the panoramas particularly of Cross Deep.

There was even a small touch of the *ferme ornée* at Marble Hill in the 1750s, where Walpole, Richard Bentley and Henrietta Howard jointly devised a sham Gothic chapel, the Priory of St Hubert, to act as a 'farm' (=farmhouse or farm building) amid a formal plot. The term 'farm' plus a sham chapel folly were also to be encountered at Portmore Park, which, along with Woburn Farm (both along the Surrey bank), constituted a more developed example of the *ferme ornée*.

Finally, there was a blossoming of the full, naturalistic landscape style in Twickenham Meadows (now Cambridge Park and built over) under the direction of Richard Owen Cambridge, and at Twickenham Park. There was also a major change-over at Kneller Hall. Thus we can see all the principal movements of the eighteenth-century garden in Twickenhamshire save the 'wild Picturesque', which would have been topographically impossible (and regretted by William Gilpin) though hinted at in the stonework of the grottoes.

Such a proliferation of gardens encouraged local resident gardeners and nurseries to supply plants. Usually a nurseryman would be a gardener as well. This was the case with Thomas Ashe, whose nursery was in a small corner of the Strawberry Hill estate. Worple Way, running north-south almost parallel to the Cross Deep road but further west, marking the boundary of Pope's garden among others, was named Nursery Lane for a while, indicating that at least one nursery was sited along it (it is thought that one existed to the west of the road). There is also the slightly mysterious matter of Pope paying the rates for the house of a John Frye, a gardener, who resided to the west of Twickenham Green. As Anthony Beckles Willson suggests, Frye probably gardened for him.

In what follows it may be a surprise that York House is not covered. It stands at the centre point of Twickenham, at the bend of the river, and is one of the few important houses remaining from the period: but it did not have a garden of any great significance, comprising a plain lawn stretching to a gravelled terrace walk. Edward Ironside in 1797 mentioned a grove of elms on one side, with serpentine walks and a small summerhouse. It was not until the late nineteenth and early twentieth centuries that fame and glamour arrived, with the Italianate bridge, riverside terrace and the erotic fountain that continues to ensure the popularity of the spot.

It is important to consider all the properties as constituent parts of Twickenhamshire rather than by themselves. We have seen, and it will be amply demonstrated in the individual chapters, how often there was input from neighbours and cross-fertilisation of ideas, plantings and design. Even where there is no evidence of such input, the owners could hardly be blind to what was going on around them and how all the estates combined to create the unique configuration of Twickenhamshire, which bound them together. It was greater than the sum of its parts.

CHAPTER TWO

The Arcadian Thames
Chris Sumner

Kingdoms may come, kingdoms may go
Whatever the end may be.
Old Father Thames keeps rolling along
Down to the mighty sea.
Old Father Thames (lyric by Raymond Wallace)

Statues of the mythical personification of England's principal river the Thames recline at their ease in the courtyard of Somerset House in the Strand and in Terrace Gardens Richmond (Father Thames, Fig. 2.1) and at Ham House. Derived from Roman and Renaissance figures of river gods, the figure of Father Thames at Somerset House designed by John Bacon is of bronze and shows him – naked and with a long flowing beard – with an empty urn and overflowing cornucopia; the similar figures in Richmond and Ham are of Coade Stone, a fine terracotta artificial stone manufactured in Lambeth, and were also designed by Bacon, in 1775. They omit the cornucopia, but in compensation the urn gushes forth petrified streams of water. A later statue made by Rafaelle Monti in 1854 for the Rivers and Oceans series at the Crystal Palace is now at St John's Lock, Lechlade, Oxfordshire, near the highest navigable point of the river.

The statues are a knowing reference to classical mythology and superstition, but since early times the Thames has played a part in religious beliefs, and that continues. The bronze shield mounts known as the Battersea and Wandsworth Shields (now in the British Museum) are outstanding works of the Celtic Iron Age of the third and second centuries BCE and are believed to have been religious tributes paid to the river. Christian symbols and figures are occasionally retrieved from the river and include many mediaeval pilgrim badges, and since 2005 the annual religious ceremony of immersing an idol of the Hindu Lord Ganesha has taken place on the river.

London of course owes its location and one-time pre-eminence as a trading port to the River Thames. Julius Caesar and his troops crossed the Thames in 55 BCE, by tradition close to the site of the modern Kew Bridge, and Londinium was founded a century later in 47 CE following the establishment of a Roman camp on the north bank. The existence of a timber-built Roman London Bridge is postulated but to date the archaeological evidence is inconclusive.

The stone-built London Bridge, once famous for its houses and the heads of traitors and with a chapel dedicated to Thomas Becket – the starting point for pilgrimages to Canterbury – was started in 1176. With its nineteen arches springing from wide masonry piers rising from the river bed it was a barrier to navigation and to the free flow of the tide until its replacement and demolition in 1832.

The Romans established a network of roads across the country that rapidly fell into decay,

2.1 Statue of Father Thames in Terrace Gardens, Richmond. Coade Stone, John Bacon, 1775. Undated photograph. (Richmond Local Studies Collection, LCF 21311)

'In that blest moment from his oozy bed
Old father Thames advanced his rev'rend head
His tresses drop'd with dew, and o'er the stream
His shining horns diffus'd a golden gleam…'
Alexander Pope, *Windsor Forest*

and even after the establishment from the seventeenth century onwards of turnpike roads, rivers – and especially the Thames – remained well into the eighteenth century the most comfortable and certain means of transport for those who could afford to be carried on them. The mediaeval and later monarchs established a chain of palaces along the river between Greenwich and Windsor – Placentia, the Tower of London, Baynard's Castle, Somerset House, Whitehall, Westminster, Kew, Sheen (Richmond), Hampton Court, Oatlands, and Windsor Castle. The Court of course followed the monarch, and so the aristocracy, princes of the Church, and fashionable society also established their residences on its banks, followed in turn by the architects, builders, gardeners, painters and writers. From Elizabethan times onwards, poets have extolled the Thames:

'Sweete *Themmes* run softly, till I end my song', Edmund Spenser, *Prothalamion* (1596).

'Earth has not anything to show more fair…
The river glideth at his own sweet will'.
William Wordsworth, *Composed upon Westminster Bridge September 3 1802*.

'… I am in paradise', Ray Davies, *Waterloo Sunset* (1967).

In 1988 the Great River Race was inaugurated to celebrate the many past generations of watermen who rowed people and goods up, down and across the river. The race, held annually in September, is open to traditional-style, coxed craft powered by a minimum of four oars or paddles and carrying a passenger. The course is from Millwall in London's Docklands to Ham House opposite Marble Hill and is rowed on an incoming tide. About 300 crews participate (they don't all finish what is a very strenuous race over 21.6 miles), and the fastest times are around an astonishing two hours.

The splendid royal barge designed for Frederick, Prince of Wales, by William Kent in 1731 is now housed in the National Maritime Museum, Greenwich. It is 63 feet (19 metres) in length, and was rowed by twelve oarsmen. The prow, cabin and stern are encrusted with gilded carvings of sea lions, dolphins, scallop shells, mermaids, the Prince of Wales feathers, and the star of the Order of the Garter. Frederick and his wife Princess Augusta, the parents of the future King George III, lived in the White House, Kew, close neighbours to but bitterly estranged from his parents King George II and Queen Caroline at Richmond Lodge, the two royal estates separated at the time only by the ironically-named Love Lane. Richmond Lodge (its site is now under the Royal Mid-Surrey Golf Course in the Old Deer Park) and Kew were favourite residences of George II and George III and their consorts – as Hampton Court had been a favourite palace of the later Stuarts – and so the stretch of the Thames between Kew and Hampton was, for the Long Eighteenth Century especially, particularly prized as a place to live (Fig. 2.2, the 'Chinese' bridge at Hampton Court).

The River Thames was the making of Twickenhamshire: 'This is very fine, but take the river away and it is good for nothing' (an unnamed Frenchman to Pope, quoted by Mavis Batey in *Alexander Pope, The Poet and the Landscape*), and Twickenham, on the Middlesex bank of the Thames upstream of central London, is best observed first from a boat on the river. Failing that it should be viewed from the opposite Surrey bank, in which case where better to start one's observation and contemplation than Richmond Terrace Walk on top of Richmond Hill, 165 feet (50 metres) above the water?

> Heavens! What a goodly Prospect spreads around,
> Of Hills, and Dales, and Woods, and Lawns, and Spires,
> And glittering Towns, and gilded Streams, till all
> The stretching Landskip into smoke decays! (James Thomson, *The Seasons*, 1727)

The gravelled terrace on top of the hill was first laid out formally as a public walk and look-out around the year 1700 and is now included at Grade II* in the Historic England Register. The artist JMW Turner celebrated the view in his painting of 1809, *Thomson's Aeolian Harp* (Manchester City Art Galleries), a romanticised view of the River Thames showing a piping shepherd boy and sheep, dancers in classical dress, and Italian pine trees and fragments of Roman ruins in the foreground, with below them the distinctive curve of the river and a generalised view of the villas and woods and gardens of Twickenham.

Turner designed and built a small villa in Twickenham as a base for his fishing and painting expeditions on the river, Solus or Sandycombe Lodge, recently restored and opened to the public by the Turner's House Trust. He was not, however, the first or last painter to record or interpret the famous view. Orleans House Gallery (see Chapter 8), which houses the Borough art collection, holds a painting of *c*.1720 by Leonard Knyff showing the less-frequently recorded view looking eastwards downstream from Richmond Terrace towards Richmond town, Isleworth and Kew, with Richmond Ferry (superseded in 1777 by Richmond Bridge)

2.2 *The First Bridge at Hampton Court*. Engraving after a pen drawing by Antonio Canaletto, 1760. (Orleans House Gallery, LDORL: 01951). The timber bridge in the chinoiserie style was built as a toll bridge in 1752 by James Clarke and replaced in 1778. The present bridge was built 1930-33.

in the middle ground. The painting *The View from Richmond Hill* (Government Art Collection) by Peter Tillemans of c.1730 shows the view looking both upstream and downstream, with the Ashe family house (Twickenham Meadows, later Cambridge Park, q.v.) prominent in the middle ground. Sir Joshua Reynolds, first President of the Royal Academy, so appreciated the view that in 1771 he commissioned the architect Sir William Chambers to build Wick House on Richmond Terrace, where he lived until his death in 1792.

It was the similarity between the views from the hill overlooking the River Thames and from the hill overlooking the James River in Virginia that inspired William Byrd to give the name Richmond to what became the capital of the one-time English colony and later the American state, a link celebrated in the twinning of the two towns and by an exhibition of modern paintings called *The View: An Exhibition about Richmond Hill*, held at Waterstones in Piccadilly and at Orleans House Gallery in 2003.

The coloured engraving by Grignion after Heckel (Fig. 2.3), *A View from Richmond Hill up the River*, shows figures, horsemen and a coach and pair in the foreground, with below them the flat river valley stretching to the distant Surrey and Berkshire hills, and the broad river, dotted with sailing barges, curving out of sight. Glover's Island and a smaller ait stand in mid-stream, and level with them on the right Middlesex shore stand The Glasshouse or Little Marble Hill (see Chapter 10); upstream are the avenues of Marble Hill House (the house is out of sight), Southend House at the end of Montpelier Row, Orleans House and, beyond, further villas along the bank. On the left Surrey bank are Petersham Meadows and the clearly defined avenues of Ham House. An earlier painting by Jan Siberechts of 1677 in the collection of Lord Hesketh at Easton Neston shows much the same view, with the river

2.3. *A View from Richmond Hill up the River.* Engraving by Charles Grignion after Augustin Heckel, *c.*1752. (Orleans House Gallery, LDORL: 03205)

broad and unembanked and evidently shallow, as cattle are shown wading in mid-stream.

If there are still cattle in Petersham Meadows – albeit no longer wading in mid-stream – only ten miles from Charing Cross, and if the view from Richmond Hill is essentially not much changed from that drawn by Heckel in *c.*1752, that is not merely a matter of chance but rather the result of conscious and deliberate policy over several centuries to celebrate and protect a wonderful and life-enhancing vista (Figs. 2.4 and 2.5):

'A beautiful prospect delights the soul', Joseph Addison, 'Essay on The Pleasures of the Imagination', *The Spectator*, 1712.

In the year 2000 a small book with the striking title *Indignation! The Campaign for Conservation,* by Mavis Batey, David Lambert and Kim Wilkie, was published. The essays start with those on John Ruskin and William Morris and go on to discuss Clough Williams-Ellis and Patrick Abercrombie and other figures prominent in the conservation movement. The book's title comes from the public meetings held in the nineteenth century to protest against what were perceived locally as threatening proposals, known as 'indignation meetings'. The book lists key events in the amenity movement starting with the foundation in 1865 of the Commons and Footpaths Preservation Society and with the campaigns in the 1870s to preserve from development and keep open to the public Epping Forest and Hampstead Heath. In 1893 was founded SCAPA – the Society for Checking the Abuses of Public Advertising – which, improbable as it may seem, helped lead to the passing in 1902 of The Richmond Petersham and Ham Open Spaces Act.

2.4. The view from Richmond Hill looking upstream over Petersham and Twickenham. Photograph by Chris Sumner, 2020

In 1898 *The Thames Valley Times* reported that Mr Glover, a boatman who owned the island that bears his name and that stands in the middle of the famous view, had threatened to sell it for the erection of advertising hoardings. In the same year the Marble Hill estate was bought by William Cunard of the famous shipping line, who had already bought for redevelopment the nearby Mount Lebanon and Orleans House estates. By the summer of 1901 machinery had been brought in and work started on laying out roads and sewers at the Richmond Road end of the park. However, under the aegis of the London County Council a meeting was held in July 1901 at the old County Hall in Spring Gardens, and Cunard and his sons agreed to suspend work and to sell the estate on the immediate payment of £3,500 – a deposit provided by the LCC – and finally sold the estate for £70,000. The purchase money came from the LCC, Surrey CC, Middlesex CC, Richmond Corporation, Twickenham UDC and other bodies and private donors. The conveyance to the LCC took place on 1st August 1901 and the park was opened to the public on 30th May 1903, events celebrated in 2002 by English Heritage with a modern art exhibition and catalogue, *Arcadia in the City at Marble Hill*.

The centenary of the 1902 Act for the preservation of the view from Richmond Hill was also marked by the publication by the Thames Landscape Strategy of *Arcadia in the City: A Hill with a View* and by *An Arcadian Miscellany* held at the Royal Star and Garter Home – a celebration in words and music of the Arcadian Thames. The Act, a pioneering piece of environmental legislation, was the first to protect a view, and in doing so acknowledged the importance of public feeling and recognised that the protection of an amenity for the benefit of the general public should sometimes override private property rights, since its aim was to prevent built development from taking place in designated areas along both banks of the river below the hill.

Arcadia was a mountainous district of the Peloponnese and the legendary birthplace of Pan, a barren rocky landscape that with the end of winter breaks suddenly into life with

2.5. The view from Richmond Hill looking upstream. Photograph by Chris Sumner, 2020

2.6. The view downstream from Radnor Gardens towards Eel Pie Island and St Mary's Church, Twickenham. Photograph by Chris Sumner, 2018

2.7. The summerhouse, formerly of Cross Deep House, in Radnor Gardens. Photograph by Chris Sumner, 2018

2.8. Eel Pie Island from the riverside terrace at York House. Photograph by Chris Sumner, 2018

green vegetation and colourful wild flowers that include tulips, anemones, cyclamen and terrestrial orchids. In poetic fantasy it represents a pastoral paradise, and was appropriated by the Elizabethan and later poets as an ideal land of perpetual spring where humankind and nature coexist in near-perfect harmony. There is always of course a snake in the grass or a worm in the bud – 'Et in Arcadia ego' (which may be translated as 'I too was once in Arcadia', or as the more sinister 'Even in Arcadia I, Death, am present'), as poets and painters have liked to remind us – but the creation of gardens is partly to do with the creation of myths, and the myth of Arcadia translated from the mountains of southern Greece to the gentle green Thames Valley is very persuasive. As the late Mavis Batey, one-time President of the Garden History Society, wrote in the opening paragraph of *Arcadia in the City*, 'The panoramic view from Richmond Hill sweeps over a stretch of the Thames that unites virtually the whole history of English landscape and garden design – it is the cradle of the English landscape movement.'

Arcadian Thames by Mavis Batey, Henrietta Buttery, David Lambert and Kim Wilkie (1994), describes the riverside landscape between Hampton and Kew. It stems directly from *The Thames Landscape Strategy: Hampton to Kew*, a long-term planning study of the river and its banks devised principally by Kim Wilkie and funded initially by the Countryside Commission, English Heritage and the Royal Fine Art Commission, which was launched by the Minister for Local Government and Planning, John Gummer, in June 1994 at the Royal Botanic Gardens, Kew.

The terms 'Middlesex bank' and 'Surrey bank' may call for some explanation; historically, Twickenham was in the County of Middlesex, and Richmond in the County of Surrey. When Greater London was created in 1965 from the older and much smaller County of London, Middlesex ceased to exist as an administrative county and along with parts of Surrey, Kent, Essex and Hertfordshire was absorbed into the newly-enlarged capital, which now comprises the City of London and thirty-two London Boroughs. Twickenham then became part of LB Richmond upon Thames, the only borough to straddle the river.

The Thames Landscape Strategy – now extended up river to Weybridge in Surrey – is supported and partly funded by the associated local authorities and by national organisations, but some of its funding and much of its strength and effectiveness derive from engagement with local communities for whom the river is an essential part of their lives and often livelihoods. The Thames has many functions; for the purposes of this book its main function is historical and aesthetic in that it unites a series of major and minor landscapes that are mostly now in the public or semi-public domain and which have been preserved for the enjoyment of the local inhabitants and all Londoners and visitors from elsewhere and abroad. It is a landscape to enjoy by boat or on foot or by bicycle. The river's tendency to flood has kept main roads to higher ground well away from the banks, so while main roads (and railways) cross it by bridge at a few points, the riverside is largely free of cars and other traffic, which is of course one of its great delights. Hammerton's Ferry links Ham House and Marble Hill for pedestrians and cyclists, Bell Hill Ferry links Hampton and Hurst Park, and there is a footbridge at Teddington Lock. Until the nineteenth century, though, the Thames was a major transport highway linking London both eastwards to the coast and westwards inland to beyond Oxford.

The river is still important as a highway, but the emphasis in the upper reaches is now on leisure, sightseeing and sport rather than on the transport of people and goods. Nevertheless, boats are still built and repaired on Eel Pie Island and next to Richmond Bridge, reminders of the earlier, hugger-mugger mixture of industry, brewing, glass-making, tanning, glue-boiling, eel and fish traps and market gardens that was largely supplanted by politer uses as fashionable society and suburbia moved in. The river is a large elemental force that has to be managed for many purposes – not least, public safety – and in the relatively short stretch past Twickenhamshire displays three quite disparate characters. The river above Teddington Lock is normally non-tidal, and generally placid although increasingly prone to flooding in wet winters. Below Richmond Lock the river is tidal, with two tides a day with a rise and fall of up to seventeen feet (5.2 metres) or more, depending on the time of year, the state of the moon, and weather conditions. Richmond Lock (Richmond Half-Tide Weir and Footbridge), opened in 1894 and managed by the Port of London Authority, was constructed to hold back a five-foot (1.5 metres) head of water to prevent the river above it from draining down completely at low tide – as it is permitted to do in December each year during the so-called 'draw down'. The speed and direction of the tide are still a significant factor in the use of the river, and were even more so when boats were dependent on wind-, horse-, or most likely, man-power. The Tillemans painting of the Thames at Twickenham (see Fig. 1.6) includes a team of five men trudging along the towing path and hauling a barge upstream, its sail hanging slack.

The demolition of the mediaeval London Bridge changed the dynamics of the river, speeding the tidal flow, and since 1984 the Thames Barrier at Woolwich has helped control flooding by holding back tidal surges driving up the estuary from the North Sea. Nevertheless, climate change has increased the frequency and severity of flooding along the Thames, exacerbated by faster run-off of storm water through the past ill-advised straightening and culverting of streams and ditches, the backfilling of ponds, and the continuing loss of open space to building and roads and car parking. The towpath between Richmond and Ham and the roadway past York House on Twickenham Riverside are regularly impassable for an hour or two.

The Thames Landscape Strategy includes projects as well as planning policies. In January 2020 a new project was introduced – Rewilding Arcadia – the purpose of which is to deliver and explain a series of nature-based flood risk management projects that are designed to restore the lost flood plain to reconnect water, people, heritage and wildlife with the natural cycles of the Thames. A *bon mot* that I recall from my school days is 'in the summer the river is at the bottom of my garden, and in the winter my garden is at the bottom of the river', and that is increasingly the case. The churchyard wall of St Mary's Church, Twickenham, bears plaques to exceptionally high floods over the centuries, but floods are becoming more and more the norm rather than the exception. Historically, Petersham Meadows and Ham Lands were flood meadows, as were Twickenham Meadows/Cambridge Park, Marble Hill and the riverside grounds of Pope's Villa, Radnor House, Strawberry Hill and most of the other riverside properties; the houses were built on land high enough to protect them from all but the most exceptional floods, but the grounds were periodically inundated before the banks were raised in the nineteenth and twentieth centuries.

Just downstream of our study area, the grounds of Syon House are still unembanked and function as traditional water meadows with their own distinctive flora and fauna. It is a remarkable sight still to see cattle wading at high tide in the meadows beyond the haha that protects the house and gardens. Syon Park and Kew Gardens (formerly Richmond Gardens) opposite exemplify uniquely a landscape, remodelled by Lancelot 'Capability' Brown in the 1750s for the Duke of Northumberland and in the 1760s for King George III, that incorporates the river as a dynamic and constantly changing feature of the landscape that unifies rather than divides the two estates.

The old Baroque formality destroyed – not without censure even at the time – by Brown to create a 'natural' landscape at Syon and Kew still prevails on a much larger scale upriver at Hampton Court, Bushy Park and Ham House (see Fig. 1.4). It was the formal network of avenues, leading out into the wider countryside and framing views of and across the river to landmarks and further gardens and estates beyond, that inspired Kim Wilkie for the Royal Fine Art Commission's Thames Connection Exhibition in 1991 and that seized the attention and enthusiasm of local groups conscious of a need for integrated policies for the river and its banks, leading in turn to the formation of a working party and the subsequent publication of *The Thames Landscape Strategy*.

It is beyond the scope of this essay to catalogue all that the TLS has achieved since its launch in 1994, and the TLS document and regular updates and reports are readily available on its website. In association with its many official partners and community groups and through its supporting charity The Father Thames Trust it has raised many millions of pounds and directed hundreds of thousands of volunteer hours for environmental improvements to the riverside and for educational projects. A very limited selection of TLS projects includes the replanting and management of the Ham avenues and encouraging a mowing regime using heavy horses rather than tractors, installing 'bat-friendly' lighting along the Twickenham bank past Marble Hill, supporting the repair and restoration of Orleans House Gallery, Pope's Grotto, Strawberry Hill, and Garrick's Temple and Lawn, and clearing and managing the water meadows at Hampton Court Home Park to improve flood control and encourage wildlife, and to act as an educational resource for schoolchildren and adults alike.

CHAPTER THREE

The Garden of David Garrick's Villa at Hampton
Suzannah Fleming

From the moment David Garrick made his astonishing theatrical debut in 1741 in the role of Shakespeare's *Richard III*, and up until his retirement in 1776, he was the dominant figure on the English stage. Through his extraordinary career as actor/manager he became the central figure in the revival of Shakespeare and his plays. Moreover, his unique professional stature was such that he rapidly rose to pre-eminence in the social and artistic life of eighteenth-century London. Always uncannily anticipating public taste he revolutionised acting technique by bringing it far closer to *nature*. In this period the shift in taste away from the old formality (and all that represented) in favour of nature and natural forms became a prevailing principle in the arts – common to both the theatre and garden-making.

Garrick (1717–1779) acquired his Thames-side villa at Hampton in 1754 and promptly proceeded to create for himself and his wife Eva Maria (née Veigel) a splendid country retreat befitting a man of his extraordinary status (Fig. 3.1 and see also Fig. 1.10). The quest for a suitable property had begun in earnest in the summer of 1753 when his two brothers Peter and George were each dispatched to search the estate market throughout various parts of England. In a letter to Peter he asked whether there was a river nearby a particular house for sale in Derbyshire 'for I must have a River' and insisted his brother consider 'what kind of a house, what Wood, what prospect?' Here Garrick set out his chief requirements: 'I own I love a good Situation prodigiously & I think the four great Requisites to make one are, Wood, Water, Extent & inequality of Ground'. In this same letter he added a playful note 'you mind Me, there must be a little Taste for Us'!

Before long the search was focused closer to London, initially Hertfordshire. In September 1753 Garrick reported he was stepping away from purchasing The Grove estate near Watford in Hertfordshire. It seems he had 'conceived Resentment & dislike against the place' having been told that 'Persons of Family & Fortune are about it' and he added 'I shall therefore not contend with my betters'. Hinting at more modest ambitions he then announced: 'I shall content Myself with ye Bank of ye Thames – I have a place in my Eye that I think will Suit us'. As to why he settled on this particular Hampton property is not recorded precisely, but it seems that it answered many of his specific requirements. From a practical standpoint, Hampton was close enough to London (i.e. to the Drury Lane Theatre and the Garricks' town house in Southampton Street) to make a convenient escape. It was also far enough away to be considered sufficiently rural and tranquil. Perhaps Garrick was cognisant of Alexander Pope's words: 'Blest Thames shores the brightest beauties yield| Feed here my lambs, I'll seek no distant field'.

By September 1754 the Garricks had already moved in and he wrote to his brother Peter from Hampton to explain: 'I agree to ye Gardiner's proposals & hope in a Day or two to

3.1. *A View of the Seat of the late David Garrick Esq. at Hampton, with a prospect of the Temple of Shakespeare in the Garden.* Engraving for *The Modern Universal British Traveller*, 1779. (Suzannah Fleming Collection)

have notice of his coming, for I should be glad to see him settled here before I repair to London to begin ye Acting Season – I hope he has a good Character in his Neighbourhood, for he will be left in trust of Every thing, house, Garden, Workmen &c &c'.

In 1777 the poet/playwright Hannah More, who stayed with the Garricks for long periods of time over many years, wrote the *Ode to Dragon, Mr Garrick's House-Dog at Hampton* in which she described the gardener known as 'Mr Bowden' in the following terms:

> Though fired with innocent ambition,
> Bowden, great Nature's Rhetorician,
> More flowers than Burke produces;
> And though he's skill'd more roots to find,
> Than ever stock'd an Hebrew's Mind,
> And knows their various uses.

Early on in his project Garrick apparently expressed an interest in the gardening of Horace Walpole at nearby Strawberry Hill – presumably after a visit. In a letter in 1755 Walpole remarked to a friend that he had 'contracted a sort of intimacy with Garrick, who is my neighbour. He affects to study my taste'. Garrick must have admired something of the novelty of Walpole's planting of a 'serpentine walk bordered by flowering shrubs' – a fashionable idea that Garrick certainly used in his walks in the grounds at Hampton.

Another of Garrick's friends, the artist William Hogarth, provided an extremely important theoretical influence in the making of the Hampton garden, as well as several other

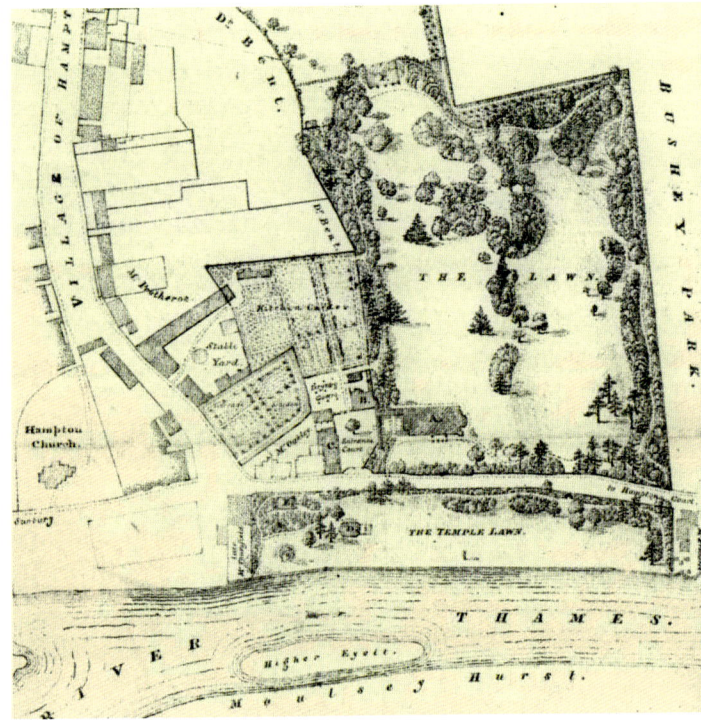

3.2. Plan of Garrick's Villa (detail) showing 'The Lawn' and 'Temple Lawn'. Drawn by J Thompson, c.1770. Lithograph, from the sales particulars published 1822. (Orleans House Gallery, LDORL: 00368)

new gardens in the area. His long-anticipated *Analysis of Beauty* was published in 1753, yet as early as 1745 Hogarth introduced into his famous *Self-portrait with Pug* the mysterious 'Line of Beauty and Grace'. In the painting, as well as subsequent prints of the image, this serpentine line was shown as a relaxed S-curve. However, rather than being a mere two-dimensional squiggle, it was painted with a shadow; therefore, Hogarth clearly intended it to have form and substance. Moreover, it was seen to *undulate*. Interestingly, in the composition of the painting, Hogarth's oval portrait rests on volumes of Swift, Milton, and Shakespeare. Here his message was that his art, like the work of the British poets, and even the 'Line of Beauty' itself, were all of indigenous origin and inspiration.

In the 1750s the layout of Garrick's garden would have been viewed as a very fashionable addition to the Twickenham/Hampton riverscape. Almost twenty years later Henrietta Pye, a local resident and author, described Garrick's walks at Hampton as 'laid out in the modern taste' (Fig. 3.2). Contemporary engravings of the garden show an *undulating* lawn with many fine trees and a serpentine path bordered by flowering shrubs and evergreens. The trees included cedar of Lebanon, fir, chestnut, elm, oak, yew, and a tulip tree. There was, of course, the famous mulberry (supposedly grown from a slip taken from Shakespeare's own mulberry at Stratford-upon-Avon), as well as the weeping willows and the cypresses.

In the summer of 1755 Garrick initiated works to erect his 'Temple of Shakespeare', a building clearly designed as the focal point of his riverside 'Temple Lawn' and prominently shown in all contemporary engravings and drawings throughout the eighteenth century. Garrick conveyed in a letter to his brother: 'We are at present over head & Ears in dirt & Mortar: how far it will be prudent to leave the Workmen in this Situation, we shall know in a little time'. By October 1756 Horace Walpole was corresponding again on the subject of Garrick – this time in anticipation of a visit to Hampton: 'John and I are just going to

3.3. Interior of Garrick's Temple to Shakespeare showing the British Museum cast of the Roubiliac statue of Shakespeare. Photograph by Suzannah Fleming

Garricks with a grove of cypresses in our hands, like the Kentish men at the conquest. He has built a graceful Temple to his master Shakespeare and I am going to adorn the outside since his modesty would not let me decorate within'. There is no doubt that from its original conception Garrick intended the Temple for a dedication to the Bard. After the building was completed, to preside over the interior, Garrick commissioned a life-sized marble statue of Shakespeare from Roubiliac, the leading sculptor in England at the time. The statue was finally finished and installed in the Shakespeare Temple in July 1758. Garrick is said to have set the pose himself showing Shakespeare at the precise moment of inspiration (Fig. 3.3).

The Temple was conspicuous not only for its dramatic riverside setting, but also its resemblance to the late Lord Burlington's much earlier Ionic Temple in the garden at Chiswick. The Burlington connection is significant, for in 1749 Garrick had married Lord and Lady Burlington's young protegée Eva Maria Veigel, the beautiful Viennese ballet dancer sometimes known by her stage name 'La Violette' or 'Violetta'. Since coming to England in 1746 she had lived under the guardianship of the Burlingtons at Chiswick and at Burlington House, and was by all accounts treated as if she were their own daughter (rumours circulated that she was an illegitimate offspring of Lord Burlington). Garrick himself eventually became a trusted member of the Burlington circle, and the newly-wed couple spent part of their honeymoon at Chiswick, having already conducted much of their formal courtship there.

It would seem plausible that the Burlingtons (along with their circle of cousins and affiliates) – and even Chiswick itself – had a significant influence on Garrick's taste in gardens and architecture. But there was something more significant – Garrick would have fully recognised Lord Burlington's role in convening a 'Committee' in the 'publick-spirited'

3.4. Garrick's Temple to Shakespeare from the Temple Lawn. Photograph by Suzannah Fleming

campaign to erect a national monument to the long-neglected Shakespeare in Westminster Abbey. This project had been initiated in 1737 by Burlington's cousin, Susanna Ashley Cooper (née Noel), Countess of Shaftesbury (founder of the 'Shakespear Ladies Club'), and was finally completed in 1741 with the raising of Shakespeare's monument in Poets' Corner. During this period Lady Shaftesbury created her own contemplative garden building dedicated to Shakespeare (and his works) in the walks of her newly laid out pleasure grounds at St Giles's House in Dorset. It was in this context that Garrick made his famous stage debut in 1741 in a powerful Shakespearean role. It may seem fitting therefore that Garrick would align himself with the Burlington realm of influence, and choose as an architectural model the temple in the grounds at Chiswick as an inspiration for his own temple at Hampton.

Traditionally, it has been assumed that Robert Adam was the architect of the Shakespeare Temple at Hampton. However, Adam was on the Grand Tour in Italy between 1754 and 1758. Adam's involvement occurred first in 1765, and finally in 1775. Garrick commissioned alterations to the villa from the designs of Adam to create a classical frontage, in addition to the erection of an Orangery at the far end of the 'Back Lawn'. Earlier, Robert Adam and his brother John both paid a friendly visit to Garrick at Hampton in 1759. John later wrote that he thought the Shakespeare Temple was 'much too large for this small piece of ground, and is not elegant either outside or inside, though the prospect to the river is most delightful.' It is unlikely that he would be quite so critical of a building that his brother had designed.

Lancelot 'Capability' Brown has also recently been suggested as a possible architect of the Temple. Brown is alleged to have advised Garrick on part of the layout of the grounds at Hampton, yet there is only anecdotal evidence for this – and nothing that even suggests that Brown had a hand in the design of the Temple.

However, Brown was certainly a friend of the actor, and it seems that a story was frequently related by Mrs Garrick herself to visitors while touring in the garden that '*Capability Brown* was consulted as to the communication of these grounds with those by the water'. She recalled that her husband 'had an idea of having a bridge to pass over the [public] road, similar to the one at Paine's Hill; but this was objected to by Capability Brown, who proposed to have a tunnel cut.' It seems her husband 'at first did not like that idea; but Dr Johnson observed Davey! Davey! what can't be over-done may be under-done!' The grotto-tunnel feature was indeed completed sometime before 1759 when the Adam brothers visited, but the extent to which Brown may have been responsible for either designing the details and/or implementing the works is unknown. The standing question then is what was Garrick's relationship with Brown – friendly or professional or a mixture of both? A clue lies in a poem Garrick wrote to Richard Owen Cambridge in August 1770 in which he says 'With the great Planner *Brown*, who's himself ye best Plan, I Envy his Genius, yet doat on ye Man'. In the only known letter from Garrick to Brown in February 1776, it becomes clear Garrick was annoyed with him (as a friend who had been discourteous by not showing up to a theatre performance): 'You make Me & my Wife mad – you shall be prefer'd to the whole body of Nobility, if you will give us Notice but one day of yr Coming – I have kept places till 12 o'Clock the two last times of my Playing […] – Don't use me so again for I love & esteem You & am moreover oblig'd to You…'. On 13 December 1780, shortly after Garrick's death, the editors of the *Gazetteer and New Daily Advertiser* commented that Mr & Mrs Garrick had in fact laid out their own grounds at Hampton, with Brown contributing only a weeping willow on the river's edge, and added: 'This single addition Brown compared to punctuation, and not without some felicity of phrase, called it a dot, the presence and operation of which, as it were, made sense of the rest'.

In an edition of Lyson's *Environs of London* it is recalled of Garrick's time at Hampton that 'the gardens were laid out with much taste, under his [Garrick's] own direction'. It is indeed entirely possible that Horace Walpole conveyed to Garrick at an early stage his belief that 'the possessor [of an estate], if he has any taste, must be the best designer of his own improvements'. And very late in her life Mrs Garrick, who outlived her husband by forty-three years, continued to maintain the gardens as they had first been laid out in the mid-eighteenth century (Fig. 3.4). It was written elsewhere that her 'greatest pride was in promenading her picturesque grounds and explaining with enthusiastic delight the age and date of every tall tree, planted by herself and Mr Garrick'.

Away from the usual theatrical season and social rounds in and around London, the Garricks are known to have occasionally visited some of the finest large landscape gardens throughout England. Hagley, Stourhead, Mount Edgcumbe, Chatsworth, Wentworth Woodhouse, and Londesborough (Lord Burlington's Yorkshire seat) were all places where they were received as welcome guests. Burlington had a yew avenue with a bowling green on one side at Londesborough that was later called 'Garrick's Walk' by the family. When Garrick visited Stourhead later in life it was recounted that 'Being particularly charmed with the Grotto, Garrick declared he should like it for his burying-place, upon which one of the company wished him to write his own Epitaph'. The resulting document is labelled 'On the death of David Garrick after being struck in the Temple at Stourhead by a great bough of the laurel'. He also wrote a poem titled *Exclamation on first seeing Mount Edgecombe*: ''Tis the haunt of the Muses, the Mount of Parnassus. Fame lies: 'twas not Stratford; this, this is

3.5. *Mr and Mrs Garrick by the Shakespeare Temple at Hampton.* Painting by Johann Zoffany, 1762. (Reproduced by kind permission of The Garrick Club, London)

the spot Where Genius on *Nature* our Shakespeare begot'.

During these visits to the great aristocratic estates there would have been a degree of formality expected in the proceedings. As a point of honour Garrick would have worked hard to charm his aristocratic hosts and oblige them … which usually meant entertaining them in some way. However, the atmosphere of the Hampton scene was always aimed at informality and rest. This was immortalised in two exquisite conversation pieces by Johann Zoffany, painted in the summer of 1762 (now in the collection of The Garrick Club). Each painting captures a tranquil moment in the garden; one shows David and Eva Maria Garrick relaxing by the Shakespeare Temple, with the Roubiliac statue of Shakespeare visible through the open door (Fig. 3.5), and in the other the couple are shown seated on the Temple lawn taking tea with family and friends (Fig. 3.6). Two additional smaller paintings by Zoffany each show different parts of the garden and villa. One of these depicts Garrick writing on the villa-side entrance of the grotto tunnel while crouched under the shade of a large tree, while his gardener, Bowden, rolls the turf in the background. In the other, Garrick's two young nieces are at play in front of the riverside entrance of the grotto-tunnel. All four intimate scenes once hung in the dining room of Garrick's London house in the Adelphi. They are perhaps most remarkable for having just exactly the right touch of the theatrical about them.

3.6. *A View in Hampton Garden with Mr and Mrs Garrick taking tea.* Painting by Johann Zoffany, 1762. (Reproduced by kind permission of The Garrick Club, London)

In 1757 Garrick introduced a new comic character, 'Lord Chalkstone', into his play *Lethe, or Aesop in the Shades*, first produced in 1740. The character of Chalkstone, often played by Garrick himself, was a sort of amalgam of the various old aristocratic 'Patriots' of the previous generation – the Cobhams and Burlingtons – whom both Garrick and Capability Brown would have encountered at the start of their careers – but freshly animated by the spirit of the new generation of landowner/improver/gardener. And no doubt Garrick drew from his own recent experience of laying out his fashionable garden. In the farce, the gout-stricken peer complains as he waits to cross the River Styx into the Elysian Fields that it is laid out without taste and should have been given a 'serpentine sweep' to improve its 'capabilities' (a clear allusion to Brown). He continues: 'You should clear the wood to the left, and clump the trees to the right: in short, the whole wants variety, extent, contrast, and inequality'. As he advances to the edge of the stage, Garrick (as Lord Chalkstone) peers down into the orchestra pit: 'Upon my word, here's a fine ha-ha!…and a most curious collection of evergreens and flowering shrubs' (Fig. 3.7).

As both a physical and comic model for the character of Chalkstone, Garrick probably had no further to look than his friend Colonel George Bodens, who was regarded as a 'great wit' and former drinking companion of Lord Cobham of Stowe. His chronic gout apparently contributed to his famous lack of 'agility'. Bodens was the son of Charles Bodens, an influen-

3.7. David Garrick in the character of Lord Chalkstone in the farce Lethe; or Aesop in the Shades. Engraving (detail), 1757. (Suzannah Fleming Collection)

tial courtier and friend of Frederick, Prince of Wales, who in 1732 penned a satire titled *The Modish Couple,* which was critical of George II and Queen Caroline. It was performed at The Drury Lane Theatre but closed immediately. In an inventory of the Garrick estate in 1779 George Bodens is identified as the gentleman with a cane seated on the 'Temple Lawn' next to Mrs Garrick in Zoffany's painting (Fig. 3.6). Someone with the initials 'G.B.' (presumably George Bodens) compiled an extensive 'List of flowering trees & flowering shrubs', along with 'evergreens' for the Hampton garden. On the list are such as catalpa, flowering ash, tulip tree, sweet almond, 'Perfumed Cherry' and 'Sweet scented Crab' and there are various sorts of lilacs, viburnums and laburnums, in addition to various 'Sumachs' and 'Dog Wood' trees from North America. There is also a section of 'pretty Evergreens' such as Italian cypress, cedar, arbutus, Portuguese laurel, hollies and '5 sorts of Laurastinus'. The document includes hundreds of available plants – some with a range of prices – and is now preserved amongst the Garrick estate papers at the Hereford City Museum. Evidently an intimate friend of Garrick the author of the list ends on a personal note: 'But for the Violetta [Mrs Garrick's former stage name], you are so happy to have that already, the finest in the world, the Beauty of your garden. *Supereminet omnes.*'

Sometime after 1757, William Hogarth designed alterations to an already elaborate chair intended to form the interior decoration of the Shakespeare Temple. These alterations included an oval relief of the Bard (supposedly carved from the wood of his mulberry tree) set into its backrest. The back of the chair was also then surmounted by a dramatic theatrical trophy. It was referred to as 'The President of the Shakespeare Club chair', and on May Day each year Garrick would distribute money, cake, and wine to the poor children of Hampton whilst seated in the Temple next to Shakespeare's statue. Over the years, various interesting Elizabethan and Jacobean relics were introduced to the contents of the Temple, such as a glove, a salt-cellar, and a signet ring with the initials 'W.S.'. Garrick apparently believed these to have once belonged to Shakespeare himself. To the display were eventually added a number of elaborately carved modern artefacts – mostly made of mulberry wood and associated with the Shakespeare Jubilee at Stratford in 1769.

Mrs Mary Delany visited the Garricks at Hampton in 1770 in the company of her friend the Duchess of Portland. Her subsequent correspondence records a most enlightening impression of the Garricks, their perceived position in society, their Villa, and the riverside garden:

> Mr Garrick did the honours of his house *very respectfully,* and tho' in high spirits seemed sensible of the honour done them … As to Mrs Garrick, the more one sees her the better one must like her; she seems *never* to depart from a perfect propriety of behaviour…I cannot help looking on her as a *wonderful creature,* considering all circumstances relating to her. The house is singular (which you know I like), and seems to owe its prettiness and elegance to her good taste… on the whole it has the air of belonging to a *genius.* We had an excellent dinner and when over went directly to the garden – a piece of irregular ground sloping down to the Thames, very well laid out, and planted for shade and shelter and an opening [the grotto-tunnel] to the river which appears beautiful from that spot, and from Shakespeare's Temple at the end of the improvement, where we drank tea and coffee, and where there is a very fine statue of Shakespear in white marble, and a great chair with a large carved frame, that was *Shakespeare's own chair,* made for him on some particular occasion, with a medallion of him fixed in the back. Many were the relics we saw of the favourite poet.

Michael Symes mentioned a perceived theatrical character of the Zoffany depictions of Garrick's garden in his article in 1986 on Garrick's villa and noted: 'The Temple at Hampton served both as a celebration of Shakespeare and also a symbol of the inspiration and cause of Garrick's success as an actor. The conflation of garden and theatre is therefore at its most potent and apparent at this point'. Along similar lines, a critic had proclaimed as early as 1757 that Garrick had rejuvenated the English stage by establishing 'Nature, Shakespeare, and himself'.

The stage-like quality of the scene would have been especially pronounced during a summer's evening in 1774 when one of the London journals reported that the Garricks had given a 'splendid entertainment, or Fete Champetre…The company included a great number of the Nobility and Gentry', who enjoyed 'a concert and an elegant firework display. The gardens, the grotto-tunnel, and the Temple of Shakespeare were illuminated with 6000 lamps.' This must have had an enchanting and highly theatrical effect. For some of the same guests, it must also have been ample compensation for the exceptionally bad weather that had spoiled Garrick's Shakespeare Jubilee at Stratford-upon-Avon five years before.

The restoration of Garrick's Temple to Shakespeare in 1998–2000, including the 'Life of Garrick' exhibition and a copy of Roubiliac's statue mounted permanently within the Temple, provides a fitting memorial to Britain's greatest actor-manager. The layout and plantings of the garden have been based on both the 'G.B.' (George Bodens) list of trees and shrubs, and on eighteenth-century illustrations. Here, in a beautifully re-created garden setting, is displayed a visual record not only of Garrick's illustrious career, his image, his garden, and his life at Hampton, but also evidence of how, by his talent, he made Shakespeare central to the British theatrical tradition.

CHAPTER FOUR

Strawberry Hill
Chris Sumner

Where silver Thames round Twit'nam meads
His winding current sweetly leads;
Twit'nam, the Muse's fav'rite seat,
Twit'nam, the Graces' lov'd retreat… (Walpole)

Horace Walpole called Twickenham his seaport in miniature: the 1755 drawing of him in his library by Johann Heinrich Müntz (Fig. 4.1) shows – through the open Gothic casement – Walpole's water meadows and the unembanked River Thames with a barge sailing downstream towards Eel Pie Island, the parish church of St Mary's and Richmond Hill.

Horace was born in 1717 and died in 1797 at the age of seventy-nine. His father was Sir Robert Walpole, First Lord of the Treasury and first minister to George I and George II from 1721 to 1742, and thus one of the most powerful men in the country. Sir Robert was MP for King's Lynn and the family home was at Houghton in Norfolk, which was rebuilt in a grand and lavish manner to designs in the fashionable Palladian style by Colen Campbell, Thomas Ripley, James Gibbs and William Kent between 1721 and 1735. Many contemporaries disapproved of Sir Robert's conspicuous extravagance, and it has been suggested that it was Walpole's Houghton rather than Canons, the magnificent but evanescent palace of the Duke of Chandos at Edgware, that was satirised by Alexander Pope in his *Epistle to Burlington*. Be that as it may, Horace's background was splendid, moneyed, and at the centre of the Whig establishment. As First Lord of the Treasury, Sir Robert lived at No 10 Downing Street and also had a house at 22 Arlington Street, St James's. Horace, as the youngest son, had no great expectations of inheriting the Houghton estate, but did eventually succeed to the title of the Fourth Earl of Orford in 1791 at the age of seventy-four on the death of his nephew the Third Earl, who died insane, having squandered his fortune and sold Sir Robert's collection of pictures to Catherine the Great of Russia.

The young Horace was sent to Eton, which he seems to have survived and even recalled with affection and nostalgia, helped – as a weedy and rather effeminate youth – by his father's powerful position, and supported by his friends – the so-called Quadruple Alliance – who included Thomas Gray, later to become the famous poet and with whom Horace travelled to Italy on the Grand Tour and with whom he was to quarrel and be later reconciled. The four members of the Alliance adopted secret names, and Horace became the pastoral shepherd Celadon. He went on from Eton to Cambridge in 1735, where he was at King's for four years and learnt Italian and studied anatomy and civil law, but left without showing much application or taking a degree. In 1741 he was elected MP for Callington in

4.1. Portrait of Horace Walpole in his library with the River Thames seen through the open window. Engraved by W Greatbatch after the *c.*1755 drawing by Johann Müntz. (Chris Sumner Collection)

Cornwall, in 1754 MP for Castle Rising, and from 1757 to 1768 he represented King's Lynn, very much the Walpole pocket borough.

His fortune, which by the end of his life was considerable, was derived from various patent places he held under the Crown into which he had been nominated during his father's years of power. The sinecures he held included the offices of Controller of the Pipe, Clerk of the Estreats, and Usher of the Exchequer (Brian Fothergill, *The Strawberry Hill Set: Horace Walpole and His Circle*).

As a Member of Parliament and a rich landowner at a time when Britain's power and wealth were expanding rapidly, he was under no illusions about the source of much of the country's wealth. In his letter to Horace Mann of 25 February 1750 he wrote,

> We have been sitting this fortnight on the African Company. We, the British Senate, the Temple of Liberty, and bulwark of Protestant Christianity, have this fortnight been pondering methods to make more effectual that horrid traffic of selling negroes. It has appeared to us that six and forty thousand of these wretches are sold every year to our plantations alone! It chills one's blood – I would not have to say that I voted in it, for the continent of America!

Three years before writing that letter, in 1747 and at the age of thirty, he took a lease on a modest brick-built house with five acres (two ha.) of land around it near the River Thames between Twickenham and Teddington. The district, a short distance upstream from London and close to the Royal Palaces of Hampton Court, Richmond and Kew, was aristocratic, fashionable, literary and artistic, with a series of grand villas in extensive grounds on the banks of the Thames. Twickenham's most famous resident, the poet Alexander Pope, had died three years earlier in 1744, but his villa with its famous garden and grotto survived only a five-minute walk away.

Informally known as Chopped Straw Hall, the property, about fifty years old, had belonged to Mrs Chenevix, a seller of trinkets with a shop at Charing Cross. Walpole changed the name to Strawberry Hill and over the following decades transformed the house into a Gothic villa and the chief setting for his collection of books, art and antiquities. It became one of the most famous English buildings of the eighteenth century. Walpole wrote in June 1747 to his friend and cousin Henry Conway:

> It is a little plaything house I got out of Mrs Chenevix's shop and it is the prettiest bauble that you ever saw. It is set in enamelled meadows with filigree hedges… Two delightful roads that you would call dusty supply me continually with coaches and chaises; barges as solemn as barons of the exchequer move under my window; Richmond Hill and Ham-walks bound my prospects… Dowagers as plenty as flounders inhabit all around, and Pope's ghost is just now skimming under my window by a most poetical moonlight. I have about land enough to keep such a farm as Noah's when he set up in the ark with a pair of each kind.

The hill at Strawberry Hill, like the hill at nearby Marble Hill, is a relative term, but provided sufficient elevation to afford a prospect from the house and to raise it above flood level. Horace continued to develop his house and garden for fifty years until his death at his town house in Berkeley Square in 1797, and in that time increased the size of his estate to forty-six acres, now reduced again to much like the original five acres. To understand the house and garden, both subjects of recent major restoration schemes, it is useful to know something of their history following Walpole's death.

Walpole never married, and initially Strawberry Hill was left for her lifetime to his cousin's daughter the sculptor Anne Seymour Damer. Mrs Damer found the house too expensive to run, and in 1810 she moved to York House in Twickenham and relinquished Strawberry Hill to Walpole's heiress Lady Waldegrave, the granddaughter of his brother Edward. Lady Waldegrave's illegitimate grandson John married Frances Braham in 1839 but died within a year of the marriage, and Frances then married John's (legitimate) brother George, the 7th Earl Waldegrave, shortly after; they had to go to Scotland to marry to avoid the 1835 Act that forbade marriage to a deceased husband's brother. George ran into trouble locally and was jailed not long after his wedding for riotous behaviour and attacking a policeman. He had the good grace to die in 1846, leaving his considerable estates to Frances, but sadly not before he had abandoned Strawberry Hill to dereliction and sold its contents out of spite and, it is said, as a reproach to the Twickenham magistrates who committed him to the Assizes.

The sale in 1842 of Horace's library, furniture, pictures and collection of antiquities and curios lasted twenty-four days at Strawberry Hill, where a temporary building was erected specially, and the sale of the rest of his books and prints at the Covent Garden auction rooms lasted a further ten days. The combined sales raised £33,450 11s. 9d, which was considered to be high at the time. Frances, Lady Waldegrave managed to buy back some of the items, mainly family portraits and stained glass, without her husband's knowledge, but the vast majority of Horace's huge collection was dispersed. Many of the items were brought together for an exhibition at the Victoria and Albert Museum in 2010, and the memorable and spectacular *Lost Treasures of Strawberry Hill* exhibition held over the winter of 2018/19 saw many of Horace's most prized possessions returned on loan to their original positions in the house.

In 1848 Frances, by then still only twenty-seven, married for a third time, and in 1856 with the support of her husband George Granville Harcourt of Nuneham Courtenay in Oxfordshire, she set about restoring and extending Strawberry Hill. Frances clearly loved the house, and the extensions were remarkably sympathetic to Horace's earlier Gothic remodelling. Reputedly acting largely as her own architect, she added a grand new drawing room and dining room to link the existing house and offices, and heightened the Round Tower by a storey to improve the architectural composition. Walpole had spent £20,000 including the initial purchase; Lady Waldegrave spent £100,000 and then 'stopped counting'. Harcourt died in 1861, and in 1863 Frances married for a fourth and last time. Chichester Fortescue, later Lord Carlingford, was a Liberal minister and Secretary for Ireland, where Frances was known as the Queen of Dublin. She became the leading Liberal hostess of her day, entertaining Palmerston, Gladstone, and the Prince and Princess of Wales. Frances died in 1879, and the estate was bought in 1883 by Baron de Stern, who sold most of the remaining contents, and from him it passed to his son Lord Michelham, who sold the estate in 1932. Much of the outer estate was sold for housing, but the house and gardens were sold to the Catholic Education Council, and the architect Sebastian Pugin Powell, a grandnephew of AWN Pugin, was employed to design a chapel, dormitories and lecture rooms as a new home for St Mary's Catholic Teacher Training College, now St Mary's University Twickenham. Walpole's house became the home of the Vincentian fathers who taught at the college. The 1930s college buildings are in a simple Gothic style, of yellow brick and stone, and are tactful and have little impact on the older house. There was extensive damage to the new buildings from firebombs in 1940 and fortunately less serious damage to the Walpole and Waldegrave wings, which were repaired in the 1950s by Sir Albert Richardson, who designed the new chapel built in 1962. The chapel is a fine building and now listed, but it truncates Walpole's Serpentine Walk, the path that wound through the woods and formed part of the original perimeter walk, and isolates Walpole's little Chapel in the Wood, built in 1772-4. More recent college buildings and the sports track are, fortunately, to the south of the garden on land that was formerly Thomas Ashe's Nursery and meadows.

The college buildings were purpose-built and the Lady Waldegrave rooms are generally of a large scale and robust enough to stand up to college use, but the interiors of Walpole's house are more domestic in scale and their details and finishes are fragile, and once the Roman Catholic fathers had moved out of the house about thirty years ago it became a problem to know how best to use it. The building had been kept heated and in reasonable condition, but it was effectively redundant as a college building, and St Mary's as an educational establishment could not afford to maintain it as an unproductive and wasting asset. Letting it out for parties and filming brought in some income but also led to theft and damage, and the house was placed on the English Heritage and World Monuments Fund registers of buildings at risk.

The very proactive Friends of Strawberry Hill helped form the Strawberry Hill Trust, a registered charity, in 2002 with a mission to restore Walpole's Gothic villa and gardens and open them to a wider public. The house and surrounding gardens are held on a 120-year lease from the Catholic Education Service and approximately £10m has been raised from the National Lottery Heritage Fund, the Architectural Heritage Fund, the World Monuments Fund, English Heritage, and many other trusts, charitable bodies and private donors to restore the house and gardens and to open them to the public as an educational resource. Walpole saw his house and garden as an entity – the heads of his windows were filled with colourful stained glass but the lower panes were clear and especially large for the period to frame views of the garden and the greater landscape beyond – and the restoration and re-presentation of the house have been accompanied by the restoration of the garden. One of the guiding principles behind the restoration of the house has been to return it as far as possible to its optimum condition in Walpole's day where there is convincing evidence to support that and where it might be achieved without destroying significant later interventions. Both house and garden were extensively recorded in Walpole's time and later, and in restoring the house and grounds the architect Peter Inskip and the landscape historians Patrick James and Mark Laird have trawled through all the known images and written descriptions of the estate as well as analysing the physical evidence of the monument.

While the building has grown in size over the centuries with additions and embellishments that have generally respected its original character, the garden has shrunk and the important views to the water meadows, River Thames, Twickenham and Richmond Hill have been lost to two-storey houses of the 1930s, themselves now largely screened by mature trees.

Walpole's passion for Gothic was romantic, patriotic and escapist, and was also antiquarian and scholarly, but as he wrote:

> In truth I did not mean to make my house so Gothic as to exclude convenience and modern refinements in luxury. The designs of the inside and outside are strictly ancient, but the decoration is modern… But I do not mean to defend a small capricious house. It was built to please my own taste, and in sole degree to realize my own vision.

When asked by his friend Horace Mann if his garden was to be Gothic too, Walpole wrote, 'Gothic is merely architecture, and as one has a satisfaction in imprinting the gloomth of abbeys and cathedrals on one's house, so one's garden, on the contrary, is to be nothing but *riant* and the gaiety of nature.'

His passion for Gothic did not preclude entirely a flirtation with China and her arts:

> I am almost as fond of the Sharawaggi, or the Chinese want of symmetry, in buildings, as in grounds or gardens. I am sure whenever you come to England, you will be pleased with the liberty of taste into which we are struck, and of which you can have no idea. Adieu! (Letter to Sir Horace Mann, 25 February 1750).

He named his goldfish pond Po-Yang after a lake in China famous for its shoals of fish, and it was in a Chinese porcelain goldfish bowl 'Where China's gayest art had dy'd the azure flowers, that blow' that his tabby cat Selima drowned in 1747, a minor domestic tragedy commemorated in Thomas Gray's *Ode On the Death of a Favourite CAT, Drowned in a Tub of Gold Fishes*, published at the Strawberry Hill Press in 1753 with inventive Gothic-*chinoiserie*-rococo illustrations by Richard Bentley.

The 1755 drawing by JH Müntz of the Shell Bench (Harney, p.257) shows a small timber bridge spanning a ditch. It is nominally Chinese, but not much different from the post-and-rail fencing with diagonal struts that separates the meadow from the pleasure garden. However, writing of his friend Richard Bateman's villa at Old Windsor, he states, 'I converted Dicky Bateman from a Chinese to a Goth… I preached so effectually that his every pagoda took the veil.' Of his neighbour Lord Radnor's house (see Chapter 5), clearly visible from his water meadows, Walpole wrote to Horace Mann (12 June 1753), 'The Chinese summerhouse which you may distinguish in the distant landscape, belongs to my Lord Radnor. We pique ourselves upon nothing but simplicity, and have no carvings, gildings, inlayings or tawdry businesses.' Radnor had given his old house a Gothic exterior shortly before Walpole set out about his much more thorough-going Gothic remodelling next door, and one senses some resentment on Walpole's part in his slighting references to what he called 'Mabland' and to its owner 'Queen Mab'.

Walpole's essay on *The History of the Modern Taste in Gardening*, written between 1750 and 1770, promotes the English landscape style of William Kent and Lancelot Brown as the modern, natural and patriotic style of gardening; Kent with his use of the ha-ha 'leaped the fence and saw that all nature was a garden', and it was a garden in the modern style that Walpole created by the banks of the Thames.

The garden was enclosed to the north and north-west by the house and offices, and to the south west and south by the wooded and underplanted Serpentine Walk, which turned through a right angle at the Chapel in the Wood. To the north east was the Shrubbery of trees and flowering shrubs, shielding the garden from the Hampton Court road, and to the east were a small meadow, the Kingston road, water meadows, and the River Thames.

The Serpentine Walk exemplifies Walpole's taste for 'Sharawaggi or want of symmetry', but the house shaded by a grove of regularly-spaced trees on a grass terrace dropping away to the river sounds faint echoes of Burlington and Kent's landscaping at Chiswick. Chiswick is an inward-looking garden with a great deal of architectural incident; Strawberry Hill, started a generation later, was conceived as outward-looking in order to capture the views of cattle on the water meadows and down the Thames to St Mary's Church, Ham House and Richmond Hill, and its built features were fewer and less ambitious – the Chapel in the Wood, a Gothic gate, a Chinese bridge, a Roman marble sarcophagus, the Gothic screen to the Prior's Garden, and the Shell Bench.

The principal flower garden was to the north surrounding the rustic cottage; the cottage survives, enlarged in the late nineteenth century and with an eighteenth-century wrought-iron gate reused when the Hampton Court Road was moved by Lady Waldegrave in order to give her house a more impressive entrance and carriage sweep. The garden cottage is no longer college property, nor is what remains of the walled kitchen gardens, now part of a garage court at the back of houses in Tower Road. A watercolour drawing of 1780 by William Pars, now in the Victoria and Albert Museum and reproduced on p.13 of *Horace Walpole's Strawberry Hill – A History and Guide* by John Iddon shows the gardener with his watering-can attending to beds containing sunflowers and hollyhocks and other less readily-identifiable flowers with dramatic foliage: 'now and then a lettuce run to seed overturns all my botany, as I have more than once mistaken it for a curious West Indian flowering shrub' (letter to Henry Conway, August 1748). Tall shrubs hide the road, and tall thin trees, their spindly trunks bare but for honeysuckle or ivy, stand against the sky and the north front of Walpole's Gothic castle. It is reminiscent of Lord Harcourt's walled flower garden at Nuneham Courtenay, designed by Walpole's friend the Rev. William Mason, author of the poem *The English Flower Garden* and inspired by Julie's garden in Rousseau's *La nouvelle Héloïse*. Lord

4.2. *Strawberry Hill chiefly taken in the year 1769 by Mr Sandby.* Watercolour by Paul Sandby, *c.*1769, showing the south and east fronts of the villa. (Lewis Walpole Library, lwlpr 31268)

4.3. *South Front of Strawberry Hill.* Watercolour by Paul Sandby, *c.*1769, looking past the south and east fronts downstream over the water meadows and river towards Twickenham. (Lewis Walpole Library, lwlpr 31267)

Harcourt's garden was painted by Paul Sandby, who also painted the gardens at Strawberry Hill (Figs. 4.2 and 4.3).

In 1777 (letter of 18 October to the Earl of Harcourt), Horace wrote:

> I have a gardener that has lived with me above five-and-twenty years; he is incredibly ignorant and a mule. When I wrote to your Lordship my patience was worn out, and I resolved to have a gardener at least for flowers. On your not being able to give me one, I half consented to keep my own; not on his amendment, but because he will not leave me, presuming on my long suffering. I have offered him fifteen pounds a year to leave me, and when he pleads that he is old, and that nobody else will take him on, I plead that I am old too, and that it is rather hard that I am not to have a few flowers, or a little fruit as long as I live. I shall now try if I can make any compromise with him, for I own I cannot bear to turn him adrift, nor will starve an old servant, though never a good one, to please my nose and mouth. Besides, he is a Scot, and I will not be unjust, even to that odious nation… I know how strong my prejudices are, and am always afraid of them…

A great advocate for the restoration of the gardens was the late Mavis Batey, who in 2005 wrote a paper for the Garden History Society (now The Gardens Trust), *Strawberry Hill. A Romantic Garden for a Gothic Castle*:

> 'Romantic', as defined by Dr Johnson, meant 'resembling the tales of romance'; it was in this sense that Walpole indulged his 'romantic inclinations'. Revelling in Chaucer, and in particular his *Romaunt of the Rose*, Walpole spent much time in trying to prove that Chaucer was his ancestor. It was, after all, Chaucer who had led the way in romanticising gardens:
>
>> It seemed a place espirituel.
>> For certes, as at my devys,
>> There is no place in paradys
>> So good in for to dwell or be
>> As in that Garden, thoughte me;
>> For there was many a bird singing,
>> Through the yarde al thringing
>> In many places were nightingales.

'We hear of Walpole, Gray and Mason sitting up far into the night, in May 1761, listening to the nightingales and intoxicated by the fragrance of lilacs and acacias.' (Batey)

Contemporary poets and friends too influenced Walpole; Thomas Gray, whose poems including his *Elegy written in a Country Churchyard* were published only at Walpole's urging; William Mason, whose *The English Garden* was published in four volumes between 1772 and 1781; and William Gilpin, whose *Remarks on Forest Scenery* had been published in 1791 and seen in manuscript ten years earlier by Walpole, Mason and Lord Harcourt.

Edmund Spenser's *The Faerie Queene*, first published in two sections in 1589 and 1596 and republished with illustrations by William Kent (of which Walpole had a low opinion despite his general championing of him in his *The History of the Modern Taste in Gardening*) in 1751 was an inspiration for Walpole, and before him for Pope:

It was Spenser's guiding hand that Walpole had sought in the garden; his 'thickets of sweets', the fragrance of flowers, joyous birds, fruit-bearing trees were for him the 'gaiety of nature'. Natural arbours entwined with sweet briar and honeysuckle ('Eglantine and Caprifole') were also one of the romantic Faerie Queene features Walpole consulted Spenser about. (Batey)

Mason reported that Kent 'frequently declared that he caught his taste in gardening from reading the picturesque descriptions of Spenser':

> Ah, see the Virgin Rose, how sweetly shee
> Doth first peep forth with bashfull modestee
> That fairer seems, the lesse ye see her may,
> Lo see soone after, how more bold and free.

John Macclary, the gardener at Rousham in Oxfordshire, one of Walpole's favourite gardens, gave an account in a letter of 1750 of how Kent taught him to plant its perimeter wood walk:

> there you see deferent sorts of Flowers peeping through the deferent sorts of Evergreens, here you think the Laurel produces a Rose, the Holly a Syringa, the Yew a Lilac, and the sweet Honeysuckle is peeping out from every Leafe, in short they are so mixed together that you'd think that every Leafe of the Evergreens produces one flower or another.

In June 1765 Walpole wrote of Strawberry Hill,

> I have just come out of the garden in the most oriental of all evenings, and from breathing odours beyond those of Araby. The acacias, which the Arabians have the sense to worship, are covered with blossoms, the honeysuckle dangles from every tree in festoons, the seringas are thickets of sweets, and the new-cut hay of the field in the gardens tempers the balmy gales with simple freshness.

The theme of scented flowering shrubs is taken up by Mason in *The English Garden*:

> ...Shrubs there are
> Of bolder growth, that, at the call of Spring,
> Burst forth in blossom'd fragrance: Lilacs rob'd
> In snow-white innocence, or purple pride;
> The sweet Syringa yielding but in scent
> To the rich Orange; or woodbine wild
> That loves to hang, on barren boughs remote,
> Her wreaths of flowery perfume.

The restoration of the garden, which is open to the public free of charge (see strawberryhillhouse.org.uk for opening times) and managed by one gardener and a team of volunteers, followed the production in 2008 of a *Landscape Management and Maintenance Plan* produced by the Landscape Agency, Mark Laird, and Peter Inskip & Peter Jenkins Architects, which was amended in 2011 and is kept under review. The Trust does not have a lease

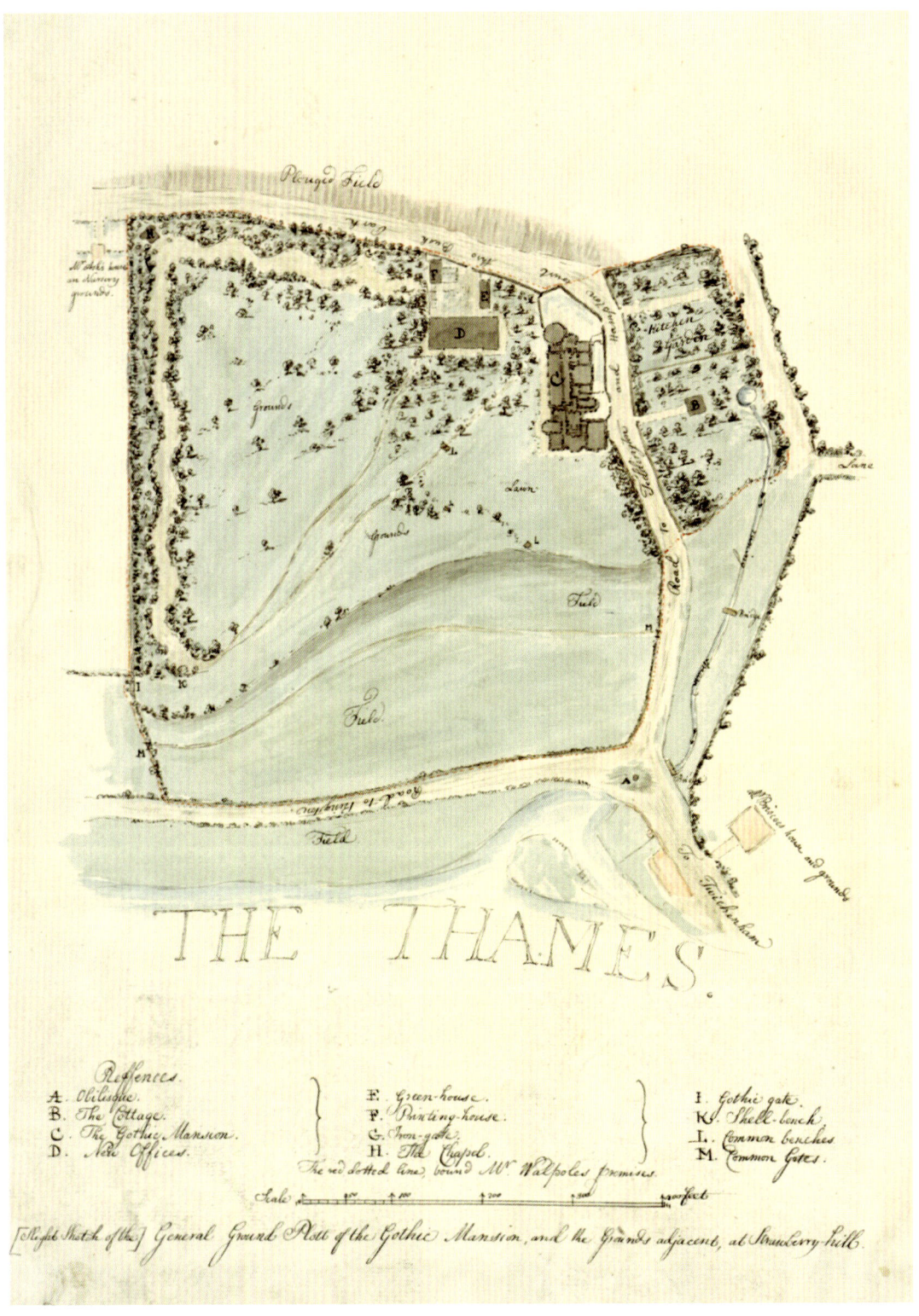

4.4. *Slight Sketch of the General Ground Plott of the Gothic Mansion and the Grounds adjacent at Strawberry Hill*. Engraving, *c.*1791. (Lewis Walpole Library, lwlpr 16005). North is to the right.

References:
A Obelisque. B The Cottage. C The Gothic Mansion. D New Offices. E Green-house. F Printing-house.
G Iron Gate. H The Chapel. I Gothic Gate. K Shell-bench. L Common Benches. M Common Gates

4.5. *Strawberry Hill from the West.* Aquatint by Joseph Charles Barrow or possibly William Pars, 1797. (Lewis Walpole Library, lwlpr 14835)

on all of the surviving grounds, most of which remain in the care of the University, but the land immediately attached to the Walpole house (about five acres) has been replanted to accord as far as possible with its historic design as recorded in the late eighteenth century. The structural planting was completed early and is maturing surprisingly fast. It comprises in the main two groves of common limes (*Tilia x europea*) planted on a regular grid to the south of the lawn south of the house, with outliers of Italian cypresses (*Cupressus sempervirens*), and a group of 'acacias' (*Robinia pseudoacacia*) in front of the Waldegrave Wing, visible from the Long Gallery on the first floor and from the cafe in the former Cloisters below. Surviving mature trees were in the main retained, including a fine cedar of Lebanon (*Cedrus libani*) of nineteenth-century date, and a large English oak (*Quercus robur*) known as the Walpole Oak, which is the only tree thought to remain from Horace's time. A (later) stone pine (*Pinus pinea*) of fine form on the edge of the Terrace above the Lower Terrace Walk had to be severely reduced in size in 2016 because of decay in the trunk. Neighbouring trees, including an ungainly but rare native black poplar (*Populus nigra*), have been retained for ecological or amenity value, screening as they do the houses built between the garden and the river in the 1930s.

The house and garden are approached from Waldegrave Road, named after Frances, Countess Waldegrave. The former Hampton Court road originally ran only twenty or so feet (6m.) in front of Walpole's house (Fig. 4.4 gives the Slight Sketch of the General Ground Plott, *c*.1791), from which it was separated by an ivy-covered wall with a scalloped top (Fig. 4.5) and a Gothic door leading to the small entrance court, now shielded by Lady Waldegrave's curving and crenellated screen wall. It leads past the Gothic Oratory and Cloisters

4.6. *View of the Prior's Garden at Strawberry Hill*. Engraving by Richard Bernard Godfrey after William Pars, *c*.1784. (Lewis Walpole Library, lwlpr 15093)

to the front door and entrance and staircase hall or, on turning right instead of entering the house, to the Prior's Garden.

Mavis Batey, quoting Walpole, writes:

'Strawberry is almost the last monastery left, at least in England.' After a visit to Gloucester Cathedral in 1753 he wrote enthusiastically to (Richard) Bentley that 'of all delight is what they call the abbot's cloister. It is the very thing you would build, when you have extracted all the quintessence of trefoils, arches and lightness'. In a letter to his friend the Rev. William Cole (who tended towards Rome), Walpole wrote, 'I like Popery as well as you and have shown that I do. I like it as I like chivalry and romance. They all furnish me with ideas and visions – a gothic church or a convent fills me with romantic dreams.'

'There was no question of Strawberry Hill gothic feeling heralding a return to Rome as the Ruskin-inspired nineteenth-century gothic revival would influence the Oxford Movement.' (Batey)

The *Oxford Dictionary of English* provides two definitions of the adjective 'camp'; 'ostentatiously and extravagantly effeminate'; and 'deliberately exaggerated and theatrical in style'. The same source defines 'gay' as 'homosexual'; or '*dated* light-hearted and carefree'; or '*dated* brightly coloured; showy'. In 2019 Strawberry Hill and St Mary's University hosted a conference on The Queer Eighteenth Century; the terms 'queer', 'gay' and 'camp' were tossed about, in the main more earnestly than gaily, alas!, and not wholly conclusively. Whatever may currently be the finer gradations of the epithet, however, Walpole was camp; '… he always entered a room in that style of affected delicacy, which fashion had then made almost natural … knees bent and feet on tip toe as if afraid of a wet floor'. (Laetitia Hawkins)

> Strawberry has been in great glory… Last Friday all of France dined there… At the gates of the castle I received them dressed in the cravat of Gibbins's carving, (the Grinling Gibbons limewood lace cravat now in the V&A) and a pair of gloves embroidered up to the elbows that had belonged to James I. The French servants stared and firmly believed that this was the dress of an English country gentleman. (Letter to George Montagu, 11 May 1769).

Camp, yes, but hard-working and scholarly; the provenance of his eclectic collection was important to Walpole, and the sources of inspiration for the Gothic details of his house were soundly researched if sometimes surprising in their application. The openwork screen to the Prior's Garden, recently renewed in painted timber to replace Sir Albert Richardson's crumbling post-War concrete, was designed by John Chute and based on a drawing by Wenceslaus Hollar of a tomb in old St Paul's Cathedral.

The Prior's Garden, beneath the windows of the Great North Bedchamber, was known from contemporary descriptions and drawings but latterly had descended to use as a staff car park. It has been recreated in accordance with the evidence (Fig. 4.6) and evokes the mediaeval *hortus conclusus*, the single and most literal Gothic reference in Walpole's otherwise *modern* and *riant* gardens. It impressed Humphry Repton, who was much charmed by Strawberry Hill and admired Walpole's essay. Repton surely recalled the Prior's Garden when he prepared his Red Book for Ashridge in 1813, where the long narrow flower beds in the Monks' Garden evoked (too literally, as they were soon removed) the monks' graves.

The Prior's Garden has been replanted with low box edging, almond trees, daphnes, hellebores, roses, wild strawberries, violets and spring bulbs, and with ivy growing on the scallop-topped fence. It is a charming garden that tends to be overlooked by visitors.

The path from the entrance car park to the front door follows the line of the old road and is planted with ferns and wild flowers to suggest a country lane outside the polite garden. Behind the close-boarded fence is the Shrubbery, replanted following the drawing produced by Mark Laird and reproduced as the plate on p. 169 of his *A Natural History of English Gardening* (2015) (Fig. 4.7).

> The Shrubbery was one of the main features of Walpole's garden… it is represented in Johann Heinrich Müntz's painting of 1755-9. At that time supple and regimented, by the time of JC Barrow's painting of 1789 it was compacted and overgrown. A wooden trellis with niches for orange tubs marking the boundary between lawn and

4.7. Watercolour drawing by Mark Laird showing his scheme for replanting The Shrubbery. (By kind permission of Mark Laird)

shrubbery is shown in Barrow's view. A flower border… seems to have been added to the trellis in the later 1770s or early 1780s… (*Strawberry Hill Landscape Management and Maintenance Plan*).

Against the fence is a line of hornbeams (*Carpinus betulus*), which are deciduous; in front of them, evergreen shrubs including variegated hollies (*Ilex aquifolium* vars.), sweet bays (*Laurus nobilis*), the strawberry tree (*Arbutus unedo*) and 'laurustinus' (*Viburnum tinus*). Broom (*Cytisus hirsutus*), butcher's broom (*Ruscus hypoglossum*), bear's breeches (*Acanthus mollis*), myrtle (*Myrtus communis*), daphne (*Daphne mezereum*) and roses (*Rosa damascena*, and *R. foetida* 'Bicolor') add to the mix, and seasonal colour is supplemented by spring bulbs and annuals and perennials including pinks (*Dianthus*). The green-painted trellis, whether originally a reference to the Roman garden paintings then being rediscovered in Pompeii and Herculaneum, or a fashionable expedient to reimpose order on overgrown shrubs, has been recreated, complete with niches for tubs of citrus trees which, swathed in fleece and bubble-wrap, now have to take their chances with the weather since Walpole's cloisters, converted to bachelor's bedrooms by Lady Waldegrave and now the café, can no longer shelter them over the winter.

A recent addition is the low-key single-storey block, clad in timber and with a green roof, that faces the car park and provides an office, meeting room and store for the gardeners, and lavatories for visitors. A bark chip path and informal steps lead from the edge of the lawn past the still-dramatic trunk of the damaged stone pine to the Lower Terrace Walk; 'Given the loss of the original relationship of the garden to the water meadows and Thames, the main purpose

4.8. *The Shell Seat at Horace Walpole's Villa at Strawberry Hill.* Grey wash and watercolour. Unknown artist, *c.*1825. (Lewis Walpole Library, lwlpr 15053)

in replanting this area is to screen the eastern boundary and adjacent housing as well as improve the quality of the existing woodland walk…' (*SH LMMP*). Given too that the surviving stretches of the Serpentine Walk are still in the ownership and care of St Mary's, the opportunity is being taken here to evoke beneath the canopy of the mature trees something of the character of Walpole's original meandering woodland walks, with evergreens and flowering shrubs, open glades, climbing roses, honeysuckle, snowdrops and spring bulbs. The walk was formally opened in 2017 by Alan Titchmarsh, who is a patron of the charity. It leads back past the Walpole Oak and children's play area to the Lime Grove, Shell Bench, and Closed Grove. The Shell Bench is a modern replacement for the seat designed by Richard Bentley, a cockleshell originally carved from green oak, that once stood at the east end of the Serpentine Walk where Lady Waldegrave's charming little octagonal summer house now stands (Fig. 4.8). 'There was never so pretty a sight as to see them (the Duchesses of Hamilton and Richmond and the Countess of Ailesbury) all three sitting in the shell.' (Walpole letter to George Montagu, 1759.)

4.9. *View of the Offices at Strawberry Hill*. Ink and watercolour by Joseph Charles Barrow, 1791. (Lewis Walpole Library, lwlpr 16483)

The planting of the Closed Grove, which partly screens the rather utilitarian Gothic of James Wyatt's and James Essex's New Offices, was influenced by William Gilpin and comprises false acacias (*Robinia pseudoacacia*), yews (*Taxus baccata*), almonds (*Prunus dulcis*), bird cherries (*Prunus padus*), and lilacs (*Syringa vulgaris*), underplanted with periwinkle (*Vinca major*), *Viburnum tinus*, box (*Buxus sempervirens*) and broom (*Citiisus hirsutus*), with snowdrops (*Galanthus sp.*). The planting evokes New Forest scenery (Fig. 4.9). A new, non-historical but nevertheless popular and successful addition to the gardens is the small community garden, cultivated on organic lines and tended by volunteers, which provides vegetables, herbs and a few cut flowers, and which is located near the café terrace next to Lady Waldegrave's wonderfully decorative wrought-iron staircase.

Today's visitor should not overlook the Chapel in the Wood, which is not part of the grounds leased by the Trust but which nevertheless was an important feature of Walpole's garden, marking as it did the south-west corner of the Serpentine Walk. It survives largely unaltered from his day in a brick-paved court in a corner of the university car park to the west of Sir Albert Richardson's much larger modern chapel (Fig. 4.10). It was designed by John Chute in 1772 and the Portland stone façade, based on the tomb of Bishop Audley in Salisbury Cathedral, was executed by Gayfere, the master mason at Westminster Abbey.

Acknowledgement
Some of this text was first published in my article 'Horace's Eclogue' in *Historic Gardens Review* (Issue 26. December 2011 – January 2012), and appears here with the kind agreement of The Historic Gardens Foundation.

4.10. *The Gothic Chapel which contains the Italian Shrine at Strawberry Hill.* Unknown artist, *c.*1822. (Lewis Walpole Library, lwlpr 15082)

CHAPTER FIVE

Radnor Gardens

Mike Cherry

Radnor Gardens is a small riverside park in Cross Deep approximately half a mile south of the centre of Twickenham. The gardens take their name from Radnor House, the major house that once stood in the centre of the park, but the gardens comprise the land of several other riverside houses.

The park consists of a narrow strip of land between the road, Cross Deep, and the River Thames. Part of the park was originally an island separated from the rest of the land by a narrow channel which was filled in in 1965. The island was at one time known as Hozier Hoop, perhaps a reference to its use for growing osiers or willows for basket-making. The riverside land was part of one of Twickenham's medieval open fields, South Field, and known as Thames Furlong, and consisted of strips of land curving gently from west to east. The line of the strips was reflected in later property boundaries in the area. To the south the land was originally crossed by a stream, Sparksmead Brook, which ran from the west and into the Thames at modern day Swan Island.

Narrow and liable to flooding, the land was originally considered suitable only for small-scale commercial activity and its transformation to a fashionable residential area had to wait until the eighteenth century.

The earliest building of any size on the site of Radnor Gardens dates to 1673 when a London tallow chandler, John Hooker, bought two adjoining pieces of land in Cross Deep, Twickenham. His will shows that he owned several properties including a large London house in St Giles in the Fields and 'my copyhold messuage or tenement situate and being in Twittenham'.

On this land he built a house. If he ever occupied it then he did so but very briefly as he died in 1674, leaving the property in Cross Deep to his wife Elizabeth. If she was living in the house at that time she clearly had no desire to remain there as she obtained a licence to let the property in 1677, and in 1699 she sold it to Edward and Elizabeth Cole who were related to the Cole brewing family of Twickenham.

The Hooker land comprised approximately the central third of Radnor Gardens together with the island. The rest of the present-day park was in other ownerships and remained so until the later nineteenth and early twentieth centuries when a piecemeal process of amalgamation took place.

Peter Tillemans' painting *The Prospect of the River Thames at Twickenham c.1724–30* provides the earliest view of part of the land comprising Radnor Gardens, and shows Radnor House in probably its original form (Fig. 5.1 – detail from Fig. 1.6). The house was an unremarkable building of three bays and two storeys with attic rooms. In the foreground is the cold bath which stood at the edge of the riverside plot on which the house was built, with the island in front of it. The riverside garden has timber piling along the frontage to the

RADNOR GARDENS

5.1. Radnor House. Detail of painting by Peter Tillemans, c.1724-30 (Fig. 1.6)

channel and in the garden are a number of statues. These, and much else, were later the subject of comment by Horace Walpole who lived at nearby Strawberry Hill.

A number of small buildings are shown to the north. These formed a riverside working community with a tannery, a malthouse, bricklayer's yard, wheelmaker, poulterer and other businesses, which were gradually replaced by much grander detached houses as Twickenham's popularity grew in the eighteenth century.

What became known as Radnor House was built hard against the road, Cross Deep, in order to maximise the riverside land and to keep the house above the river which was then, as now, liable to flood. This practice was followed by the neighbouring properties built later in the century.

Ownership of Radnor House passed to various descendants of Edward and Elizabeth Cole and in 1718 a lease was taken by Gabriel du Quesne from Thomas Vernon. Du Quesne was the grandson of Admiral Abraham du Quesne who had been made a Marquis after naval service for France. The family were Huguenots and Gabriel had been sent by his father Henry to England to plead the cause of French protestants with Queen Anne. He was naturalised in 1711 and joined the army becoming Lt. Colonel of the First Regiment of the Grenadier Guards in 1717. He married a widow, Elizabeth Yates, in 1714 and one of their sons, Thomas, was christened at St Mary's Church in Twickenham.

Du Quesne acquired at the same time, or a year or two before 1718, two parcels of land at what was to become twenty years later the famous landscape garden of Painshill, Cobham, Surrey. However, it was too early for any landscaping, and while du Quesne may conceivably have initiated some formal garden areas and is likely to have had the Vanbrugh-style house built which survived long after its successor was erected, his residence was brought to an abrupt end as it was at Twickenham.

Gabriel du Quesne extended the Radnor estate in 1719 adding some adjacent land and seven acres on the other side of the road. A tunnel was later added under the road, as Pope had done, to give private access from the riverside and house to the main grounds.

Du Quesne's stay was brief. Barely four years after taking the lease he suffered great losses in the South Sea Company crash and had departed for Jamaica having been found employment there by the Duke of Portland. This did not prove to be the financial cure he had sought and he returned to England in 1726 under a cloud and in debt.

The house built by John Hooker soon found a new occupant and one who would change the landscape considerably. By 1722 John Robartes was recorded as paying rates for the estate. He was to live there until his death in 1757 having succeeded to the title of 4th Earl of Radnor in 1741 and giving the house its name from then on.

Robartes was born in London in 1686, possibly in Danvers House or Radnor House, both Robartes family houses in Chelsea. He was the grandson of the 1st Earl of Radnor and his second wife, Letitia, and son of the Honourable Francis Robartes (1649/50 – 1718) and his second wife Lady Anne Boscawen. Francis was a Member of Parliament for Bossiney in 1673 and represented various other Cornish constituencies. He was also a Teller of the Exchequer (a sinecure also held by another member of the Robartes family), and Vice-President of the Royal Society.

The founder of the Robartes family fortune was Sir Richard Robartes, a banker, merchant, mine-owner and landowner based in Truro. He was created a Baron in 1624 and his son, John, became 1st Earl of Radnor in 1679.

Despite the Cornish ancestry and the family's ownership of Lanhydrock House near Bodmin, there is no evidence that John Robartes ever visited the county although he did own estates there. Educated at Eton and Christ's College Cambridge, he seems to have had some talent for mathematics. He studied under Nicholas Saunderson at Cambridge who left Robartes his papers when he died. Robartes's application for election to the Royal Society (something of a family tradition) in 1731 stated that he was 'very well qualified in Mathematical Learning'.

It may well be that Robartes's inheritance following his father's death in 1718 enabled him to establish his own estate but why he chose Twickenham is unclear. However it was by then a fashionable place to live so he may just have been attracted by the setting and the company – Alexander Pope's villa was nearing completion a few hundred yards up the road; additionally it was within easy reach of London, which he must have known well.

His father and grandfather may have been prominent public figures but John Robartes seems to have been a more retiring character. By no means reclusive he nonetheless seems to have led a quiet life on his estate on the banks of the Thames. He wrote, much later, in 1746, that: 'These parts afford little news. It will not be any to tell you that I still continue to add to and alter my little house and garden. My collection of pictures also, such as they are, are at this time many. I have some few that I think are very good.' His collection included a Canaletto, several paintings by Samuel Scott, and works by a number of seventeenth-century Dutch masters. Scott drew Radnor House and garden (Fig. 5.2).

In 1741 Robartes's cousin Henry, 3rd Earl of Radnor, died and the title passed to John. The only known portrait of him (now at Lanhydrock House) shows him in his Parliamentary robes and was probably painted soon after he succeeded to the title. The money he inherited enabled him to continue his passions for gardening, collecting paintings and, above all, building. He enlarged and refaced the house in the gothic style in the 1740s as shown in this detail from a print of 1750 based on a drawing by Augustin Heckel (Fig. 5.3 – detail of Fig. 1.3). There is a Chinese summerhouse to the left and the cold bath to the right.

This detail from John Rocque's map of 1744–6 (Fig. 5.4 – detail from Fig. 1.4) shows the

5.2. *A view of Mr Hindley's formerly Lord Radnor's at Twickenham*. Watercolour by Samuel Scott, 1758. (Lewis Walpole Library, Yale University lwlpr 16661)

5.3. 'A View of the Earl of Radnor's House at Twickenham'. Detail of engraving by Anthony Walker after Augustin Heckel, 1750 (Fig. 1.3)

5.4. Detail of Rocque Survey (Fig. 1.4), showing the formal quadripartite layout of Lord Radnor's 'inland' garden contrasted with the more 'natural' layout of Pope's garden immediately to the north

Thames on the right, the road running from top to bottom and the main part of Radnor's gardens in the lower middle. The formality of Radnor's garden contrasts with the more natural and fluid lines of Pope's just above it.

In 1745 Radnor bought the land he had previously leased from the Vernon family which included a tunnel under the road, Cross Deep, which gave him access to the major part of his estate. The entrance can just be seen in Fig. 5.3 to the right of the summerhouse behind a small group of trees. Unlike Pope, Radnor created a 'grotto' only by decorating the tunnel. The land transfer of 1745 states '…there is lately made a passage or way under the said road…' A report of 1937 states:

> The grotto situated on the south of the house formed a subway which passed under the lane 'Cross Deep' to give access to the gardens. It is constructed of brick covered with flints, and portions of glass slag may be seen in the east wall…There are small recesses with semi-circular heads on either side of the subway…It was filled up when the modern road was made.

The bricked-up entrance is now covered by landscaping and planting.

Contrasting descriptions survive of the house and gardens. Horace Walpole, who arrived at nearby Strawberry Hill in 1747 when Radnor's rebuilding was well-advanced, could not resist the temptation to amuse his correspondents at Radnor's expense. As early as 5 October 1747 he wrote: 'The autumn is in great beauty, my Lord Radnor's baby houses lay eggs every day, and promise new swarms…' In 1752 he wrote to George Conway: '… or have you any Lord Radnor that plants trees to intercept his own prospect, that he may cut them down again to make an alteration…' The following year he wrote to Horace Mann: 'The Chinese summerhouse which you may distinguish in the distant landscape, belongs to my Lord Radnor. We pique ourselves upon nothing but simplicity and have no carvings, gildings, paintings, inlayings or tawdry businesses.' This is indeed rich coming from a man who devoted much of his life to collecting paintings, books and historical artefacts of all sorts, genuine and of less than certain provenance. It may perhaps be that Walpole was piqued because Radnor had already gothicised his house.

In 1754 Walpole wrote to Richard Bentley: 'From Mabland I have little news to send you, but that the obelisk is danced from the middle of the rabbit warren into his neighbour's garden, and he pays a ground-rent for looking at it there. His shrubs are hitherto unmolested.' (Mabland was Walpole's name for Radnor House, referring to Shakespeare's Queen of the fairies.)

Walpole was however appreciative of the setting of Radnor House. Much later in life, in 1791, and perhaps in a mellower temper, he wrote to the Berry sisters: '…and it is true that hay-carts have been transporting haycocks from a second crop all the morning from Sir Francis Basset's island opposite to my windows. The setting sun and the long autumnal shades enriched the landscape to a Claude Lorraine.' (Basset was then owner of Radnor House.)

A more disinterested commentator, Henrietta Pye, wrote in *A Short Description of the Principal Seats and Gardens in and about Twickenham* published in 1760:

> The Earl of Radnor's Villa is situated in an open romantic country with as fine a view of the river as any in those parts. The rooms are small but elegantly fitted up and there is an excellent collection of pictures. A noble gallery runs the whole length of the house adorned with paintings of great value. If there is any fault it is that of being too much ornamented but this is greatly atoned by the exquisite taste that is displayed throughout the whole. The garden is not equal to the house for there is not one view [i.e. from the main garden over the road] except that of the river through the subteranneous passage which his Lordship cut under the road for a communication to his garden from the fine lawn at the back front of the house by the riverside.

She continues:

> But that which surpasses every other beauty is the Cold Bath, a small building open to the river with an alcove at each end one of which contains the water and is adorned with the finest shell work. From a piece of rock a perpetual rill of water drops with an agreeable murmur in many little streams into the bath. Over the alcove is this inscription from the 6th satyr of Horace (…). The other contains a sideboard and the middle is a pretty square room adorned with pictures. There is also a beautiful Chinese tower which stands near the water.

The Cold Bath also caught the attention of Batty Langley, a Twickenham born and based architect who states: 'The most beautiful pavements of marble that I ever saw are that of… Mr Scawen at Carshalton…and that of the Honourable Mr Roberts at Twickenham…'

The setting of Radnor House and the adjacent riverside is captured by a print by JH Müntz published in 1756, *A View of Twickenham* (Fig. 5.5), which shows the view from Walpole's grounds with Radnor's Chinese summerhouse on the left, the island in the foreground with Radnor House framed by the trees in the centre.

John Robartes died in 1757. By that time the neighbouring land along the river in Cross Deep had already changed considerably.

To the south, in 1743/4 Robert Parsons, a Twickenham carpenter living in Church Lane, built a new house on the far side of the road. Known as Cross Deep House, the building can be seen in this detail of the 1750 Heckel print (Fig. 5.6). It is a square five bay, three storey house with a hipped roof fronting the Cross Deep road. The main gardens were behind the house – on Rocque's map (Fig. 1.4) they can be seen immediately below and

5.5. *A View of Twickenham*. Engraving by J Green after Johann Müntz, 1756. (Orleans House Gallery, LDORL: 03222). From left to right, the summerhouse to Cross Deep House, Lord Radnor's Chinese tower, house and bath house, Thomas Hudson's, Mr Pope's (Sir William Stanhope's), Lady Ferrers' Summer House, and Mrs Backwell's (Crossdeep).

adjacent to the gardens of Radnor House. There was a shallow riverside meadow which, in the 1750 print, has a roadside border of two groups of trees pleached to form arches. The meadow seems not to have been initially landscaped as sheep can be seen grazing on it. At this time Cross Deep House was leased to George Jones, and from 1754 to Robert Cramond. By the time of the Müntz print of 1756 (Fig. 5.5) a small Gothic summerhouse/verandah can be seen in the riverside garden. Part of this still stands in Radnor Gardens against what had been the boundary wall with the grounds of Radnor House. At about this time Cross Deep House was leased to Isaac Fernandez Nunez who suffered financial disasters and gambling losses which led him to take his life in August 1762 in the summerhouse. The next lessee was Stafford Briscoe, a goldsmith, who was to stay for some 20 years. In a lease of 1776 the property is described as:

> …Messuage…at a place called Cross Deep…fronting…on the King's Highway leading from Twickenham…to Teddington…and also that piece of garden ground lying behind the said Messuage…containing by estimate 2 acres…more or less with a wall erected on the northern side…together with…coach houses stables yards backsides buildings and appurts…and also those two roods of land lying in a Field called South Field next adjoining the garden…and also all that Lands End lying and being next the River Thames opposite to the said Messuage…and containing by estimation half

5.6. Cross Deep House. Detail of Fig. 1.3.

an acre…together with the Barge house thereon erected and built…Also all that…half part of an Ayte or Island lying and being in the River Thames opposite to the sd. Lands End and containing by Est. One Acre…as the same is now railed off.

The barge house, shown on the left in the Heckel print was earlier leased by Alexander Pope (see Fig. 1.3).

Stafford Briscoe died in 1789 and his nephew John Briscoe took on the lease and eventually bought the estate in 1801.

Land on the riverside to the north of Radnor House was also rapidly redeveloped. In about 1750 a house in the Palladian style was built and, from 1754, occupied by the celebrated portrait painter Thomas Hudson (1701–1779). Roger Morris, an architect with other Twickenham associations, is thought to have been the designer. The house can just be made out in Müntz's print (Fig. 5.5). Hudson also leased land on the opposite side of the road Cross Deep on part of which he built a gothic style house (see Fig. 1.13).

Shortly afterwards, in 1756, Joseph Hickey, lawyer and father of the scandalous diarist William Hickey, bought the tan yard on the riverside. It was a substantial brick and tiled building dating from the early 1700s. Hickey sold a piece of the land to Samuel Scott and on the remainder he built himself a house. Joseph Hickey's wife died in 1768 and he sold the house to Richard Holden. The riverside house eventually came into the ownership of Samuel Prime who in 1777 had inherited Kneller Hall in Whitton from his father.

On the land Samuel Scott bought from Joseph Hickey, he built a house which became known as Cross Deep Hall. Scott was a landscape painter particularly known for his marine and river scenes, as in Fig. 5.2. He later lived briefly in the Manor House in Church Street

5.7. Cross Deep Hall. Early twentieth-century photograph. (Mike Cherry Collection)

Twickenham. In 1759 Scott obtained a licence to let Cross Deep Hall, eventually selling it to Frederick Atherton Hindley in 1765. Hindley had inherited nearby Radnor House from the 4th Earl when he died in 1757 (Fig. 5.7 shows Cross Deep Hall in the early twentieth century).

Hindley had held various government appointments and at some time had become Steward for the Earl of Radnor's Twickenham estate. He was a Deputy Teller of the Exchequer, a post of considerable responsibility carrying out the duties of the Teller, which carried a varying but substantial income. Hindley's father had been a clerk in the Teller's office at the same time as Francis Robartes, father of the 4th Earl, had been one of the four Tellers. It is possible that the association between Frederick Hindley and Lord Radnor may have begun through the employment connection of their fathers.

By 1765 Hindley's appointment as a Deputy Teller was revoked and, subsequently finding himself in ruinous financial difficulties, he fled abroad, dying in exile in Brussels in 1781. As a result of the complications surrounding Hindley's downfall, ownership of the Radnor House estate was disputed and it finally passed into the possession of Henry Hoare, a wealthy banker, in 1783. Hoare, the owner and designer of Stourhead, was elderly and unwell by this time, and unlikely to have had any ideas for altering the garden, but may have been attracted by the location. By 1784/5 he had sold it to Sir Francis Basset, later Lord de Dunstanville, who, like John Robartes, was from a very wealthy Cornish family. From Walpole's records Basset was a regular summer visitor to Strawberry Hill House from 1784 to 1787. By 1793 Radnor House was in the possession of, in Walpole's words, 'the neat old Lady Murrays': they were Lady Anne and her younger sister Lady Margery Murray, nieces of William Murray, 1st Earl of Mansfield who had been appointed Lord Chief Justice in 1756.

5.8. Baroness Howe's House (*Pope's Villa*) (detail). Aquatint by C Bentley after William Westall, 1828. (Orleans House Gallery, LDORL: 00334)

A major change in the architectural landscape of the riverside in Cross Deep came with the arrival of Sophia Charlotte, Baroness Howe of Langar, daughter of Admiral Earl Howe. By 1803 she had bought Thomas Hudson's house and in 1807 she bought Alexander Pope's villa and gardens. In 1810 she added Hickey's house. Having bought up this row of properties she proceeded to demolish them – Pope's in 1808 and Hudson's in 1810. She left the site of Pope's villa undeveloped apart from the basement grotto and tunnel, but on the land immediately to the south, now cleared of houses, she built a long and somewhat disjointed house (Fig. 5.8). Here, with her second husband Sir Jonathan Wathen Waller, oculist to George III, she entertained royally – and royalty, both British and French (Louis-Philippe, Duc d'Orléans was an acquaintance) – in the lavishly furnished and decorated house. Mary Berry wrote in 1824: 'Walked with Mrs Damer to Sir Wathen Waller's to see the wonderful collection of old Sevres china at his house in Twickenham, to which he had added I know not how many rooms, all filled with china, the finest I have ever seen, even in France; he had also a quantity of valuable French furniture of all sorts.'

It is perhaps only fitting that the Baroness's buildings would last barely 30 years, being largely demolished in 1840. The remaining part was divided into two: 'River Deep' and 'Ryan House'. The latter survives and now marks the northern boundary of Radnor Gardens.

In 1840 Francis Lind bought Cross Deep Hall and extended its gardens with the land on which Hickey's house had been built.

The nineteenth century saw little further change to Cross Deep House and Cross Deep Hall but Radnor House underwent a major transformation in 1847 when the owner, William Chillingworth, a wine merchant, commissioned Henry Kendall Junior to remodel the house in the newly fashionable Italianate style. At the same time the central part of the Cold Bath

5.9. Radnor House and War Memorial. Postcard, 1920s. (Mike Cherry Collection)

house was resited from the riverside of the garden to its present position near the entrance from the road.

A new house, Pope's Garden, was built next to Cross Deep Hall in 1864. It was later renamed Beechcroft.

For the rest of the nineteenth century modern Radnor Gardens consisted of the riverside garden of Cross Deep House, Radnor House and Cross Deep Hall and their riverside gardens, Pope's Garden, and River Deep.

The dawn of the twentieth century saw the beginning of the creation of Radnor Gardens by name, a piecemeal process that was to take over fifty years.

In April 1901 Twickenham Urban District Council received an offer to sell Radnor House and 'a proportionate part of the island in front for £4,500' on behalf of the trustees of the late Mrs Stearns, William Chillingworth's daughter who had died in 1900. The estate had previously failed to sell at auction. A lengthy correspondence ensued and eventually the Council agreed terms and came into possession in October 1902. The Council's interest was laudable: to secure a public recreation ground and public access to the Thames. However it was also clear that the Council's interest did not extend to the house itself. A contemporary report of the discussion noted in respect of the house: '…if the cost of repairs and maintenance were found to be too expensive the house and buildings might be pulled down and other new buildings erected or the site added to the pleasure ground.'

The Council wasted no time in preparing the site for public access and on 11 April 1903 the house and grounds were formally opened by Mrs JHS Lawton, wife of the Chairman of the Council. Radnor Gardens initially comprised about half the modern area – the riverside grounds of Cross Deep House (the house was demolished shortly after in 1906), Radnor

House itself and its grounds, and the island. This was to remain the extent of the gardens until after the Second World War.

Later in 1903 the island was raised by the addition of 7,000 cubic yards of material from excavations at nearby Teddington Lock. The Council considered filling in the channel at the same time but decided against this course, and the channel remained (Fig. 5.9 shows an early twentieth-century view of the gardens).

The Council made regular improvements to the gardens with tree planting, benches and fencing, and Radnor House was used for exhibitions and meetings. It became the base for the local Public Health Department in 1912 until 1926 when Twickenham acquired Borough status and took on York House as its headquarters. In 1920 the Strawberry Hill Bowling Club was established on the island, and in 1921 the island was selected as the site for a 1914–1918 war memorial. Designed by Mortimer Brown (and Grade II* listed in 2017) it was unveiled on 2 November 1921.

It became increasingly clear that Radnor House was a building in search of a purpose and its later history is a lengthy battle of wills between conservation groups with heavyweight supporters (Queen Mary visited the house in 1936 in support of its preservation) and a Council that was reluctant to spend ratepayers' money on a building it had never wanted.

The future shape of Radnor Gardens fell to the course of the Second World War. On 16 September 1940 a 250kg delayed action high explosive bomb fell on Radnor House and penetrated to the cellars. It exploded two hours later and completely destroyed the house. The site of the house was landscaped. A further bomb dropped in the same raid caused damage to neighbouring Cross Deep Hall, Beechroft and River Deep. The demolition of the Pope's Grotto Hotel on the other side of Cross Deep by a V1 flying bomb in 1944 added to the damage and saw the destruction of River Deep. Cross Deep Hall was eventually demolished in 1954, Beechroft in 1955 and, with the grounds of River Deep, the sites were incorporated into Radnor Gardens taking the northern boundary up to Ryan House and completing the park.

The only subsequent major change was the in-filling of the channel in 1965. Part of the Earl of Radnor's bath house, and the little gothic summerhouse that stood in the grounds of Cross Deep House remain as echoes of the eighteenth-century houses that once lined the riverside.

CHAPTER SIX

Pope's Garden and Grotto
Chris Sumner

*Pope's ghost is just now skimming under my window
by a most poetical moonlight.*
(Horace Walpole to Henry Conway, June 1747)

*Happy the man whose wish and care
A few paternal acres bound,
Content to breathe his native air
In his own ground.* (Pope)

In 1718 Alexander Pope (1688–1744) took out a lease from Thomas Vernon of Twickenham Park (see Chapter 10) on three small cottages and some land in Cross Deep, the road from Twickenham to Kingston and Hampton Court. The cottages were between the road and the River Thames but the greater part of the land was on the other, west, side of the public highway.

Pope commissioned the architect James Gibbs to build him a new villa on the riverside (see Fig. 1.6), with the river front in 1735 shown in Fig. 6.1. In 1719 he obtained a licence to construct a brick tunnel under the road to connect his new 'inland' garden with the basement of his house, thus commencing on his famous grotto:

> A grotto is not often the wish or pleasure of an Englishman, who has more frequent need to solicit rather than exclude the sun, but Pope's excavation was requisite as an entrance to his garden, and, as some men try to be proud of their defects, he extracted an ornament from an inconvenience, and vanity produced a grotto where necessity enforced a passage. (Samuel Johnson)

Pope was born in the year of the 'Glorious Revolution', which saw the Roman Catholic King James II deposed and replaced by the Protestant King William III and Queen Mary II. As Catholics, Pope's family were restricted by the various Test Acts passed in the seventeenth century that excluded them from holding public office and by legislation that forbade the ownership of property within ten miles of central London and precluded a university education. Pope was further disadvantaged – and Dr Johnson's jibe may have been an unkind reference to it – by Pott's disease or tuberculosis of the spine, which left him stunted at only four feet six inches (1.4m) tall and hunchbacked.

Pope's ghost is fainter now than it was in Horace Walpole's day. It is unlikely that the two men ever met, given the differences in their ages and political and religious backgrounds, but they most certainly knew one another by repute, and Pope's villa and garden still

6.1. *An Exact Draught and View of Mr Pope's House at Twickenham.* Engraving by Nathaniel Parr after Pieter Andreas Rysbrack, 1735. (Orleans House Gallery, LDORL: 00084)

survived largely unaltered when Walpole moved to Strawberry Hill in 1747, three years after the older poet's death.

Pope's poetry is arguably no longer much to the public's taste – who but garden historians and students of social and political history or English literature reads him now? – but in many ways he was a very modern man, and is said still to be quoted more frequently than any source save the Bible and Shakespeare.

He was a self-made man and, in his own time and for long afterwards, a celebrity. Excluded by his parents' religion from receiving a formal education and precluded by his physical frailty from undertaking the Grand Tour, he nevertheless learned Greek, Latin, Italian, and French, and became the pre-eminent English poet of his period.

His verse translation of Homer's *The Iliad*, published in six volumes undertaken to commission between 1715 and 1720, earned him 200 guineas per volume and enormous fame and critical acclaim both in Britain and on the continent. It also provided the means for him to construct his house, garden and grotto at Twickenham, to which he continued adding for much of his life and which became as famous as he and a place of pilgrimage for a generally adoring public.

Pope cultivated his public image carefully – Dr Johnson said that he 'never drank tea without a stratagem' – and Voltaire, who was to visit him in his grotto in 1726, wrote of seeing Pope's portraits in as many as twenty houses in England. An exhibition held at Waddesdon Manor in 2014 entitled *Fame and Friendship: Pope, Roubiliac and the portrait bust* focused on a series of eight portrait busts of the poet sculpted and modelled by Louis François Roubiliac (1702–1762).

Roubiliac's busts of Pope were in the classical tradition of busts of authors and represented the poet with short hair and antique drapery. However, Roubiliac used the mode in a thoroughly modern way. While the bust was a public form of representation, these images of Pope have an intensity that assumed more private viewing by the sitter's friends… Pope was said to have the 'countenance… of a person who had been much afflicted by headache' … Emphasising the taut angularity of Pope's face, with its bony cheeks and pursed lips, Roubiliac's images have a delicacy that heightens our sense of the poet's fragility. (Exhibition handlist – Yale Center for British Art and Waddesdon Manor: The Rothschild Collection)

Pope's father had been a prosperous linen draper in the City, who on retirement in 1700 when his son was twelve, moved to an old house with about 16 acres of land at Binfield on the edge of Windsor Forest, where his young son rode for exercise and pleasure. Alexander's poem *Windsor Forest*, a political georgic composed to celebrate the Peace of Utrecht, was published in 1713:

> Thy forest, Windsor! and thy green retreats,
> At once the Monarch's and the Muse's seats…
>
> Where order in variety we see,
> And where, tho' all things differ, all agree.
> Here waving groves and checquer'd scene display,
> And part admit, and part exclude the day…
>
> There interspers'd in lawns and opening glades
> Thin trees arise that shun each other's shades.
> Here in full light the russet plains extend:
> There wrapt in clouds the blueish hills ascend…
>
> See Pan with flocks, with fruits Pomona crown'd,
> Here blushing Flora paints th'enamel'd ground,
> Here Ceres' gifts in waving prospect stand,
> And nodding tempt the joyful reaper's hand;
> Rich Industry sits smiling on the plains,
> And peace and plenty tell, a STUART reigns…

The rhyming couplets may now sound relentless, and the admixture of classical allusion and ingratiating political commentary appear too tied to its period to hold much appeal for an audience no longer on familiar terms with the gods and heroes of antiquity, but interspersed with it all is a painterly recognition of the beauty of the natural and agricultural landscape – a beauty that Pope aimed to conjure up in his own garden and in the gardens of his more alert contemporaries. His sensibility was not new; Spenser and Milton had been comparably responsive in their poetry, but Pope found a fresh and receptive audience in the circle that gathered around Lord Burlington at his town house in Piccadilly and his estate at Chiswick.

Richard Boyle, 3rd Earl of Burlington (1694–1753), undertook the Grand Tour twice, returning in 1719 after his second trip – during which he had made a special study of the buildings in and around Venice and the Veneto designed by the architect Andrea Palladio

(1508–1580) – with a large collection of Palladio's drawings and accompanied by the Yorkshireman William Kent (1685–1748), who had been studying painting in Rome. Burlington made it his mission to promote the cool Roman Classicism of Palladio as the new English national style, in deliberate contrast to the then-current Baroque manner, and between 1726 and 1729 built his famous villa at Chiswick as a free-standing addition to the old Jacobean house.

Burlington was not the first Englishman to discover Palladio; Inigo Jones (1573–1652) had designed and built the Queen's House at Greenwich and the Banqueting House, Whitehall, for James I in a remarkably pure Italian style more than a century earlier, and Jones's assistant and kinsman John Webb had built Gunnersbury House as a Palladian-inspired villa in the 1650s but, to quote Mavis Batey from her *Alexander Pope: The Poet and the Landscape*, 'Chiswick Villa was the centre of the arts in Augustan England. It was Lord Burlington who brought Pope the poet and Kent the painter together, an introduction which would lead to the new art of landscape gardening.'

Pope's family had left Binfield in 1716 and moved under Burlington's patronage to Mawson's New Buildings (now Mawson's Row) in Chiswick, where a Blue Plaque records the poet's residence there. Burlington offered Pope a house in Mayfair near Burlington House, but with the financial independence achieved through his translation of The Iliad, Pope was able to move with his mother and his nurse (his father had died in 1717) to Twickenham in 1720, there to create his famous and influential garden and grotto tunnel.

The Rome of Augustus was to be the inspiration for the new style of building and gardening, but while the ruined buildings of ancient Rome could still be seen and measured and brought to England in drawings, prints and paintings, the landscapes and gardens could be known only through the ancient poets and other writers or through the imagination of much later painters like Nicholas Poussin or Claude Lorrain, whose evocations of classical landscapes with heroic or mythical figures and temple ruins bathed in an Italian light hung on the walls of the wealthy across Great Britain and Ireland.

In 1728, the architect Robert Castell published *The Villas of the Ancients Illustrated* with a dedication to his patron Lord Burlington. In addition to an extensive text, the volume contained two engraved plates depicting Castell's fanciful recreation of the plans of the villas and estates belonging to Pliny the Younger at Laurentium on the coast near Ostia and at Tusculum in the Apennines and described in his letters.

The combination of formality and 'natural' informality as described and depicted by Castell was to be given expression at Chiswick, where Burlington laid out an essentially inward-looking and small-scale landscape of loosely-related formal geometrical features based on an existing avenue and vista running north west past the Jacobean house. William Kent, first brought to Chiswick in 1719 and working on the gardens there largely in the 1730s, – and who, in Horace Walpole's memorable phrase, 'leapt the fence and saw that all nature was a garden' – continued to design in a formal Roman or Italian Renaissance manner but also introduced a softening of the existing layout, removing fussy details and simplifying the relationship between the villa and the canal or 'river' formed from the earlier boundary ditch or Bollo Brook.

Pope wrote in 1732, 'I assure you Chiswick has been to me the finest thing this glorious sun has shined on', but already by 1720 he was in a position to commence on his own garden in Cross Deep. Drawn and painted representations of Pope's garden are rare. The British Museum (BM 1872-11-9-879) owns William Kent's drawing of *c*.1725–30 of the garden at Twickenham, which shows the artist with his palette in one hand and his other hand on the poet's shoulder, standing at the east end of the garden. An octagonal shell temple is flanked

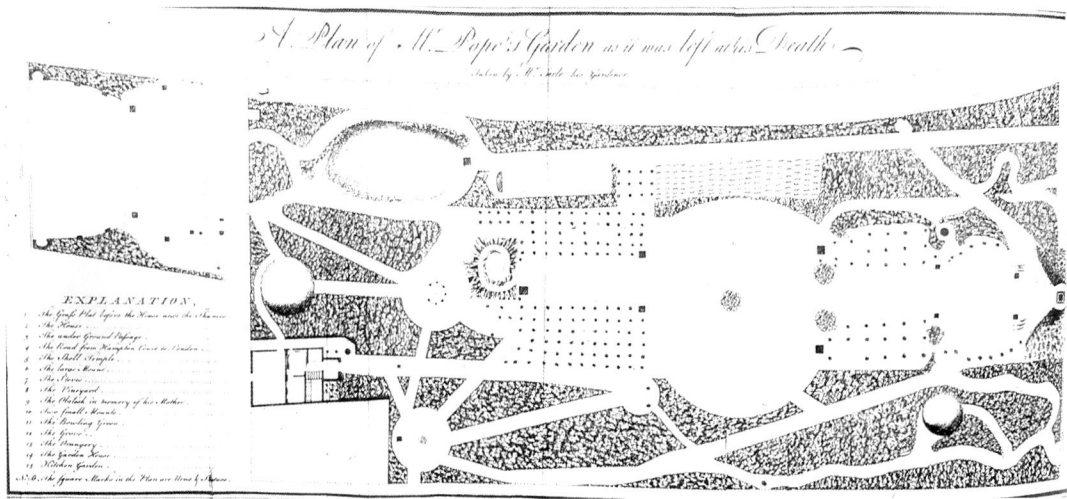

6.2. *A Plan of Mr Pope's Garden*. Engraving after John Serle, 1745. (Richmond Local Studies Collection, LCP 3623)

by rockwork niches; there are a Roman altar and a bust of Homer on a plinth, and between the splayed columns of the temple a framed vista down through the grotto tunnel reveals a boat on the river. At the end of an arc of rainbow – a characteristic Kent caprice – classical deities and tritons disport themselves amid jets of water: 'Descending gods have found Elysium here'.

The plan of the garden is known from John Serle, 1745 and John Rocque, 1744–6 (Fig. 6.2 and see Figs 1.4 and 5.4). John Serle was Pope's gardener from about 1724, and the plan 'published a year after the poet's death was to illustrate a guidebook intended for tourists who had begun to visit the gardens and grotto during Pope's lifetime and who made pilgrimages to Twickenham in increasing numbers throughout the century.' (Catalogue to exhibition *Alexander Pope's Villa. Views of Pope's villa, grotto and garden: a microcosm of English landscape* held at Marble Hill, July–September 1980. Greater London Council.)

The fullest description that we have of the grotto is from an anonymous account published in *The General Magazine of Newcastle* in January 1748, four years after Pope's death:

> Between the River and the House ascends a Parterre or Piece of Grass near Square; on the uppermost Verge of which is the House, fronting the River, and backing against the Wall of the high Road…This Grass Plot is joined to the Garden by a subterraneous Passage, or Cavern… Mr Pope, you may observe, in a letter to Mr Blount, says, that in forming the subterraneous Way and Grotto, he there found a Spring of the clearest Water, which fell in a continuous Rill that echo'd thro' the Cavern Day and Night… The Grotto is an irregular Vault and Passage, open at both Extremities, and further illuminated by two Windows to the Front…here (the stream) gurgles in a gushing Rill thro' fractur'd Ores and Flints; there it…rushes out in Jets and Fountains…To multiply this Diversity, and still more increase the Delight, Mr Pope's poetic Genius has introduced a Kind of Machinery…this is effected by disposing Plates of Looking Glass in the obscure Parts of the Roof and Sides of the Cave…while the other Parts, the Rills, Fountains, Flints, Pebbles, &c. being duly illuminated, are so reflected by the various profited Mirrors, as, without exposing the Cause, every Object is multiplied… Cast your Eyes upward, and you half shudder to see Cataracts of Water precipitating over

your Head…Thus, by a fine Taste and happy Management of Nature, you are presented with an undistinguishable Mixture of Realities and Imagery…

The anonymous journalist was clearly much impressed by the theatrics of the grotto, and after his somewhat exaggerated account of the rocks and water and mirrors his description of the garden is less sensational. What he describes is an inward-looking woodland garden sheltered from the outside world by trees and shrubs, with open lawns, groves and winding walks, the land-form modulated to include a spiral mound with a seat shaded by a tree and other mounds and declivities. Contrasts of light and shade, of openness and enclosure, and of 'nature' and artifice, were carefully balanced; Italy was recalled with a small vineyard, groves and orange trees, and practicalities were catered for by a strip of kitchen garden and 'stoves'. Formal elements were few in number (certainly compared with Chiswick), and included the Shell Temple and flanking rockwork niches, a handful of classical busts, statues and urns, and the obelisk erected to the memory of his mother.

> As this Obelisk terminates the longest Prospect of Mr Pope's Garden, it shall also put a Period to my Description; which is not of a Place that bears the high Air of State and Grandeur, and surprises you with the vastness of Expence and Magnificence; but an elegant Retreat of a Poet strongly inspired with the love of Nature and Retirement…
>
> It is not here,
>
> That – Grove nods at Grove, each Alley has a Brother,
> And half the Platform just reflects the other,
> But – Pleasing Intricacies intervene,
> And artful Wildness to perplex the Scene.

(The description continues – for the full text see Hunt and Willis, *The Genius of the Place*)

'Grove nods at Grove…' and 'Pleasing intricacies…' are (mis)quotations from Pope's *An Epistle to Lord Burlington* (1731), the famous and influential poem that expresses Pope's call for a 'natural' style of gardening:

> … To build, to plant, whatever you intend,
> To rear the Column, or the Arch to bend,
> To swell the Terras, or to sink the Grot:
> In all, let Nature never be forgot.
> Consult the Genius of the Place in all…

The 'natural' style was also seen as a patriotic English style (a sentiment echoed later by Horace Walpole), and the Epistle goes on to attack the artifice and symmetry of the Baroque style of Versailles, represented as Timon's Villa:

> At Timon's Villa let us pass a Day,
> Where all cry out, 'What sums are thrown away!…
> No pleasing Intricacies intervene,
> No artful Wilderness to perplex the Scene:

> Grove nods at Grove, each Ally has a Brother,
> And half the Platform just reflects the other...

Pope's witty but sharp pen won him many admirers but also enemies, one of whom was James Brydges, 1st Duke of Chandos, whom many identified as Timon – a charge that the poet denied. Brydges had built a vast palace, Canons, at Edgware between 1713 and 1720 at a cost of £200,000, but such were his debts that his heir sold off the contents and demolished the house in 1747.

Pope wrote of his own more modest estate in Twickenham:

> Know, all the distant Din the World can keep
> Rolls o'er my Grotto, and but soothes my Sleep.
> Content with Little, I can piddle here
> On Broccoli and Mutton round the Year;
>
> But ancient Friends (tho' poor or out of Play)
> That touch my Bell, I cannot turn away.
> 'Tis true, no Turbots dignify my boards,
> But Gudgeons, Flounders what my Thames affords:
>
> To Hounslow-Heath I point, and Banstead-Down,
> Thence comes your Mutton, & these Chicks my own:
> From yon old Walnut Tree a Show'r shall fall:
> And Grapes long-lingring on my only Wall,
>
> And Figs from Standard and Espalier join:
> The Devil's in you if you cannot dine.
> Then chearful healths (your Mistress shall have place)
> And, what's more rare, a Poet shall say Grace.

The picture he paints of himself as a welcoming host is an attractive, even loveable one, and his espousal of localism and self-sufficiency has a modern appeal. The engraving by Parr after Rysbrack (Fig. 6.1) shows a party of visitors arriving by boat at the riverside lawn. Pope stands with his dog Bounce, a Great Dane, at the arched entrance to the grotto; by that date (1735) the villa had acquired a projecting porch and a single-storey portico with four Tuscan columns supporting a balcony at first-floor level. The Tillemans painting (see Fig. 1.6), composed before the porch and portico were added, suggests that the house was of yellow brick with white stone dressings. An interesting detail of the Parr engraving is the cold frames flanking the porch or ante-room to the grotto. Trees – probably fruit trees – are trained against the garden walls.

Alexander Pope came to see his grotto in the 1730s as the classical Egerian grotto where statesmen could philosophise in the lap of the Muses. By tradition the legendary philosopher king, Numa Pompilius, had learned to cultivate good government through the inspiration of the nymph Egeria, who dwelt by the spring in her sacred grotto outside Rome. When Joseph Spence brought Pope a piece of marble from the Egerian grotto after his Grand Tour a poetic link between Twickenham and classical

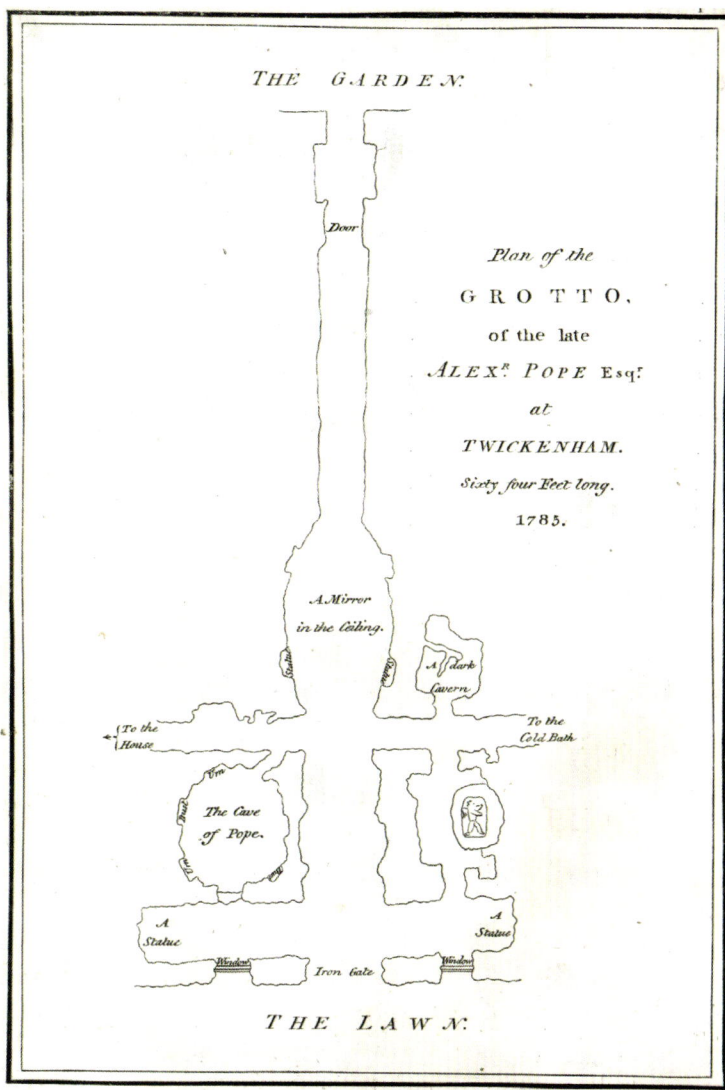

6.3. *Plan of the Grotto of the late Alex. Pope Esq. at Twickenham*. Engraving after Samuel Lewis, 1785. (Orleans House Gallery, LDORL: 00345)

Rome was forged. (Mavis Batey, unpublished note)

Figs. 6.3 and 6.4 give the plan and perspective view from Serle, 1745.

Following a visit to Hotwell Spa in Bristol in 1739 where he was impressed by the Avon Gorge and its geology, Pope undertook with advice and gifts of minerals from Dr Oliver in Bath and Dr William Borlase in Cornwall to redesign his grotto as a museum of mineralogy rather than simply as a cabinet of curiosities. His collection displayed over 140 different mineral and geological specimens from Britain and abroad and included a stalagmite from Wookey Hole in Somerset, ore from Cornish tin mines, and two hexagonal joints of basalt from the Giant's Causeway in Ireland, given by Sir Hans Sloane.

> When you shut the doors of this grotto it becomes on the instant from a luminous room, a Camera obscura on the walls of which all the subjects of the river, hills, woods, and boats are forming a moving picture in their visible radiations; and when you have a mind to light it up, it affords a very different scene. It is finished with shells

6.4. *A Perspective View of the Grotto.* Engraving after John Serle, 1745. (Richmond Local Studies Collection, LCP 3623)

> interspersed with pieces of looking glass in angular forms; and in the ceiling is a star of the same material at which when a lamp, of an orbicular figure of thin alabaster, is hung in the middle, a thousand pointed rays glitter and are reflected over the place. (Letter from the Swedish Minister Gyllenborg to Edward Blount, 2 June 1725)

Pope died in 1744 at the age of fifty-six and was buried in the parish church of St Mary's, where stand memorials to him and to his parents, and where his long-term nurse Mary Beach is also commemorated with a memorial tablet. The estate was bought by Sir William Stanhope, who added a central pediment and wings with canted bay windows to the house and acquired more land to enlarge the garden, creating a further grotto at the west end, decorated with shell- and pebble-work and known as Stanhope's Cave, which survives in private ownership.

Horace Walpole wrote to Horace Mann (20 June 1760):

> (Stanhope) has cut down the sacred groves themselves! In short, it was a little bit of ground of five acres, enclosed by three lanes and seeing nothing. Pope had twisted and twirled and rhymed and harmonized this, till it appeared two or three sweet little lawns opening and opening beyond one another, and the whole surrounded by thick impenetrable woods. Sir William, by advice of his son-in-law Mr Ellis, has hacked and hewed these groves, wriggled a winding gravel walk through them with an edging of shrubs, in what they call the modern taste, has desired the three lanes walk in again – and now is forced to shut them out again by a wall, for there was not a muse could make a little maid's water, but she was spied on by every country fellow that went by with a pipe in his mouth.

'The dilapidations of time and the pious thefts of visitors, who select the spars, ores, and even the common flints, as so many sacred relics, have almost brought it to ruin...' (Description in *The Ambulator*, 1796).

6.5. *Pope's Villa.* Engraving by John Pye, 1811, after the painting *View of Pope's Villa at Twickenham During its Dilapidation, 1808,* by JMW Turner. (Orleans House Gallery, LDORL: 00459)

Worse was to follow. In 1807 the estate was bought by Baroness Howe of Langar (1762–1835) who 'being inconvenienced by the continuing flow of visitors to Pope's garden and grotto' demolished the house and stripped out much of the remaining decoration from the grotto, an act of iconoclasm that earned her the title of Queen of the Goths. The obelisk and vases that Pope had erected at the west end of his garden in memory of his mother were moved to Penn House in Buckinghamshire, where they remain. (Baroness Howe's first husband was the Hon. Penn Assheton Curzon of Penn House). George Mason's *Essay on Design in Gardening*, published in 1795, is dedicated to (Sophia) Charlotte Curzon (Baroness Howe), whom Mason praises as an 'excellent judge of landscape'. Mason died in 1806, so had no need to rue the irony of his words. Howe retained the grotto tunnel to provide access to the garden, and built a new villa slightly upstream – part of which survives as Ryan House. Lady Howe's Villa in 1809 is shown as Fig. 5.8. In November 1807, Horace Walpole's old friend Mary Berry, who lived at Little Strawberry Hill, wrote in her journal: 'went into Pope's back garden, and saw the devastation going on upon his quincunx by its now possessor, Baroness Howe. The anger and ill-humour expressed against her for pulling down his house and destroying his grounds much greater than one would have imagined.'

The painter JMW Turner was one of the many outraged by the vandalism, and his painting *View of Pope's Villa at Twickenham During its Dilapidation, 1808* (Fig. 6.5) shows the house under demolition as viewed from one of the aits upstream, with figures and sheep in

6.6. Pope's Villa. Photograph by JS Catford, *c*.1897. (Chris Sumner Collection)

the foreground. Turner composed sibilant verses on the subject, 'Invocation of Thames to the Seasons upon the Demolition of Pope's House':

> Dear Sister Isis tis thy Thames that calls
> See desolation hovers o'er those walls,
> The scatter'd timbers on my margin lays
> Where glimmering Evening's ray yet lingering plays
> There British Maro sang by Science long endear'd
> And to an admiring country once revered
> Now to destruction doom'd thy peaceful grott
> Pope's willow bending to the earth forgot…

Despite the Baroness, Pope was not totally expunged. The name Pope's Villa was given to the 'Elizabethan Structure with Campanella Tower' built in 1842 for Thomas Young, a tea merchant, by HE Kendall Jun., which later became St Catherine's Convent and now houses Radnor House School. A photograph of *c*.1897 (Fig. 6.6) shows the house from across the river, embowered in trees and creepers, with to the left a boathouse built in line with the grotto tunnel.

The grotto's final visual link with the river was severed in the 1930s when a red brick chapel and teaching block were built immediately in front of it, reducing the tunnel to little more than the 'passage' about which Dr Johnson had been ironical two centuries earlier. It served to link the school and convent buildings, which by that time also occupied The Lawn, a pleasant mid-Victorian brick villa constructed on part of the former garden and later enlarged with other school buildings. The tunnel had been extended to accommodate twentieth-century

6.7. Entrance to grotto following conservation. Photograph by Damian Griffiths. (Courtesy of Pope's Grotto Preservation Trust and Donald Insall Associates)

6.8. Interior of north chamber of grotto following conservation. Photograph by Damian Griffiths. (Courtesy of Pope's Grotto Preservation Trust and Donald Insall Associates)

road widening, but when the two parts of the school were separated to become St Catherine's School and St James's (now Radnor House) School, the tunnel became functionally redundant and was put on the English Heritage (now Historic England) Heritage at Risk register.

Radnor House School, with the support of the Pope's Grotto Preservation Trust, the National Lottery Heritage Fund, Historic England, the Heritage of London Trust, the Thames Landscape Strategy, and other trusts and individual sponsors has commenced on the repair and re-presentation of the grotto. The project includes:

◆ Stabilisation and careful cleaning of the Grotto and its collection of minerals and fossils;

◆ Replacing the cement floor with Pope's original concept of natural stone paving;

6.9. Memorial garden to Alexander Pope. Photograph by Chris Sumner, 2018. The Parish Church of St Mary's, Twickenham, in the background is Pope's burial place and contains memorials to him, his parents, and his nurse Mary Beach

- Installing floor-level lighting and sound effects to provide sequenced focus on the features described by Pope;

- Creating a digital interpretation, re-imagining Pope's garden, that can be hosted on the web for the many followers of Pope in other parts of the world;

- Increasing opportunities for education, volunteering and access for people of all ages and abilities.

Details of the works proposed can be found on the Trust's website.

At the time of writing, the project budget is approximately £300,000, some of which has already been secured, and the work of cleaning, consolidating, lighting and interpretation was started in 2019. The digital interpretation – entitled *A Virtual Arcadia* – is being overseen by Prof Paul Richens of the University of Westminster and provides a fascinating tour of the Twickenham riverside, grotto and garden as in Pope's day.

Figs 6.7 and 6.8 show the interior of the grotto following recent conservation work.

Pope is also commemorated in a charming riverside garden (Fig. 6.9) created in 2015 by the London Borough of Richmond upon Thames close to St Mary's Church, on the site of a demolished warehouse and as an extension to the wholly delightful (although outside the period of this work) gardens of York House. There, an inventive modern interpretation in Corten steel of a classical urn on a plinth designed by Pope for the gardens at Hagley Park, Worcestershire, is dedicated to the poet, and is accompanied by a mini-grove of plane trees and benches inscribed with some of his best-known though often uncredited aphorisms:

> Fools rush in where angels fear to tread…
> Eternal sunshine of the spotless mind…
> To err is human, to forgive divine…
> A little Learning is a dangerous thing…
> Hope springs eternal in the human breast…
> Blessed is he who expects nothing, for he shall never be disappointed.

CHAPTER SEVEN

Poulett Lodge

Mike Cherry

Poulett Lodge stood on the riverside of the road Cross Deep, close to the junction with King Street and Heath Road, Twickenham. It takes its name from a later eighteenth-century owner of the property, but its origins go back to the very early 1700s. Prior to that time the riverside in Cross Deep was largely undeveloped. Moses Glover's map of 1635 indicates only one property, not on the site of Poulett Lodge, but there may have been isolated buildings associated with riverine and artisan occupations. As Alexander Pope found when he settled a few hundred yards upstream in 1719, his neighbours were a fisherman, a tanner, a wheelwright and a poultry keeper rather than the gentry.

In 1701 Sir Thomas Skipwith bought from Edward Wintour a copyhold property by the Thames including a house and orchard, known as the Osier Ground, of about ¾ acre in extent. In 1707 he bought additional land from Mary Birkhead.

Sir Thomas Skipwith, 2nd Baronet, of Metheringham, Lincolnshire, lived in Twickenham only briefly – from 1701 until 1709. He died in June 1710. At some point he also acquired an adjacent freehold property; this is recorded in a sale of 1741 by his son, Sir George Skipwith to Dr William Battie which refers to a 'parcel of ground on which a house lately stood… but is now burnt down, and various barns, stables, outhouses and buildings…and gardens, orchard, fruit trees and plants.' This describes the substantial and well-ordered estate that had been Sir Thomas Skipwith's, was then known as Lord Denbigh's, and from later in the eighteenth century as Poulett Lodge.

After Sir Thomas's death his son, Sir George, inherited the Thames-side estate. He lived only very briefly in Twickenham and the estate was occupied in the early 1710s by John Erskine, 11th Earl of Mar. He had married Margaret Hay in Twickenham in 1703 and, after her death, married in 1714 Lady Frances Pierrepont, daughter of the Duke of Kingston and sister of Lady Mary Wortley Montagu who was a later resident of Twickenham and close friend and later bitter enemy of Alexander Pope. Mar was an enthusiastic amateur architect and may have been responsible for enlarging Skipwith's original house. But Mar's residence in Twickenham was short; he was a prominent Jacobite and was driven into exile in France in 1715.

John Macky, writing in his *Journey Through England* (1722), describes 'a little house, which belonged formerly to Sir Thomas Skipwith and was improved and inhabited by that great architect, the Earl of Mar, with its hanging gardens to the river…well worth the curiosity of the traveller.'

The estate was in the occupation of William Feilding, 5th Earl of Denbigh in the 1720s and early 1730s, and it is as Lord Denbigh's house that it appears in Peter Tillemans' painting (Fig. 7.1 – detail from Fig. 1.6).

The painting shows a substantial house set in formal gardens on the banks of the Thames.

7.1. Lord Denbigh's House. Detail of painting by Peter Tillemans, *c*.1724-30 (Fig. 1.6)

The gardens descend in terraces to the river and are adorned with statuary. The house is flanked by long hedges to each side terminating in garden pavilions. In front of the hedges is a long row of small trees, alternately columnar and round. Further rows of trees stand on the lower terraces and there are another four pavilions at intervals. At the riverside there appears to be a dock, capable of accommodating a large boat, over the entrance to which is an elegant and decorative footbridge. To the right hand side is a range of stable buildings with a cupola and a cottage.

Not surprisingly the house was thought suitable for the French Ambassador to Britain, M. Chauvigny, to whom it was lent. He had occupied it for less than a year when it burnt down, his cook dying in the fire.

Sir George Skipwith seems not to have made any effort to rebuild on the site and in 1741 it was sold to Dr William Battie. He is first recorded as paying rates on the property in 1743. Battie (sometimes Batty) had a long career in medicine and was appointed President of the College of Physicians in 1764. He built a new house as seen in a later print of *c*.1770 (Fig. 7.2). This shows a more modest house than its predecessor: three storeys each of three bays with the first floor central bay extending and supported on pillars. The ground floor wings extend on each side. The house retained gardens with a formal layout. A fenced lawn extended from the front of the house to the river with a small landing stage in the centre. The rest of the considerable river frontage was also fenced behind which were very neat lateral rows of small trees and shrubs. Clearly the influence of Alexander Pope's 'natural' gardening philosophy had not spread the few hundred yards downstream.

Battie lived in the house on Cross Deep until 1759 when he sold it to Nathaniel Lloyd whose niece Mary had married Vere Poulett in 1755. The couple were living in Battie's house from 1759 and Vere took ownership in 1761. He became 3rd Earl Poulett in 1764 and died in 1788. His widow Mary continued to live in the house until 1819 and was succeeded by another dowager Countess Poulett, Margaret, widow of the 4th Earl. In between Poulett widows the house was let to tenants until the 5th Earl sold the estate in 1839 to Andrew

7.2. Dr Batty's House at Twickenham as Viewed from the opposite Shore of the River Thames. Engraving, unknown artist, *c.*1770. The house to the left is Crossdeep shown without the wings added by James Gibbs

7.3. Poulett Lodge Twickenham (Dr Punchard's). Early twentieth-century postcard. (Mike Cherry Collection)

Maclew. It was sold by a later owner, Mr C Martin, to William Henry Punchard, in 1870.

Punchard was a civil engineer with the building of railways a speciality. This clearly brought him considerable wealth because he is reputed to have spent £70,000 on a completely new, and much larger, house on the site of Poulett Lodge. The gardens were also completely remodelled, with a terrace, stone balustrade, boathouse and stable block still surviving (Fig. 7.3).

However, two garden structures from the later eighteenth/early nineteenth century remain: a grotto and a loggia. Both are located against the southern boundary wall between the grounds of Poulett Lodge and the house known simply as Crossdeep, which still stands. The grotto is listed Grade II* for the following principal reasons:

Architectural interest: shell house decorated in a precise geometric pattern to resemble a coffered vault which is separated by a deep horizontal band from the more randomly decorated vertical walls, and is possibly applied to an earlier garden structure; Materials: created using scallops, winkles and other native shells, coloured slag and stone, fragments of glass and ceramic, set in cement on a brick base; Rarity: rare

7.4. Interior of the Grotto. (Mike Cherry Collection)

example of a once common building type, where two thirds of the decoration remains in situ; Historic interest: Poulett Lodge was one of a group of substantial houses and gardens fronting the River Thames at Twickenham, associated with the literary and dilettante circles which included Alexander Pope and Horace Walpole. (©Historic England 2020, List Entry 1080812.) (Fig. 7.4)

The loggia (Fig. 7.5) is listed Grade II and links the grotto to the riverside along the boundary wall. The principal reasons for listing are:

Architectural interest: Portland stone Tuscan loggia leading to the rare surviving grotto or shell house (separately listed at Grade II*) and built against the boundary wall where there have been garden structures since at least 1725; Historic interest: Poulett Lodge was one of a group of substantial houses and gardens fronting the River Thames at Twickenham, associated with the literary and dilettante circles which included Alexander Pope and Horace Walpole; the Tuscan loggia, which is typical of the early to mid-C19 development of the garden, reflects a C19 phase in the continuing development of the gardens where the historic and architectural interest ranges from the early C18 to the late C19. (©Historic England 2020 List Entry 1401819)

Grottoes and other garden structures were fashionable in the eighteenth century and were mainly intended as showpieces for friends and visitors. Certainly Pope's grotto, in the basement of his villa a few hundred yards upstream, and other local structures such as the shell grotto at Hampton Court house, were designed to make an impact. The grotto or shell house at Poulett Lodge is, in contrast, a small structure. The internal dimensions are 2.3m square and 2m high and the brickwork is buried under an earth mound and tucked up against the boundary wall. It seems to be hiding away and this may support the suggestion that it had originally been constructed as an ice house and was only later converted to a decorated

7.5. The Loggia.
(Mike Cherry Collection)

7.6. Arched opening to the Grotto.
(Mike Cherry Collection)

grotto. The original arched opening was partly in-filled at a later date (Fig. 7.6).

The loggia and grotto are not referred to in any early documents that have so far come to light. The first representation of the loggia appears on the Ordnance Survey map of 1863, which also shows two small structures in the neighbouring garden, whereas the Twickenham enclosure map of 1818 shows these structures but not the loggia. This suggests the loggia was erected after 1818 and before 1863, probably when it was in the ownership of the 5th Earl of Poulett or Andrew Maclew. In style, the buildings seem to be of the eighteenth century. The grotto was presumably present under the final bay of the loggia when it was shown on the 1863 map, but is mentioned for the first time by name on a map of 1890 as a 'temple & grotto'. It is very likely that the grotto existed before the loggia, which seems to have been erected to lead to it. Its brickwork shell is quite clearly distinct from the structure of the loggia. The listing suggests that the grotto started life as an icehouse and its shape, size and siting on the edge of the property make this a possibility although as it stands today there is no sign of any underground chamber. The present grotto stands at ground level, is roughly square in plan, and seems to have had an open arch towards the river (now partly bricked up). It has a semi-circular vault ornamented with coloured pebbles or stones of blue and brown, and shells, all set in geometric patterns with a circle and star at the centre. The back wall seems to have been ornamented at one time, although now it is mostly lined with flints. Such grotto chambers were being built as early as the seventeenth century, many created from the early eighteenth onwards, and through into the nineteenth century, but there are very few clues by which to date this one. The only shred of evidence is the two-storey pavilion seen in the Tillemans painting in roughly the position of the present grotto. This may have been damaged in the fire, or otherwise demolished, since it is not present in any subsequent illustration, but its lower storey may have survived to become the grotto. Early occupants of the house, especially the Earl of Mar, had gardening interests. The dating of both grotto and loggia are evidently very problematic and a number of other theories have been proposed. *Blest Retreats* (1984) suggested the loggia might date from the occupancy of WH Punchard, but its depiction on the OS map of 1863, seven years before Punchard moved in, precludes this. The construction of the loggia on the wall side indicates that it may have originally been a free-standing structure that has been moved to its present location and it has been suggested that it came from the Poulett family seat in Somerset, but this seems unlikely since the Somerset branch of the family had little to do with the house at Twickenham after 1788. In the absence of any documentary evidence, Historic England (HE) suggest that the grotto dates from the period 1770–1800 when grottoes were fashionable following the publicity given to the famous Pope's Grotto just up river from Poulett Lodge. HE also suggests that the Poulett family added the loggia and grotto in the late eighteenth century. Michael Lee suggests that the grotto and loggia date from 1780–1820, but also without documentary evidence. However, it is quite possible that one or both are of an earlier or later date.

Both structures are on Historic England's register of buildings at risk and are fenced off to prevent access, and the loggia has recently been shored-up with scaffolding to prevent it collapsing.

The later history of the estate is complicated and not untypical of large houses in the area: a series of owners and tenants and increasing difficulty in finding a practical use for such a large property.

The grounds of the estate on the other side of the road Cross Deep which had been in use as a market garden and nursery by William Bates, who had been head gardener at Poulett Lodge, were sold for housing in the 1920s. The house was the subject of two attempts to launch it as a social club – first as the Monte Carlo Sports Club and then the Newborough Club; neither proved successful and in around 1930 the house and grounds were bought by Ernest Skull, a local butcher, as an investment. He gained permission to demolish the house and replace it with Thames Eyot, a block of sixty-eight service flats in the Art Deco style.

It should be noted that the grounds of Thames Eyot including the loggia and grotto are private and there is no public access.

CHAPTER EIGHT

Orleans House Gallery
Chris Sumner

> 'Here is an admirable prospect of the most charming part of the
> Thames, where the eye is entertained by a Thousand Beauties not
> to be conceived but from this station'.
> (Colen Campbell, *Vitruvius Britannicus Vol. I*, 1715)

Orleans House Gallery owes its name to the estate's early-nineteenth-century tenant Louis Philippe, duc d'Orleans, but the documented history of the site and of its sequence of gardens stretches back to at least the seventeenth century. Along with the neighbouring Marble Hill the Gallery retains the distinction of being approachable by boat in the eighteenth-century tradition of Twickenham's riverside properties, connected as it is to Ham House and the Surrey bank by Hammerton's Ferry. However, while Marble Hill still has a distinguished presence when viewed from the Thames – supporting the river's claim to being England's Brenta – Orleans House Gallery is now self-effacing to the extent of invisibility.

The Gallery, owned by the London Borough of Richmond upon Thames and open to the public, houses the borough's art collection, which includes a large number of topographical images recording the changing character of the riverside over the centuries. A striking change is in the degree to which tree cover along the stretch of river through Twickenham has increased since it was first recorded in any detail four hundred years ago. Moses Glover's very large and beautiful map of the Manor of Sion of 1635 (displayed at Syon House) shows that while the aits in the river were generally wooded (probably with osiers), the riverside comprised unembanked water meadows indicated as pasture, with arable land and the occasional orchard away from the water's edge and with only a scatter of field boundary trees. John Rocque's maps of London and ten miles around (1744–46, see Fig. 1.4) and Middlesex (1754) show the network of avenues stretching out from Hampton Court, Ham House and other major houses planted from the 1660s onwards, but the now-familiar long narrow bands of woodland partly lining the riverbanks are a twentieth-century phenomenon, resulting from changes in the ownership and management of the land and consequent upon embanking the sides and suppressing the towing path as such; the waterside was traditionally clear of trees to prevent fouling the boat hauliers' tow ropes (see Fig. 1.5). Ignoring – which one easily can – the low concrete flood wall, the view across Petersham Meadows from the Middlesex bank, with the wooded slopes of Petersham Common and Richmond Park in the background and grass and wildflowers and a few stunted elder bushes and ash trees in the foreground, remains not too far removed from the traditional open view unconstrained by trees (Fig. 8.1).

By contrast, Orleans House Gallery now presents unbroken woodland to the river, a mixture of horse chestnuts and willows in the main, with a few London planes and poplars.

8.1. View downriver towards Glover's Island, Richmond Hill and Petersham Meadows from the Surrey bank opposite Marble Hill. Photograph by Chris Sumner, 2020

A silver-grey tidemark running through the lowest foliage indicates the level to which the water rises, and of that archetypal Twickenham riverside tree the weeping willow (*Salix babylonica*) – which adds so much to the character of Radnor Gardens – there is only one example, on the upstream boundary with the neighbouring gardens of Riverside House, the former home of the Gallery's great benefactor Nellie Ionides.

As recently as 1926, when the southern half of the estate was sold and the major part of the house demolished for gravel excavations, the area between the river and the public road – now a children's playground with a small cafe and lavatories and known as Orleans Gardens – was still unembanked, called on a sales plan of the time River Meadow (Fig. 8.2) and bisected towards the east by a creek leading to a boathouse. The excellent guide book published by the borough – *Orleans House: A History* – illustrates with a series of maps and paintings the estate's development, virtual vanishing act, and Sleeping Beauty-like return over the past three centuries; la belle au bois dormant indeed.

The *Parliamentary Survey of Twickenham* of 1649–50 records formal gardens north and south of the old mansion, surrounded by brick walls and subdivided by gravel paths. The walls were planted with

> rare Duke and May Cherreyes Vines and Peach with a Gravily Walk with Arbors at each corner… several borders… planted with rare and Choyce Flowers and with divers small Trees as Cipres Trees… alsoe one open Kitchen garden or piece of ground

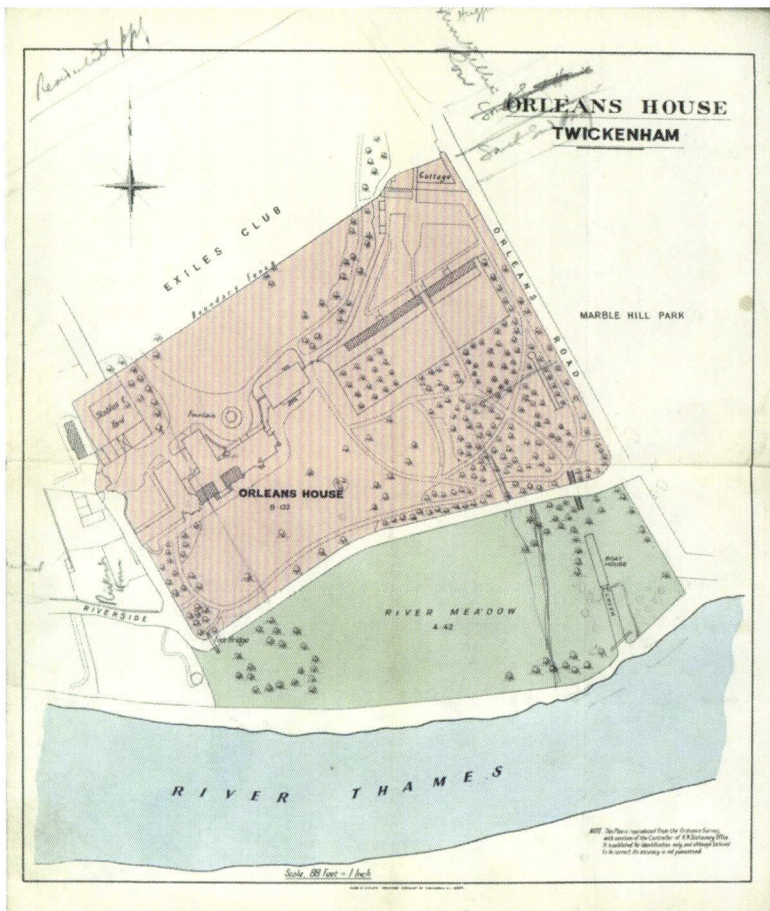

8.2. Orleans House. Extract from sales plan, *c*.1925. (Orleans House Gallery, LDORL: 02697)

Lyeing between the River Thames and the first above menconed garden beinge very plentifully planted with Cabidges Turnipps and Carretts and many other such like Creatures.

That house was rebuilt by James Johnston, who procured a lease in 1702 and commissioned the architect John James to design him a new mansion, the plans and elevation of which were published in Colen Campbell's compendium of fashionable architecture *Vitruvius Britannicus* in 1715 (Vol. I plate 77, Fig. 8.3): 'the gardens are extreme curious, the Plantations most artfully disposed; and everything contributes to express the refined Taste, and great Politeness of the Master. Designed by Mr James, 1710.'

James Johnston (1655–1737) was a Scottish diplomat and, later, English MP of mixed fortune and political success. His father Archibald Johnston, Lord Warriston, was executed in 1663 on the orders of Charles II for having served under Oliver Cromwell and the family fled to the Dutch Republic. Johnston came to England in 1688 following the 'Glorious Revolution' as a supporter of the new monarchs William III and Mary II. He was appointed joint Secretary of State for Scotland in 1692 but fell from favour with William and was dismissed in 1696, in which year he married Catherine Poulett, daughter of 2nd Baron Poulett. He returned, briefly and unsuccessfully, to Scotland in 1704 in the reign of Queen Anne, and became the MP for Ilchester in Somerset in 1708.

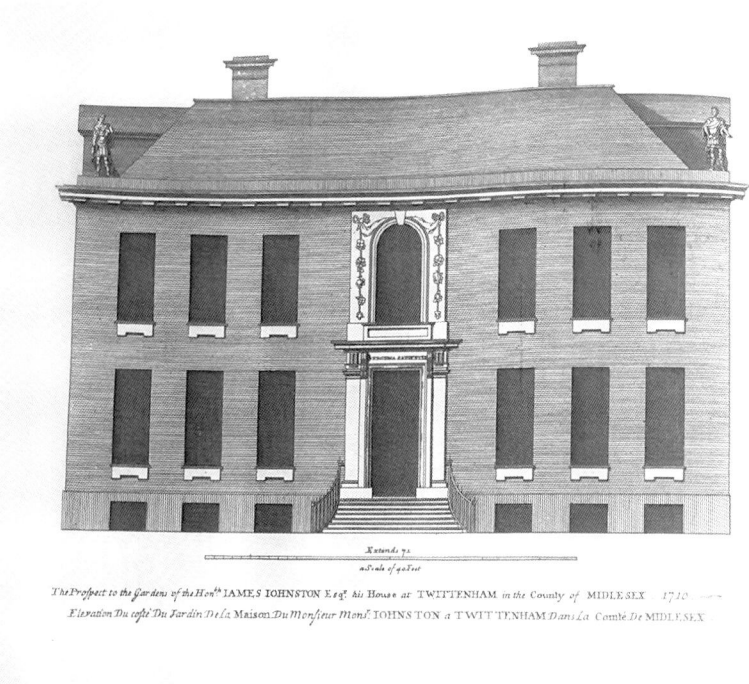

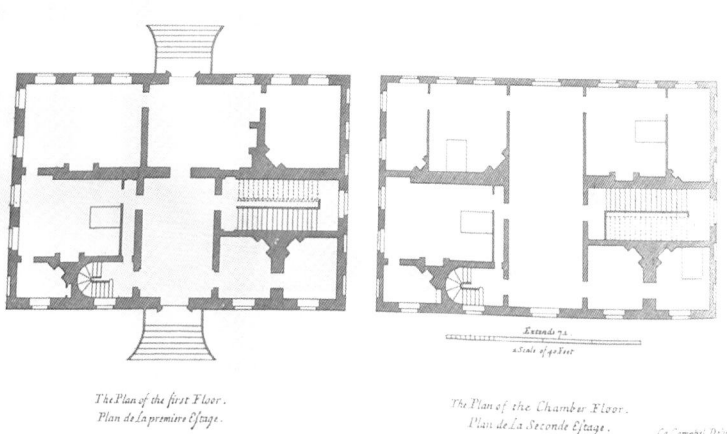

8.3. *The House of the Hon. James Johnston Esq. at Twittenham in the County of Middlesex 1710.* From *Vitruvius Britannicus, or The British Architect* by Colen Campbell, 1715. 'The Prospect to the Gardens' and plans of first floor and chamber floor. (Chris Sumner Collection)

His architect John James had worked with Sir Christopher Wren and Nicholas Hawksmoor, and in 1716 replaced James Gibbs as one of the two architects to the Commission for the Building of Fifty Churches. His surviving works include St Mary's Church, Twickenham (rebuilt except for the tower in 1714–15); St George's, Hanover Square; and Appuldurcombe House, Isle of Wight. The house he designed for Secretary Johnston was externally austere, of brick except for the central doorcase and first-floor window surround of Portland stone, of two storeys above a semi-basement and with a hipped roof. The river front was seven-windows wide, the north front five. In 1712 John James published *The Theory and Practice of Gardening*, translated from AJ Dezallier d'Argenville's 1709 French publication, with a long list of distinguished subscribers including Johnston, to whom the work is dedicated. The work contains much practical advice on surveying, the laying out of gardens and construction of steps and terraces, the management of water, planting and cultivation, and includes many engraved plates showing suggestions for parterres, borders, walks, counter-walks, palisades, woods and groves, bowers, arbours, trellis work, vases, fountains, basons, and cascades – in fact, designs for all the formal French Baroque elements that Alexander Pope, less than a generation later, was to condemn in his *Epistle to the Earl of Burlington*, 1731.

The general layout of Johnston's garden is known from a sketch plan made by John Erskine, 11th Earl of Mar, in 1711. The estate then stretched from the river to the main road (now Richmond Road), and then as now a minor public road (Riverside) bisected the southern part. The house stood on slightly rising ground set back from the river and was approached by coach from the Richmond Road along a private drive on the western boundary adjacent to the Earl of Stafford's estate. A long grass walk and avenue of trees stretched north on the central axis of the house, flanked by a pair of parallel canals, beyond which were vines and a mount and ice-house. John Macky (*A Journey through England*, 1722/3) wrote:

> Secretary Johnstoun's House may be more properly call'd a Plantation, being in the middle betwixt his Parterre, his Kitchen-Garden, his Fruit-Garden, and Wilderness… He has the best Collection of Fruit, of all sorts, of most Gentlemen in England. His Slopes for his Vines, of which he makes some Hogsheads a year, are very particular; and Doctor Bradley of the Royal Society… ranks him amongst the first-rate Gardiners in England.

Among the formal elements of Johnston's garden was a pair of lead statues of bulldogs modelled by John Van Nost and now in the Musée Condé at Chantilly. Pope could not – perhaps just for the sake of the rhyme – resist a bathetic dig at his neighbour:

> And Twick'nam such, which fairer scenes enrich
> Grots, Statues, Urns and Jo-n's Dog and Bitch.
> (*In Imitation of Spenser: The Alley*, 1727)

Batty Langley (1696–1751), the son of a Twickenham jobbing gardener, took to designing gardens and to architecture and published a number of works on both subjects illustrated with plates engraved by his brother Thomas. His architectural works include *The Builder's Complete Assistant* (1738) and *Gothic Architecture, improved by Rules and Proportions* (1747), which attempted to 'improve' Gothic architecture by imposing classical proportions, and about which Horace Walpole was scathing: 'All that his books achieved, has been to teach carpenters to massacre that venerable species' (*Anecdotes of Painting*, 1780).

Langley evidently had a taste for 'improvement', and in 1728 published *New Principles of Gardening*, which contains as plate IX 'An improvement of a beautiful Garden in Twickenham' (see Fig. 1.12). The plate is printed in reverse, but is clearly of Secretary Johnston's house and garden shown with many embellishments in the 'artinatural' style promoted both by Langley and earlier by Stephen Switzer in his *Ichnographia Rustica* of 1718, and comparable to the two plates of recreated Roman gardens in Robert Castell's *Villas of the Ancients Illustrated*, published in 1728, the same year as Langley's book. The style is still highly artificial, combining strong formal elements inherited from the French Baroque tradition with freer sinuous paths and mazes; it avoids strict symmetry, but there is as yet no nod towards the 'natural' English Landscape Garden style that Pope and Kent and others were starting to promote at the time.

8.4. *The Octagon Room*. Plan, elevation and section. Engraving by E Kirkall after James Gibbs. Plate 71 from Gibbs's *A Book of Architecture*, 1728. (Orleans House Gallery, LDORL: 00857)

It seems unlikely that any of the 'improvements' were implemented by Johnston, but the plan shows one feature that was built and that survives, and which is the main reason that the site is still so significant. The Octagon Room, commissioned from the architect James Gibbs and built between 1716 and 1720 as a garden pavilion and grand entertainment room, is an important example of English domestic Baroque architecture. James Gibbs (1682–1754) was a Scot, a Tory and a Roman Catholic who had trained in Rome with the architect Carlo Fontana. He was, briefly from 1713 to 1715, one of the two architects to the Commission for Building Fifty New Churches, but was replaced in the following year by John James, his religion and politics having weighed against his continued appointment. Nevertheless, he was the architect for many prominent public buildings including the churches of St Martin-in-the-Fields and St Mary-le-Strand, St Bartholomew's Hospital, and the Radcliffe Camera in Oxford. His publications *A Book of Architecture, containing designs of buildings and ornaments,* 1728, and *Rules for Drawing Several Parts of Architecture,* 1732, were major influences on buildings in Britain and Ireland and in North America and the colonies. Gibbs was the architect for Pope's new house in 1719, and also added the wings to the nearby house called Crossdeep, which survives. Across the river in Petersham he built Sudbrook Park for the Duke of Argyll and Greenwich.

The Octagon Room was attached to earlier buildings called 'Out Offices' on the Langley plan but detached from the house to which it was later linked by a long brick-built wing (see the Heckel/Mason view, Fig. 10.9), rebuilt in 1842 as a glass-roofed Conservatory designed by John Buonarotti Papworth (1775–1847). The design for the Octagon Room was published in Gibbs's *A Book of Architecture* and it survives much as shown there (Fig. 8.4). Externally it is of two storeys, of yellow brick with finely-gauged orange-red brick Doric pilasters at the angles, with five tall round-headed windows (one now altered to a doorway) with blank circular *oeil-de-boeuf* windows above. The architectural dressings are of white-Portland stone, and the tall windows have so-called 'Gibbs surrounds' with raised voussoirs

8.5. The Octagon Room. Photograph of exterior after 2018 restoration.
(Orleans House Gallery, IMG 0065)

8.6. The Octagon Room. Photograph of interior after 2018 restoration.
(Orleans House Gallery, Photography 179)

8.7. *Orleans House from across the River.* Watercolour by Auguste Garnerey *c.*1815. (Orleans House Gallery, LDORL: 00141)

and quoins projecting from the architraves. There is a deep stone cornice and brick parapet, and the angle pilasters are crowned by bulbous stone vases.

Johnston was on friendly terms with the new ruling dynasty from his time spent in Hanover, and the Octagon Room was built for entertaining King George I and the Prince of Wales (later George II) and his wife Caroline of Ansbach, portrait busts of whom are incorporated into the interior plasterwork. While the materials of the exterior are very English, the interior with its black and white marble floor, marble fireplace with semi-draped figures reclining on the pediment, and painted and gilded plasterwork is by contrast much more Continental in character and of a style familiar to the royal guests. The walls are articulated with Corinthian pilasters supporting the cornice, above which is a complex plaster vault modelled by the Swiss-born stuccadores Giuseppe Artari and Giovanni Bagutti, who also worked for Gibbs at St Martin-in-the-Fields (Figs. 8.5 and 8.6 give modern photos of exterior and interior).

Caroline of Ansbach (1683–1737) was a patron of the sciences and natural philosophy and of the arts including literature, architecture, and gardening. At Richmond Gardens, Kew, and at Kensington Palace she employed Charles Bridgeman and William Kent to landscape the grounds and design garden buildings; Kent's eccentric 'Merlin's Cave' at Kew, with a thatched roof and peopled with waxwork figures, attracted much derision, but the Serpentine in Hyde Park, formed by Bridgeman in 1731 by damming the shallow valley of the River Westbourne, is an early example of the deliberate creation in the landscape of a 'natural' lake of the kind promoted later in the century by Lancelot 'Capability' Brown and his followers. Caroline convened a conference on gardens at Kew in 1719, attended by Bridgeman, Pope and others. She was a forceful woman, albeit an educated and cultivated one. Pope disapproved of her treatment of her son Prince Frederick, and Walpole said of her she 'made great pretensions to Learning and Taste with not much of the former and none of the latter'. A fine life-size painting of Queen Caroline with her young son William Augustus, later Duke of Cumberland, is displayed in the gallery.

Johnston died in 1737, and subsequent owners included George Morton Pitt, MP, and Sir George Pocock, KB, who both had links to the slave trade. Pocock remodelled the house, moving the main entrance to the north front and adding a central three-storey bay window to the river-facing elevation (Fig. 8.7 shows Orleans House from across the river in a watercolour by Auguste Garnerey c.1815). The house remained in the ownership of the Pocock family until 1837, and in 1815 was let for two years to Louis Philippe, duc d'Orléans, later king of France. In 1846 it was purchased by 2nd Earl Kilmorey (who now lies entombed with his mistress in an Egyptian-style mausoleum nearby at St Margarets), and in 1852 was bought by Louis Philippe's son Henri, duc d'Aumale.

Henri had inherited the remains of the château at Chantilly (largely destroyed during the French Revolution) and what was left of its art collection from his great-uncle the duc de Bourbon, and proceeded to extend his house at Twickenham to accommodate his books and artworks, building a large new library and adding new stables for his horses. His father was proclaimed King of the French in 1830 and in 1844 paid a state visit to England to meet Queen Victoria, who accompanied him on his nostalgic visit to Twickenham and to Orleans House, at that time still owned by the Pocock family. The King's visit to England was recorded by the artist Edouart Pingret, and a coloured lithograph shows the King and his party on the front lawn at Orleans House, with the Octagon Room, conservatory and house in the background. By that time (plan by JB Papworth 1846), the area north of the house as far as Richmond Road was informal parkland dotted with trees and crossed by a curving drive from a lodge in the north-east corner. The ice-house mound apparently survived in a clump of trees, but only one of two earlier parallel canals remained, widened into a rectangular pool surrounded by trees.

Louis Philippe was forced to abdicate in 1848 and died at Claremont in Surrey in 1850. Henri returned to France in 1871, taking his large and important collection – plus Johnston's dog and bitch and some carved fireplace surrounds and mirrors and other items from Orleans House – with him, and installed it in the rebuilt château at Chantilly (Musée Condé). Orleans House remained empty until 1877, when it was bought by John Dugdale Astley and turned into a sports and social club, which failed and which was bought by William Cunard in 1882. By 1910 it had been acquired by the Ladies of Compassion, a Roman Catholic organisation, for an orphanage, and in 1926 was bought by a firm of ballast merchants. The northern part of the estate, now occupied by Orleans Park School, was sold in 1919 to the Exiles Club as a sports field.

The house, conservatory and library were demolished in 1926 and their site excavated for sand and gravel, but the Octagon Room was purchased and saved by Nellie Ionides, who used it as a grand entertaining annex to her house next door. Mrs Ionides died in 1962 and bequeathed the Octagon Room and outbuildings and stables and the surrounding land to the then Borough of Twickenham, together with some 450 portraits and local topographical views that now form the basis of the Richmond Borough Art Collection. The buildings have since been restored and extended to house and display the permanent collection and to accommodate changing exhibitions of old and new works. The most recent project, completed in 2018 at a cost of £3.7m with grant aid from the National Lottery Heritage Fund and many other sources, saw the creation of a new entrance building and display space, and the restoration of the Octagon Room with new gilding to the plasterwork, a new gilded chandelier, and the recreation of an overmantel painting of an architectural capriccio by Giovanni Panini that had gone missing in the 1960s.

Orleans House Gallery, which houses the borough Arts Service, is managed by the Orleans House Trust established in 2011 and comprises in addition to the Octagon Room and Gallery, the stables courtyard, which encompasses the Coach House Education Centre, Stables Gallery and Café. The gallery website provides details of the wide range of exhibitions, services and education programmes provided by the Arts Service supported by staff and a team of volunteers.

The site of the old house is now covered by regenerated woodland, which is managed to encourage wildlife and is especially notable for the birdsong and for the extensive ground-cover of cow parsley or Queen Anne's lace (*Anthriscus sylvestris*) in May. The grounds complement those of Marble Hill and York House nearby, which are less 'wild', but there are a few remaining specimen trees including a line of small-leaved limes (*Tilia cordata*) planted along the modern entrance drive, and an evergreen oak (*Quercus ilex*) and a golden Indian bean tree (*Catalpa bignoides aurea*) on the grass slope south of the Octagon, which regrettably no longer has a view of the river. Flower beds edged with low wicker hurdles and planted with annuals and herbaceous perennials echo the flower beds shown in the Pingret lithograph.

CHAPTER NINE

'Fair Howard's Elegant Retreat':
The Garden and Landscape at Marble Hill

Emily Parker

Today the park at Marble Hill is a popular local amenity, managed and cared for by English Heritage. It welcomes hundreds of thousands of families, dog-walkers, sports enthusiasts and picnickers each year. Its very survival as a green space is extraordinary in this popular corner of London and it was, in fact, saved from becoming a housing estate following a public campaign in the early 1900s. The pure white Palladian house (see Fig. 1.2) overlooks the playing fields and lawn, sitting within a landscape with almost exactly the same boundaries as it had at the end of the lifetime of its most famous owner. Henrietta Howard, later Countess of Suffolk (Fig. 9.1), was part of Georgian court society, mistress of the Prince of Wales (later George II) and a member of an elite circle of influential cultural, intellectual and political friends. She created Marble Hill house in the 1720s as a retreat from court life and as a place to entertain these friends. The location of Marble Hill right in the centre of Twickenham, with its large frontage on the river, cemented Howard's position in the heart of this fashionable neighbourhood. Three of Howard's Twickenham neighbours were involved at Marble Hill and are of particular interest owing to their concern with fashionable garden design and their prominent status in the area – Alexander Pope, Archibald Campbell (Lord Ilay or Islay and, from 1743, the 3rd Duke of Argyll) and later Horace Walpole.

It has been argued that the 'Golden Age' of Twickenham was in the eighteenth century, and this is undoubtedly the case for Marble Hill; however, its prominence in local life continued beyond this. After Howard's death, the estate was inherited by her nephew John Hobart, 2nd Earl of Buckinghamshire (1723–93): he had lived with Howard at Marble Hill during periods of his childhood so would have known the house and garden well. Some of his changes can still be traced in the landscape today – including new approaches and lodges – as can the changes of one of its later owners, Jonathan Peel (1799–1879), who added the current stables. The purchase of Marble Hill Park for the nation in 1902 saved it from development and allowed the structure of Howard's garden to survive into the twenty-first century. Unfortunately, this did not prevent the destruction of significant historic buildings in the park, including the China Room (a garden building created to showcase Howard's china collection) and the Green House.

A Location on the Thames
Howard and her advisors were not the first people to consider that this spot on the banks of the River Thames would provide an ideal location for a country retreat. A sketch of the plot by John Erskine, Earl of Mar, drawn in 1719 shows an area of land edged in yellow which was proposed to be purchased. A flap on top showed a plan for a new house set within

9.1. *Henrietta Howard*. Painting by Charles Jervas, *c*.1724. English Heritage, Marble Hill. (Copyright Historic England Archive)

a formal landscape. Whether this proposal was intended for the Earl of Mar himself, or was only ever an idle thought on paper, is not known. The proposal itself demonstrates the potential for and importance of connections between the houses and landscapes at this part of the Thames as the design ensured the garden and avenues created links with Ham House opposite and James Johnston's house (later Orleans House) to the west. About the time Mar completed this proposal, he and Lord Ilay were working together on Scottish ministerial business. It has been suggested that the subsequent purchase of this land by Lord Ilay for Howard was not purely a coincidence; the land and location were discussed by Lord Ilay and the Earl of Mar and the information stored away by Lord Ilay until Howard's opportunity arose. But as Lord Ilay had been born at Ham House, it would also have been a location he would already have known well.

Howard's position as woman of the bedchamber to Caroline, Princess of Wales, as well as her role as mistress to the Prince of Wales (later George II) meant that a location on the Thames would be important. However, she only actually moved into Marble Hill permanently in 1734 when she retired from court. The following year Pope wrote: 'There is a greater court now at Marble-hill than at Kensington, and God knows when it will end.' Howard had certainly forged her new role amongst the intellectual, cultural and political elite which centred on her home on the bank of the Thames at Marble Hill. In 1726, while Howard was still at court, Princess Caroline visited Marble Hill. Lady Bristol describes how, 'the Princess with all her children went by water last Thursday and landed to go to see Mrs. Howard's house at Marble-hill, and just at landing there is some very course new gravell laid, where my Lord Selkirk was awkward enough to throw me down (in helping me out of the boat)'. This is the only known reference to visitors arriving at Marble Hill by river in Howard's lifetime, but as a popular and fashionable way to travel in Twickenham it is likely it happened frequently. The mention of gravel probably refers to the newly built terrace that was created along the Thames for Howard when she needed to provide a new right of way to replace one that ran through the area that was to become her garden. It also shows that visitors were able to access and visit Marble Hill in 1726, even before the works to the house were finally finished in 1729.

A Design for a Garden

Once the location for her house and garden had been chosen and the land had been purchased, Howard must have started to consider how she wanted it to be designed and laid out. For the house, the builder-architect Roger Morris was employed and probably incorporated design advice from Henry Herbert, 9th Earl of Pembroke and possibly also the leading eighteenth-century architect Colen Campbell. It was designed at the forefront of modern fashion in the new Palladian style. When it came to the layout of the garden, the first known correspondence about the design is between Lord Peterborough and Alexander Pope. In the summer and autumn of 1723, Lord Peterborough was asking for measurements of the land at Marble Hill, as well as trying to organise a visit with Pope to discuss planting. A later letter from Lord Peterborough to Howard herself perhaps indicates that his advice was unsolicited as he stands aside for his design 'rivals', betraying some bitterness, 'I can ever wish well to the house, and garden under all these mortifications, may every Tree prosper by whatever hand'. Pope's involvement is clear even from this very early correspondence. In autumn 1724, conversations seem to have been progressing: Pope writes to his friend saying that his mind is more focused on the works in Howard's garden than his own garden or even his writing. In September 1724, Pope met with Charles Bridgeman and Howard at Marble Hill to discuss the garden and Bridgeman writes that he is working on a plan. This plan is not thought to have survived. A year later, Howard and Pope's mutual friend Martha Blount describes how Pope is 'very full of plans for buildings and gardens which I find is not owing so much to the beautys of Lord Cobhams as the desire he has of being serviceable to you at Marble Hill'. His involvement, therefore, obviously continued as work progressed: he even visited Marble Hill in Howard's absence, writing to her in 1726 to congratulate her on the birth of her new calf and describing her as a 'pastoral lady'.

An early garden plan for Marble Hill, however, does survive. In 1724, Pope wrote about Howard's garden design saying that he had 'spent many hours in studying for hers & in drawing new plans for her'. A plan (Fig. 9.2), attributed to Pope, shows a garden designed around a series of straight axes yet at the same time with asymmetrical areas. It includes a wilderness of fruit trees, flowering shrubs, tightly winding walks and various different heights of hedges in 'yew' and 'elm'. Also shown on this plan are two semi-circular areas labelled as 'parterre of flowers' surrounded by what seems to be a semi-circular arbour and a square shaped 'mount'. The existence of a plan attributed to Pope is highly significant as, although sketches for garden features are found among his writings, this would be his only known surviving plan for a whole garden design. Pope assisted in the design of only a handful of gardens, although his role in advocating design inspired by classical and 'ancient' influences had a much wider impact. Pope's inspiration came from the classical texts he was

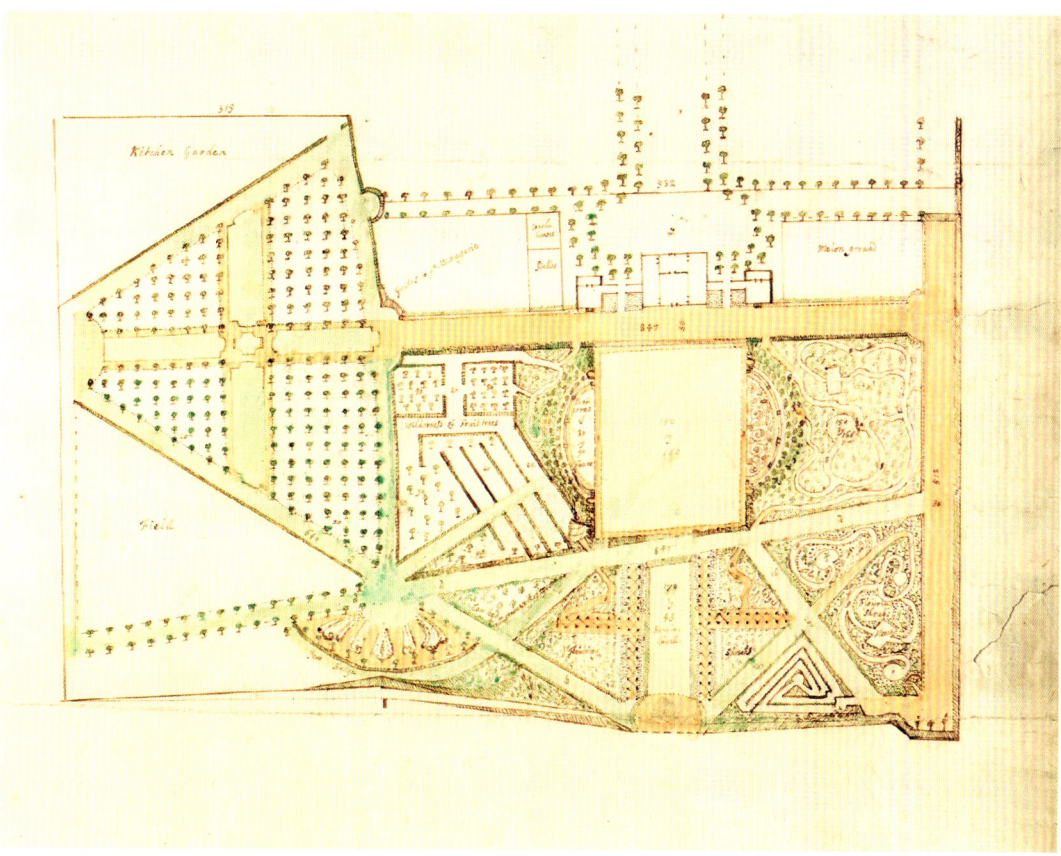

9.2. Plan of Marble Hill attributed to Alexander Pope, 1724. (Copyright Norfolk Record office, MC184/10/3 [rights reserved])

translating, such as the *Odyssey*, alongside principles taken from painting. He was probably also familiar with the letters of Pliny the Younger (*c*.AD 61–112) about his villas at Laurentum and Tusculum. Therefore, the involvement of Pope and his innovative approach to landscape design and theory in this period are particularly relevant for understanding the approach to the garden layout at Marble Hill. The garden at Marble Hill was also being designed at the same time as Pope and Lord Burlington were contemplating and implementing these ideas in their own gardens. In fact, many of Pope's 'ancient' and classical principles can be seen at Marble Hill, including the axial yet asymmetric design, with winding wilderness areas and the layout of the groves. This provides an appropriately 'ancient' setting for the Palladian villa and the classical garden buildings. The terraces, referenced at the time as aspiring to 'ancient' taste and the creation of the grottoes and mount, showcase the continuing influence of this 'ancient' style of design in the garden.

Howard's Gardening Friends

Howard was surrounded by friends who were knowledgeable about garden design and she also enlisted the help of a professional, Charles Bridgeman. It seems likely that the garden that was created at Marble Hill was an amalgamation of different ideas, as often was the case in early eighteenth-century architecture and garden design, especially when the owner was fashionable, well connected and at the forefront of taste. From the letters between Pope and Bridgeman, Howard's involvement can be glimpsed as she participated in the initial discussions, meeting with them both at Marble Hill in 1724. Without more evidence we can only ever hypothesise on the extent of her involvement in the design, but as a fashionable and well-connected 'client', it is hard to imagine she did not have her own ideas to bring to the discussion. The building of Marble Hill and the layout of the garden was made possible after a large gift of stock, jewels, plate, mahogany and furniture to Howard from the Prince of Wales in 1723. This settlement was held in trust, managed by a group of trustees, which included Lord Ilay and it was directly stipulated that the gift was to be free from any interference from Howard's estranged husband. Lord Ilay was a close friend of Howard and lived nearby at his estate at Whitton. He was an enthusiastic collector of exotic plants and created a garden to showcase these (see under Other Gardens). Although Lord Ilay's involvement in Howard's financial affairs is clearly documented, it is harder to establish if he had a role in the design ideas for the garden at Marble Hill. A clue might come from a letter from the Earl of Peterborough in which he writes to Howard about no longer being involved with the development of the house and garden at Marble Hill: 'I dislike my rivals among the living…must I yield to Lord Herbert and Lord Ilay'. This implies that Lord Ilay may have offered architectural or horticultural advice to Howard or both. His enthusiasm for gardening increases the likelihood of his involvement in some capacity in offering advice on the garden.

Understanding Lord Ilay's role in providing garden advice is further complicated by his involvement as a trustee, as he bought land and made contracts and payments on Howard's behalf. An example of this is a document from *c.*1757 which appears to describe Lord Ilay (now Duke of Argyll) as owner and patron of Marble Hill: 'About thirty three Years since, The Present Duke of Argyll purchased a Field call'd Marble Hill, upon part of which his Grace erected An House, and planned out the rest for a Garden continuing possessed there of till the year 1748, or 1749'. Although this reflects the fact that Lord Ilay had bought the land in trust for Howard and had paid bills for the house and garden on her behalf in the 1720s, it does not diminish the fact that Marble Hill was Howard's home and establishment. This land was then transferred from Lord Ilay to Howard in 1748. This provides a possible reason for the production of the plan thought to have been created at a similar time in either 1748 or 1749; it is possible that it is a record of Howard's estate after it had been consolidated with the transfer of the land held in trust by Lord Ilay. The draughtsman and surveyor of the plan has been identified as James Dorret, who was a land surveyor in the service of Lord Ilay, adding further evidence that Lord Ilay was involved in the production of the plan. Howard and Lord Ilay also employed the same gardener, Daniel Crafts. He received a year's wages in Lord Ilay's will on his death in 1761. As the agreements between Howard and Daniel Crafts for Marble Hill are undated, it is impossible to determine whether he started working at Marble Hill after Lord Ilay's death in 1761, before he was employed by Lord Ilay, or whether he worked at both gardens simultaneously.

Recording the Garden
The design drawn by Pope only included the small parcel of land which was part of the initial negotiations in 1724. Throughout her lifetime Howard would continue to acquire more land resulting in the extent of the existing park today. Access to the land which led down to the river, probably acquired in late 1724, and advice from Bridgeman in the autumn of that year, is thought to have led to adaptations to the proposed Pope layout. A series of plans in the late 1740s, probably from 1748 or 1749, showing 'The House Garden & Inclosures of Marblehill 10 Miles West from London Belonging To the Right Honourable The Countess of Suffolk' records the layout of the garden twenty-five years after the initial

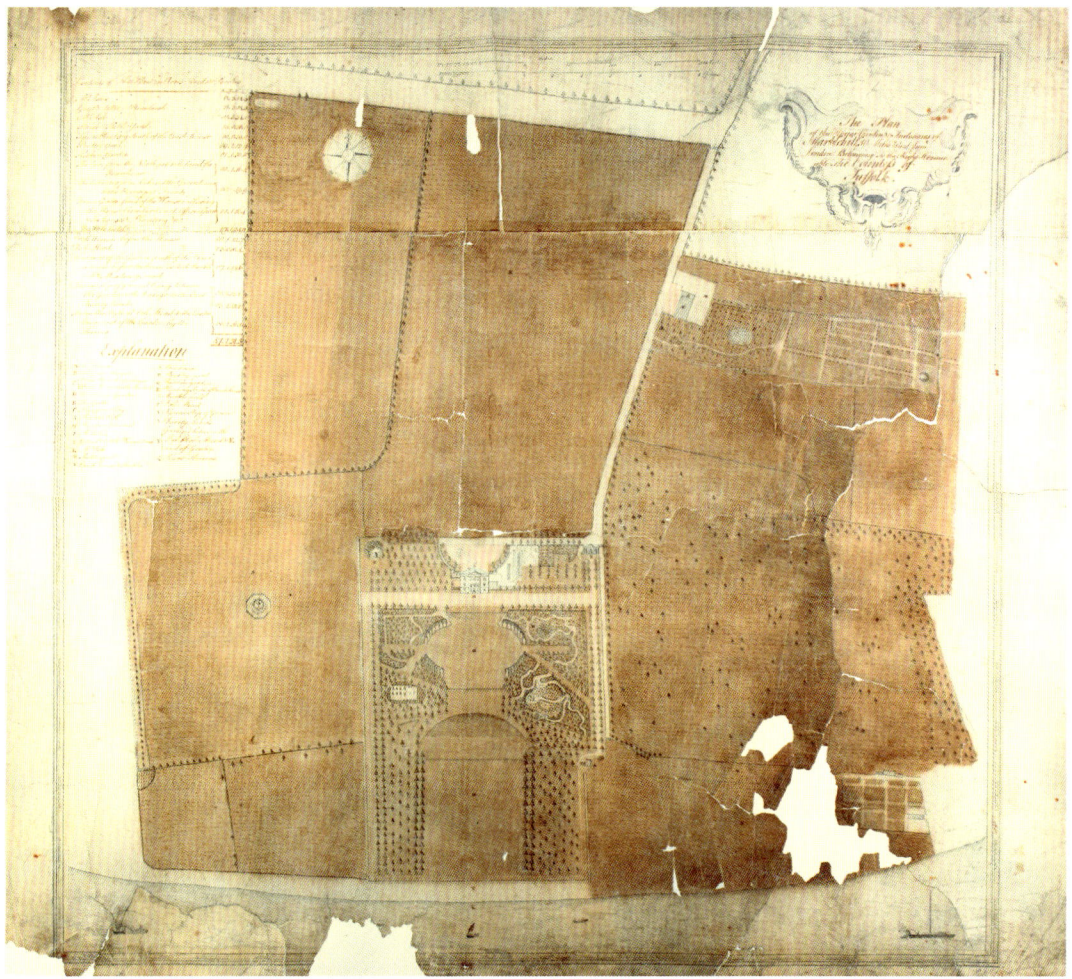

9.3. Plan of 'The House Garden and Inclosures at Marblehill 10 Miles West of London Belonging to the Right Honourable the Countess of Suffolk', c.1749. (Copyright Norfolk Record Office, MC184/10/2 [rights reserved])

discussions (Figs. 9.3 and 9.4). At this time, the garden included several garden buildings such as a Green House and Grotto, alongside serpentine paths, a Flower Garden, groves of trees and a Ninepin Alley. The axial layout, including an oval lawn with arbours as shown on the plan attributed to Pope, is evident in these later plans, as are the serpentine paths in the woodland areas. Known additions to the estate after the c.1749 plan but during Howard's lifetime included a 'Chinese' fence and a 'sweet walk' nursery in the north of the estate. A gothic farm or folly was also added, probably the result of encouragement from Horace Walpole, called the 'Priory of St Hubert'. In 1758, he described how Howard had 'at last entirely submitted her barn to our ordination'.

Although Howard made changes to both the house and garden during her lifetime, most of the substantial work appears to have taken place in the 1720s. Bills in 1724 and 1725 refer to a mount and Bolling [sic] green as well as a yew hedge. Equipment for the gardeners is also being purchased including a garden roll 'by the order of Mr Pope'. In 1727, Jonathan Swift published his poem *Pastoral Dialogue between Richmond Lodge and Marble Hill* which described the garden's ice-house, walks, plantations, groves and wildernesses. Even allowing for some poetic exaggeration, Swift's description mirrors the type of garden shown on the c.1749 plan over twenty years later. In 1728, Roger Morris, the architect of the house, is paid

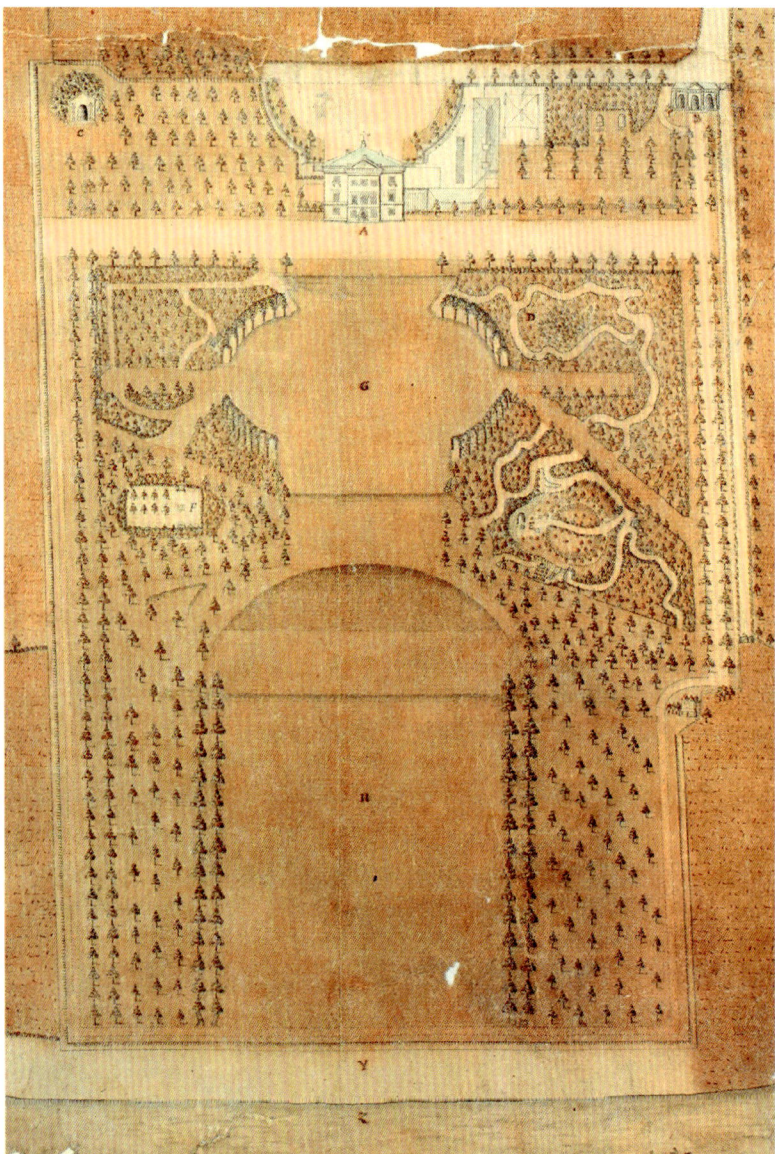

9.4. Detail of Fig. 9.3.

£200 for '4 buildings in the garden at Marble Hill'. They are likely to have been the icehouse seat, Green House, and China Room; the fourth, however, is less easily determined. It could be the icehouse itself or possibly the Coach House, although its location in a separate corner of the estate begs the question of whether this could be described as 'in the garden'.

Photos of the greenhouse and China Room before they were demolished in the early twentieth century show they were built in a classical style to match the house. The probable use of the same architect and builder Roger Morris at the same time the house was being built indicates that the garden and house were considered as a unified design concept. Marble Hill also drew the attention of another landscape designer who was born in Twickenham – Batty Langley. He was involved in the design of Thomas Vernon's garden at Twickenham Park in the early 1720s (see under Other Gardens), as well as producing, a perhaps unsolicited, design for Orleans Park (see Chapter 8), next door to Marble Hill. Langley's comments about the garden at Marble Hill, which he published in his book *New Principles of Gardening* in 1728, were not complimentary. He wrote, 'observe the error in the slopes of the Garden of the Honourable Mrs Howard at Twickenham, being view'd at the river Thames at Richmond'. He attributed this error to Howard's desire to imitate ancient architecture in her terraces, although Langley's criticism of the design was possibly motivated by professional jealousy on not being consulted as a garden designer.

Creating and Decorating a Grotto

The grotto at Marble Hill was decorated by Howard and her niece probably with advice from many of her knowledgeable friends. Exactly when the grotto labelled on the *c.*1749 plan was constructed is not known. There is no documentary evidence for the grotto until 1739 when Howard writes that she is 'head and ears in shells'. Progress on the grotto was on-going in 1742, when a friend hoped it continued 'prosperously' and it was still being altered in the 1760s when Howard's great niece, who also lived at Marble Hill, wrote to her parents saying that she was working hard in the Grotto. It is probable that the creation of the grotto was taking place over a period of thirty, perhaps even forty years. This time frame, however, is further confused by contemporary references to two grottoes at Marble Hill. A poem called 'Marble-Hill' by Anne Chambers, published in 1764, describes a 'grotto' as well as a 'rustic grot'. The poem goes on to describe the difference between them, one is the shell grotto – the remains of which are visible in the park today – and the other is more hidden with large rocks. The location of this second grotto has caused much debate, but its description in the poem and in other contemporary accounts locates it close to the other grotto. On the *c.*1749 plan, directly below the labelled grotto, there is a rock arch and rock wall, which is probably the second grotto or 'rustic grot' as described in the poem.

An idea of the kind of decoration that probably would have been found in the grotto is explained in an intriguing letter from Mary Lisles (Fig. 9.5). In the undated letter, she writes to an unknown woman, providing a practical description of how certain grotto elements can be created, including recipes for cement and artificial coral. The whole letter appears to have been written as guidance for Howard on grotto decoration, and it reads as though Howard is at the very beginning of her project as it starts with very basic concepts, which may allow a provisional date of the 1730s. In particular, two parts of the letter reflect this: 'if lady Suffolk has a design to put any icicles in her grotto' and 'I think Madam, I have answar'd [answered] all the quarrys [queries] you gave me & if I can be of any Service to Lady Suffolk , next Spring when I shall be in town, I shall with Pleasure obey her commands'. The letter provides a fascinating glimpse into grotto building in the eighteenth century as it also describes how to wash shells and how to stick shells and cinders to brick or board walls. Mary Lisles was born in 1699 and, along with eight of her sisters, decorated a grotto at Crux-Easton, Hampshire. It is thought that Pope stayed with the Lisles family in 1733, and wrote the lines described as an 'Inscription on a GROTTO of Shells at CRUX-EASTON the Work of Nine young Ladies' the same year, although the first known record of the poem is not until 1748. As Pope is known to have contributed to the design of Marble Hill garden in the 1730s and he was passionate about grottoes, it would not be unrealistic to assume his involvement. The link between Pope and Mary Lisles, and her letter to Howard, raises even more questions about how the grotto was designed and decorated and the advice that Howard was receiving. It is widely known that grotto decorating was a fashionable pastime for women in the eighteenth century, but this letter provides clear evidence that the skills required to do so were also being discussed and shared amongst a network of female grotto decorators.

9.5. A page from the letter from Mary Lisles describing how to decorate a grotto. (The National Records of Scotland, GD/40/9/139/19)

By 1800, only one grotto is being mentioned. The gardens are described as 'very pleasant, and have a beautiful grotto, to which you are conducted by a winding alley of flowering shrubs'. Moving onwards into the nineteenth century, a record of 1819 notes 'a grotto, once celebrated for the beauty of its spars, and the taste with which they were arranged is now dilapidated and forsaken'. Again, only one grotto is mentioned and the one that remains appears to have been in a very poor state. A sonnet published in 1834 decries the neglect that the garden at Marble Hill is suffering, albeit 'still delightful'. It describes one of the grottoes in the verse saying, 'In yon dim grot, by shady elms o'spread, Methinks I see the pensive Pope reclin'd.' Here again we can see the use of the word 'grot' to describe one of the grottos. It also creates another, although tenuous, link between Pope and the grotto. The poems language also gives an idea of the atmosphere created in the garden and grotto including 'sacred', 'hallow'd' and the 'haunts of poesy and love!'. By 1839, a travel guide is describing how the gardens at Marble Hill 'formerly contained a beautifully-constructed grotto'. It is possible, then, that if the grotto was constructed in the 1730s that it only lasted for a century and had been removed or was completely dilapidated by the time of this guide. The fall of a tree in 1941 broke through the roof of the grotto but the chamber was filled in and grassed over without any further investigation. In 1983, subsidence to the east of the grotto area provided an opportunity to excavate which was undertaken in 1984.

9.6. Marble Hill (Earl of Buckingham). Watercolour, attributed to John Spyers, *c*.1780.
(Orleans House Gallery, LDORL: 01001)

Marble Hill after Howard

After Howard's death, the estate passed to her nephew the Earl of Buckinghamshire (Fig. 9.6). His changes appear not to have been substantial, although a summerhouse was built on the west side of the pleasure grounds, probably during his ownership. The eastern edge of the pleasure ground was also probably extended at this time; both of these changes are shown on a map from 1786–7. After his death in 1793, the house was leased to his niece Henrietta Hotham, who had lived at Marble Hill during her childhood and helped with decorating the grotto. She decided not to live in Marble Hill house but leased it out to a succession of different tenants. The next owner thought to have made any determinable changes to the garden or landscape is Jonathan Peel, brother of Prime Minister Robert Peel. He purchased Marble Hill in 1825 and immediately created a new stable block to the north-west of the house (Fig. 9.7). Although the layout of the garden remained remarkably consistent throughout the nineteenth century, Peel did add a fashionable Italianate garden to one of the terraces in the pleasure ground. A description from 1850 describes how 'to the south front is a terrace walk, a lawn as smooth and level as a bowling green, encompassed on each side by masses of evergreen shrubs retiring amongst the groves: on a lower level is a flower garden on grass thence the park slopes down for a considerable distance to the banks of the Thames'. In 1887, the last resident of Marble Hill, Lady Peel, died. It stood empty for ten

9.7. Visitors outside the stable block. Early twentieth-century postcard. (Richmond Local Studies Collection, LCF 13212)

9.8. Marble Hill House. (English Heritage photograph)

years until it was finally purchased in 1898 by the Cunard family with an eye to development. They started building roads and sewers and felling trees, but this prompted public outcry and in 1902 Marble Hill was purchased and has been open to the public as a park ever since. As a significant historic landscape, as well as a much loved local amenity and green space, the management of Marble Hill today requires careful balance and consideration. In the twentieth century, the survival of the historic structure of the garden was threatened by the removal of historic buildings such as the Green House and inappropriately placed public amenities. This, combined with a lack of resources, meant that the significance of the garden was little recognised. This is currently being rebalanced following funding from the National Lottery Heritage Fund, which aims to improve park facilities, the ecological potential of the park and restore the historic design. One of the primary aims of restoring the garden is to unify the house and garden which, although designed as a coherent scheme, have become separated by different management priorities. The revival of the landscape at Marble Hill will ensure it survives as a recognisable and important historic landscape for future generations to enjoy and that it continues to warrant its prominent position amongst the historic houses along the Thames and its enduring place in the heart of Twickenhamshire (Fig. 9.8).

CHAPTER TEN

Other Gardens
Michael Symes

There were several other estates of interest that exhibit garden developments of one sort or another. Less research has been carried out in some cases, but that is not to say that they lacked importance at the time or are unworthy of our attention now. As with the preceding individual studies, these gardens have some elements in common with their neighbours and follow contemporary trends but each has its own character. Much of the material is derived from the past work of local historians, as acknowledged in the sources and reading list at the end.

Twickenham Meadows (Cambridge Park)
Richard Owen Cambridge's display of open landscaping has, sadly, been buried beneath nineteenth- and twentieth-century urbanisation, with a rash of houses and roads spreading from 1863 and a second wave on the eastern side, obliterating the house, from 1897. The present name of Cambridge Park for the western half is in later tribute to him and was not used in his lifetime. An informative booklet by Maureen Bunch of the Twickenham Local History Society, *Cambridge Park, Twickenham and its Owners 1616–1835* (1989) gives a detailed account of ownership and developments before, during and after Cambridge's time, but here the focus will be on Cambridge and his garden interests and achievements.

The earlier history of the site reveals an ownership by the intertwined Ashe and Windham families for almost a century from 1657. An engraving of 1726 (Fig. 10.1) shows a very formal, and mostly plain, layout with avenues and other rows of trees, possibly including orchards. The substantial area sloping down to the river is kept simple, with a curving path the main feature, indicating that it was in part a water meadow subject to regular tidal flooding, as happened on both sides of the river. But that would nonetheless have permitted grazing. Parterres can be seen near the house, protected by a long and high wall. This is corroborated by a painting by Antonio Joli of *c.*1749 (see Fig. 1.8). John Rocque's plan of 1744–6 (see Fig. 1.4), showing the estate stretching from Ferry Lane as the northern boundary to Marble Hill (and Little Marble Hill) to the south-west, confirms the formality of planting. There was, however, a new arrival, which was not recorded before the painting of 1745 by Joli or his circle (see Fig. 1.7), which therefore would appear to date from the early 1740s and which consisted of a long single-storey orangery with a cupola, in addition to the gardens adjoining the main house.

Such was the estate when Cambridge acquired it at the end of 1751. He came from a Gloucestershire family, where his father was a merchant trading with Turkey, as did Thomas Vernon. He had an early love of nature and the countryside, instilled both at home and at school, which was Eton, where contemporaries included Lord Bute, Pitt the Elder, Thomas Gray and Walpole. He himself claimed that it was on the playing fields of Eton that he

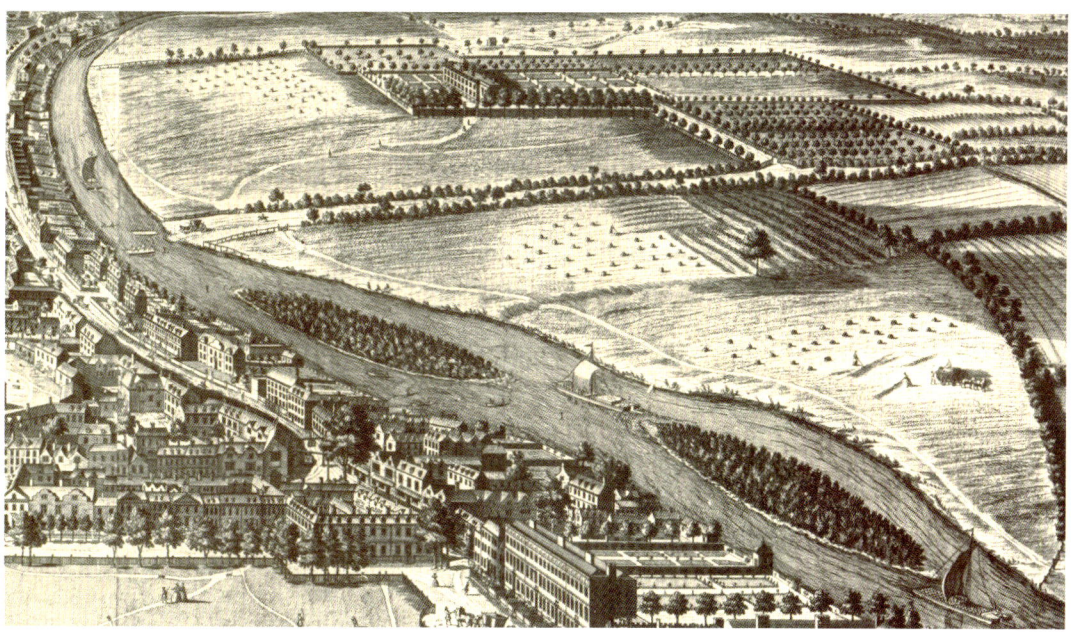

10.1. Extract from *The Prospect of Richmond in Surry*, 1726 (Fig. 1.15)

acquired 'his taste for the varied combinations of wood, water and lawn, which was exercised with great success first at his seat in Gloucestershire, and afterwards in the meadows of Twickenham'. While at Oxford he toured Norfolk in the vacation with Walpole, who was therefore a close friend when Cambridge appeared on the Twickenham scene.

In 1741 Cambridge married Mary Trenchard, a union that was to prove long and happy. They lived at his family seat of Whitminster near the Severn for seven to eight years up till 1748. This period proved crucial for forming his taste and developing his skills as a practical gardener. It lay on the banks of the River Stroud, and, in the words of his son, 'my father's first object was to introduce the more distant landscape, and open to the view those beautiful and lofty hills which bound that extensive valley; and, by a judicious disposal of his buildings and plantations, he greatly embellished the place, and gave to the whole the appearance of a garden.' He cut away trees and shrubs that obstructed his view of the Cotswolds, and carried out significant building and rebuilding, including a grotto, together with some ingenious waterworks involving a waterfall. So we can see the object was to bring in the distant landscape – 'calling in the country' as Pope put it – making the whole estate appear like a garden, as Addison had suggested; and making the garden look more natural, with lawn, wood and gravel paths. In other words, creating a landscape garden at a time when the idea was still relatively new. An interesting connection with Pope is that Cambridge, having used sparkling mundic from the Severn bank for his own grotto, sent some to Pope for *his* grotto. Among other acquaintances was Sanderson Miller, who designed a Gothic(k) stable front for him in 1748, though it was probably not built. A significant friendship was with Lord Bathurst of Cirencester Park: he wrote about the forest gardens there, in which Pope had had a hand.

Cambridge's son wrote about his water feats: 'The stream, which ran through the grounds, he made navigable for boats, not only as far as his own property extended, but, by the permission of his neighbours, for a distance of near three miles.' In this, Cambridge displayed a talent for water engineering worthy of Brown. There was both a practical benefit – he could bring by water the materials he needed for developing the estate – and he could exercise his mechanical bent in devising pleasure craft to reach the Severn. The largest was a Venetian-style 'state barge', accommodating up to thirty people in the cabin, which was decorated with eight paintings by the marine artist Samuel Scott of Twickenham. He had a twelve-oared barge in addition, and a 'double boat' with a 'flying prow', based on those seen by Admiral Anson in the Pacific. Two boats in parallel were lashed together with transverse beams. On one occasion he entertained Frederick, Prince of Wales (who had a royal barge designed by Kent), the Duchess of Brunswick and Lord Bathurst on the Venetian barge.

While Cambridge was at Whitminster he made frequent excursions on horseback into Wales, and developed a taste for its dramatic and picturesque scenery, especially the Wye valley, thereby anticipating Gilpin and Arthur Young, whose Wye tours were a decade or so later. He was thus an early advocate of the Picturesque. In 1748 his uncle died, having asked Cambridge to adopt the name of Owen, and he began to consider a move from Whitminster. Here the story becomes uncertain, largely because of the unreliable memoirs of Cambridge by his son, George Owen Cambridge, rushed out in 1803 after Cambridge's death the previous year. Some facts appear distorted, or, to take a charitable view, misunderstood. This is particularly true of the account of the connections between Cambridge and the exceptionally picturesque site of Piercefield on Wye, near Chepstow, which had some of the most spectacular scenery to be found. He was 'captivated with its bold and romantic character', where the sight of the Wyndcliffe, part rock, part wood, stunned all visitors. According to George, he considered purchasing it, but it was never publicly for sale: the *de facto* owner was Valentine Morris, although it was held in trust for him for many years. Cambridge accordingly would not have had the chance to buy it, nor would he have recommended its purchase to Morris (as George wrote) since Morris was already *in situ*. Perhaps Cambridge had told his son he *wished* he could have bought Piercefield. At all events he knew Morris and visited his seat. Further, George tells us that Cambridge 'had some share in making those improvements which showed the peculiar and striking features of the place to their proper advantage', though that has not been corroborated elsewhere. If it was indeed the case, it referred to the arrangement of the walks and seats so as to provide optimum views of the scenery in differing directions.

However, the warm-hearted and sociable Cambridge felt he might be too cut off in Monmouthshire, and in 1748 came the transfer to London for the winter months, where Cambridge moved in exalted circles, including several who were known for their garden interests – Pitt the Elder, Lyttelton of Hagley, Grenville of Wotton, Lord Hardwicke of Wimpole, Anson and Henry Fox. During the summer months the couple continued to reside at Whitminster. However, Mary found the air of London unwholesome, so after two years they looked for a base out of town, which led them to Twickenham.

Cambridge came to Twickenham a somewhat split man. On one hand he had a view of garden-making and a taste for the Picturesque that were ahead of their time, together with practical experience: but intellectually he represented something of a throwback to Pope, Addison and Steele and the golden age of the essay. The very title of Richard D Altick's biography, *RO Cambridge: Belated Augustan* (1941) indicates that he had been born a couple of generations too late and was trying to live the life of a dilettante man of letters that was out of date. But it explains why he was such an enthusiastic contributor to the periodical *The World*, which attempted to capture in its duration, 1753–6, the earlier spirit of inculcating taste through the medium of the essay. And his connection with Pope when he was a young man surely led him to model his mock-heroic poem *The Scribleriad* on Pope's *Dunciad*, quite apart from taking its title from Pope's *Memoirs of Scriblerius*. Henrietta Pye, in proclaiming Cambridge as the king of Twickenham, saw him as the successor to Pope in that role, treading in the steps of his predecessor.

Essays in *The World* were anonymous, though we now know who wrote what, including Cambridge and Walpole. A number of essays were on garden topics, such as Francis Coventry's satire on a Squire Mushroom, who compressed everything possible into a tiny garden, including a stagnant yellow 'river' in a valley almost twenty yards long. That was in 1753 and clearly inspired Cambridge to produce his finest piece of work the following year. Cambridge wrote three essays on gardens in all, the first and best satirical, the other two serious.

The first essay, appearing in June 1754, is still highly amusing to read. It sends up the notion of the Improver (a label often attached, sometimes disparagingly, to Brown), who always has to be altering something, is never satisfied, and who, in his enthusiasm, insists on dragging his visitor immediately after breakfast, unshaven and still in slippers, on what was promised to be a brief walk round the bowling green but turns out to be a complete tour that takes so long that lunch is spoiled. Among the delights encountered are temples, pagodas, pyramids, grottoes, bridges, hermitages, caves, towers and hothouses: the Improver 'knows that if you had apprehended a walk of half the distance, he never could have moved you from your easy chair'. This essay influenced his friend Garrick's play *The Clandestine Marriage*, a garden satire based heavily on Francis Coventry as well as Cambridge.

Less than a year later Cambridge returned to the fray but this time in serious vein, providing some garden history in which he supported the claim made by Walpole and others that Milton presaged the landscape garden in *Paradise Lost*, and robustly refuting the idea, harboured principally by the French, that China influenced it. The third essay, a week later, is a follow-up, exhorting designers to follow nature not straight lines. Theirs is not a simple task: the landscape gardener must study optics, hydrostatics, mechanics, geometry and trigonometry as well as architecture, plants and trees. This sounds like the voice of experience.

Cambridge pursued his garden interests in drawing up a short account of the Ranelagh Pleasure Gardens (1762). A decade later he submitted verses for Philip Yorke to use on the (mock) ruined castle at Wimpole, but they were twice rejected in favour of more heavily propagandist lines. Cambridge's verses are rather strange: they contain references to the nymphs of Kew, Richmond and Sheen as well as to the imagined episode of King Henry's adulterous affair at the Wimpole castle. Cambridge commented that he had drawn on Walpole's verses on the estate of Ampthill as an inspiration.

Brown visited Twickenham Meadows, but not to work on the grounds. He complimented Cambridge on their transformation, whereupon Cambridge told him that he hoped he would die before Brown so that he could see heaven before Brown had 'improved' it. This visit had been arranged by Garrick, who addressed a poem to Cambridge with the lines, 'I left thee…With the great planner Brown, who's himself the best plan,/I envy his genius, yet doat on the man'.

What Cambridge achieved at Twickenham Meadows was twofold. He opened up the grounds in landscape style to an extent unmatched elsewhere in the locality apart from the slightly later Twickenham Park, and made the bulk of the estate accessible to the public. First he erased the formal gardens around the house and demolished the walls and hedges; then he landscaped the area between the house and the Thames (Figs. 10.2 and 10.3). He allowed the public to enter from the river, and, in the words of Henrietta Pye, 'he leaves the Enjoyment of his Meadows and Grove to his Subjects, which has much encreas'd his Popu-

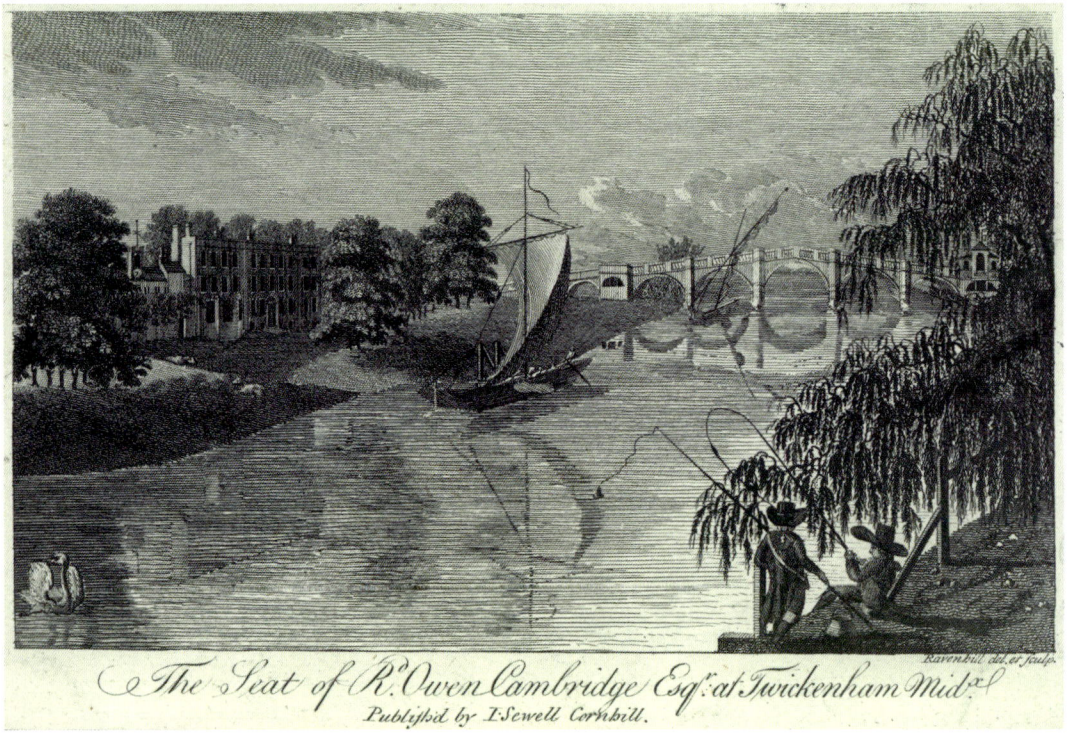

10.2. *The Seat of R^d. Owen Cambridge Esqr. at Twickenham Mid^x*. Engraving by Ravenhill, *European Magazine*, 1787. (Orleans House Gallery, LDORL: 02045)

10.3. *East Front of Twickenham Meadows and Richmond Bridge*. Engraving by J Landseer after J Webber, 1803. (Orleans House Gallery, LDORL: 01271)

larity, and has also put up many Seats and Benches, for the Ease and Satisfaction of his People, whose Esteem he makes it his Study to acquire; and indeed has succeeded as much as any Monarch can expect: For, like the Britons, they love and revere him.' The place became popular both with locals and visitors from London, who would bring a picnic with them and consume it on a cloth spread on the great lawn coming down from the house. Sadly, Cambridge's hospitality became abused, and later on 'the lawns before the house continually exhibited scenes of riot and disorder', with the private areas of the grounds invaded by those who turned them into 'a haunt of the grossest licentiousness and indecency'. Eventually Cambridge was forced to put up notices on the river front banning boats from landing.

Henrietta Pye describes his landscaping. The water meadows were open and flat, but as the ground rose towards the house there were swells and spots shaded by lofty trees. A grove ran along the upper part of the lawn, about three-quarters of a mile in length according to her account. The grove was fairly narrow and wound in and out in a serpentine line: 'it is covered with a green Turf, as soft to the Feet as Velvet, and fenc'd on each Side by thick Bushes of Roses, Orange-Flowers, Honey-Suckles, Lilacs and Sweet-Williams, and shaded by the finest tall Trees that grow'. It was thus part-grove, part-shrubbery. There were numerous small rustic seats plus two large ones which would provide shelter. There were strong scents of plants, and much birdsong. The extensive meadows themselves were grazed by oxen and sheep. Richmond and its hill formed the background, looking from the grounds. So we can see that the clearance work Cambridge undertook in order to provide fine views at Whitminster was echoed in his demolition of the walls and hedges round the house at Twickenham for the same reason.

In 1777 a further embellishment was added to the view, after seventeen years of wrangling. The ferry to Richmond was replaced by Richmond Bridge, designed by the well-known architect James Paine with the assistance of Kenton Couse, causing Walpole to dub Cam-Bridge 'Mr Foot-of-the-Bridge.' He grew old a contented and hospitable man, still the centre of many of the great names of the time. Infirmity and a degree of deafness slowed him up, and a celebrated repartee is reported when George III spotted him riding down Richmond Hill: 'Mr. Cambridge, you do not ride as fast as you used to.' 'Sir, I am going downhill.' He died in 1802 at the age of eighty-five, his last words to the family grouped round him being, 'How do the dear people?'

George succeeded him but in 1824 built, and moved into, a villa, Meadowbank, on the western side of the meadows set back a little from the river, much in the spirit and style of Twickenhamshire. As we have seen, the estate was split in 1835 into Cambridge Park and Cambridge House.

Twickenham Park

Twickenham Park has a long and distinguished history, but is unrecognisable now as formerly the most important estate in the district, with just some fragments and a few trees remaining as a reminder of past glories. Early occupants included Francis Bacon and Lucy, Countess of Bedford, who bought the property from him in 1608. Her garden was recorded the following year by Robert Smythson, a striking design centred on four raised corner mounts enclosing six concentric circles of trees and a small central lawn. There was also a terrace overlooking a lake which may or may not correspond to the site of the lake that survives in the (private) grounds of the St Margarets Trust. In the wider park there were two great avenues of trees. This arrangement remained broadly into the eighteenth century. However, by that time Twickenham Park was somewhat on the periphery as regards what was becoming Twickenhamshire. Not only was it on the northern tip of the area and half in the next parish but the house (still basically Jacobean) was set back some way from the river, thus excluding it from being considered (or depicted) as a riverside villa. It was not a charismatic garden in comparison with some of the others and lacked a transformational hand in the eighteenth century, such as that of William Kent, who doubtless would have used the considerable space to create at least a moderate-sized pictorial circuit garden. As a consequence we lack accounts from visitors who went on garden tours.

Thomas Vernon, the owner from 1702 until his death in 1726, brought in local designer and plantsman Batty Langley, who was planning the gardens at Orleans House at about the same time. In his *New Principles of Gardening* (1728) he wrote that 'About ten Years ago [i.e. c.1718], I planted a Wilderness of Oaks, Elms, Limes, Planes &c for the late Hon. Thomas Vernon, at his Seat in Twickenham Park', at which date he would have been only twenty-two. A wilderness meant a grove of deliberately planted trees with winding paths within it. Of Langley's abundant planting of planes (the London Plane), a couple remain in the St Margarets Trust garden.

Langley mentions what he planted at Twickenham Park in two publications in addition to *New Principles*. They are *Practical Geometry* (1726) and *A Sure Method of Improving Estates by Plantations* (1728). Hedges of hornbeam appeared, under the assiduous care of the gardener Henry Timberlin, and in 1722 Langley formed a spiral mount of 100' or more in diameter to mask a large sand pit. He also mentions experimenting with the tap-roots of oaks, although this comes under 'ilex', so may just refer to the evergreen holm oak.

Thomas Vernon's own chief claim to fame in the garden sphere concerns the weeping willow. The story about its introduction into England has assumed almost mythic proportions. One account attributes it to Pope, who was said to have seen a parcel from Spain (or Turkey) bound up by withies. He took one and planted it, and it turned out to be a weeping willow. This account, though, is not recorded until 1801. Secondly, the botanist and classifier Tournefort had brought it to France at the end of the seventeenth century, and it may have reached England as a result. Another account tells of it being at Hampton Court in the 1690s, but this has been queried. However, Langley speaks in *New Principles* of: '…the weeping or mourning willow that was brought from Babylon, and now in great Plenty and Perfection in England. Particularly, in the Gardens of the late *Thomas Vernon* Esq; at his Seat of *Twickenham Park* in Middlesex.' Langley suggests that the species was suitable for wilderness planting, not waterside as we might expect. So if it was established in plenty and perfection by 1728, it must have arrived and been planted some years earlier, presumably obtained through Vernon's trading connections. Even if the precise date of introduction cannot be pinned down, it can at least be claimed that Twickenham Park was the pioneering location for establishing this attractive tree.

The ramifications for Twickenhamshire as a whole were considerable. It became something of an icon, like the state trees of the USA. From Twickenham Park in the north, through Pope's Villa in the middle, where it became a cult despite not featuring in illustrations of his garden in his lifetime, to Garrick's Villa at Hampton in the south, the weeping willow encapsulated the lure of riverside gardens. Walpole singled it out as a special agent for transforming the appearance of the English garden generally.

As we have seen, landscaping in a more natural style was gathering momentum by mid-century. Why Twickenham Park did not become a noteworthy landscape garden, although it had the potentiality, could have been due to various factors: location, no memorable follies or other features, but mostly because the property ran through a number of owners and

10.4. *Twickenham Park House in Middlesex, the Seat of Lord Frederick Cavendish*. Engraving by William Angus, 1795. *Seats of the Nobility in Great Britain*, Plate XL. (Orleans House Gallery, LDORL: 01667)

tenants, which did not make for continuity or stability. After Mrs Vernon died, the property was acquired by the Earl of Mountrath who owned it for only a year, when it passed to his widow, described memorably by Walpole (who else?) as 'Rich and tipsy…What a jumble of avarice, lewdness, dignity and claret!' In the same vein he commented on her will: 'as drunken a Will as you could expect.' That was in 1766, and two years later the Duchess of Newcastle was in residence, but only for the summer months. After her death in 1776 the Duchess of Montrose held it for twelve years. Finally, Lord Frederick Cavendish, a younger son of the Duke of Devonshire (of Chatsworth and Chiswick), acquired the property and lived there until his death in 1803.

It was Cavendish who seems to have accelerated the conversion of the spacious grounds (140 acres) from old-fashioned to modern. He made numerous alterations to both house and grounds. Rocque in 1744 shows the still largely formal layout (see Fig. 1.4), which suggests that Langley may have planted extensively but did not design on a broad scale. We can compare Rocque with Sauthier's map of 1786–7 (see Fig. 1.14), which shows a loosening up. This is reflected in a print of 1784 that shows the grounds becoming more naturalised, but the house, though altered, is still in its basic twin-turret form.

Angus engraved a print in 1795 (Fig. 10.4) that is most revealing as to Cavendish's changes. The towers of the house are heavily modified, and the gardens have a ha-ha, lawn, shrubbery and grazing for horses. The text accompanying the print proclaims that 'The Grounds are extensive and ornamental, and by judicious Disposal may properly be termed Pleasure Grounds, blending Beauty with Utility.' However, it also makes the ludicrous assertions that some trees survive from William the Conqueror's time and that the Earl of Essex in 1594 planted some of the cedars (a species not introduced until 1648). But the text does comment on the picturesque views over the Thames and Richmond.

It has been claimed that the long, narrow lake in Lake Gardens today is a remnant from the eighteenth century, but it does not appear in Sauthier. It may have been fashioned from a ditch or even what had been a canal at some point, but much more likely is that it was created as a lake only after developments in 1854. Other possible remains include three mounds or mounts, viz. at the south end of the lake, probably spoil from the nineteenth-century remaking of the lake, which could be on the site of Bacon's or Lucy's mount garden; on Kilmorey Road, possibly the remains of Batty Langley's; and near the river, just south of Gordon House, the site corresponding to the rising ground on which the Gothic pavilion at Lacy House (see Fig. 1.11) was situated. Some old trees survive from early times, including planes, with oaks that may even date back to medieval deer park days.

Little Marble Hill

This estate stood to the east of Marble Hill, comprising fields stretching to the north and a dwelling close to the river – much closer than Marble Hill House. It was developed gradually from a modest house in a fairly basic style from the early 1750s. There is no question that it was later ornamented and enhanced to constitute what Edward Ironside in 1797 called 'a sweet little box'. In the later eighteenth century it was known as 'Spencer Grove' after the residence of Lady Diana Beauclerk, née Spencer, and then Marble Hill Cottage. The name in use today, Little Marble Hill, did not appear until 1831. It was demolished in 1873 and the land, after being purchased and added to Cambridge Park, was subsequently united with Marble Hill.

There is some mystery surrounding the history of the house. The Bartlett family owned the land, and lived in that location, from 1686. Their holding amounted to 13 acres which became known as Glasshouse Meadow. The name referred to a particular building, the Glass House (first mentioned as such in 1718) and its function, being a manufactory. It is likely that Pope used it for some of his grotto materials, since he refers to obtaining them from 'the Glass House'. In 1722 Sarah Bartlett obtained a wayleave to allow her to move the products down to a landing point on the river. The property passed out of the family in 1747. Rocque's plan of 1744–6 (see Fig. 1.4) shows four buildings given a prominent overall label of The Glass House: the oblong on the right is likely to be the manufactory. Early in the 1750s it was said that two dwellings were rebuilt, one of which may have been the subsequent Little Marble Hill, while the other was occupied by a John Fridenberg until 1757. Confusion has been caused by artists depicting only one building, from Tillemans in c.1724–30 and Joli in c.1745 (see Fig. 1.7) onwards. What Collert showed in 1753 (Fig. 10.5), the downstream view from Marble Hill, was probably one of the buildings in Rocque, with the summerhouse in Collert being the smaller building shown in the plan near the river. Presumably the Glass House itself disappeared soon after Rocque since it does not feature in any later views.

Little Marble Hill, through its various manifestations, assumed the character of a *cottage orné*, with 'a rustic verandah, completely covered by the jessamine, woodbine, clematis and rose, and its lawn bedecked with lovely flowers'. It was regarded as far more attractive a scene than Marble Hill itself, with its trees, terrace, sloping lawn, shrubbery and the cottage set back just a little from the public riverside path (Fig. 10.6). It abutted Cambridge's decorative grounds, which lay on its eastern border, so closely that a number of prints mislabel it as Twickenham Meadows. This seems to have started in 1784, with the publication of a view of Lady Diana Beauclerk's house drawn by the surveyor John Spyers, who also sketched

10.5. *A View of Richmond, taken near Twickenham*. Engraving by Collert, 1753. (Orleans House Gallery, LDORL: 03174)

10.6. *Little Marble Hill* (wrongly captioned *Twickenham Meadows*). Engraving by S Middiman after William Watts, 1794. (Private collection)

10.7. Cliveden near Strawberry Hill, Twickenham, formerly the Villa of Mrs Catherine Clive the Comedian, and now of Miss Mary and Miss Agnes Berry. Watercolour by Joseph Charles Barrow, 1792, showing Little Strawberry Hill behind hedges and the fence that indicates the lane between the villa and the garden of another property in the foreground. (Lewis Walpole Library, lwlpr 16014)

Marble Hill, and engraved by J Wells. The mistake was compounded by the drawing by William Watts engraved by Samuel Middiman for Harrison and Co. three years later, reproduced again in 1794. That may possibly indicate that Twickenham Meadows was thought of as part of the area generally even though the strict border determined that it was within its own curtilage. It foreshadowed the *cottages ornés* of a slightly later period, that of the Regency garden, ushered in by Humphry Repton and others.

Little Strawberry Hill

Kitty Clive provides the link with Little Marble Hill, where she lived previously, moving into the cottage and land that Walpole assigned to her at the southern end of his estate, thus constituting something of a pair with the 'sweet little box'. Walpole gave her a life tenancy from 1754 to her death in 1785: after a gap it was then bestowed on Walpole's young friends the Berry sisters. The cottage was not remarkable in itself and lacked the ornamentation lavished on its cousin at Little Marble Hill, but had a balcony and was apparently more elegant inside than the exterior appearance would indicate (Fig. 10.7). Mrs Pye commented that 'Her Prospect is equal, if not superior to any of that Part of the Country, and is perfectly rural; her Gardens are laid out in an excellent Taste, and are of considerable extent [more than eight acres].' Although buried in meadows, the house would have afforded a view of the river, especially from the balcony.

As soon as Kitty Clive moved in, she and Walpole started jointly planting 'the green lane that leads from her garden to the common', which suggests that she was capable of planning the garden itself, no doubt with Walpole's advice. The lane, which Walpole christened Drury Lane, extended the still-existing Clive Road. Both names therefore commemorated the actress.

Mr Hudson's Villa

The villa, according to Mrs Pye, was 'situated in the happiest Spot imaginable, though small, its Beauties are numerous and striking'. Just upstream from Pope's Villa, it was a riverside property dating back to the seventeenth century, its most famous occupant being the portrait painter Thomas Hudson, who lived there between 1753 and 1779. It appears that Hudson had a new house built, probably to the designs of the recently-deceased Roger Morris, a small Palladian villa with upward pediment projections at each end (see building in the centre of Müntz's view, Fig. 5.5). The design slightly echoed Morris's enchanting Palladian bridge at Wilton. It became known as Mr Hudson's Villa. Mrs Pye described the confined garden leading down to the river: '[the villa] stands in a Lawn of the finest and most verdant Turf…on the right Hand of the Lawn is a little Shrubbery, where blooms every fragrant Flower, and many curious Exotics'.

There was a tunnel under the road, in the manner of Pope's and Lord Radnor's, to link the property with land on the other side, augmented by the acquisitive Hudson over the years. This included a strip of land almost opposite his villa on which the bizarre 'Hudson's Gothic House' arose (see Fig. 1.13). Whether this strange concoction was a house, a façade or a garden building is not clear. It is attributed, again, to Morris posthumously, but Hudson evidently had no long-term use for it, for he leased it in 1759 to Sir William Stanhope, by then owner of Pope's Villa. One can see the influence of Walpole both in the Gothic style of the building and in the decorative shrubbery on the lawn by the river.

Countess Ferrers' Summer House

Although the Shirley family owned a large tract of land north of Pope's Villa, it was not remarkable as a garden except for one outstanding feature, the Summer House, which tends to draw the eye in all the views of the surrounding dwellings (see Figs. 1.1 and 1.6). Sir Robert Shirley was created 1st Earl Ferrers in 1711 and three years later acquired the Heath Lane Lodge estate, adding further land in 1716 and 1717, in which year he died. His first wife had given him seventeen children and died in 1693 (presumably of exhaustion), and his second wife, Selina, provided ten more. She was thirty-six at the time of his death, and continued to live there until her own demise at eighty in 1762.

The Summer House was built on higher ground, in fact on a terrace, on the far side of the Cross Deep road, and this vantage point secured it high visibility, since there was nothing between it and the river. It is likely to have been planned by Earl Ferrers but not erected until after his death. The designer is not known (Gibbs is the most likely candidate), nor its exact date. It was a substantial building of brick with stone ornamentation and a lead-covered dome, topped by a figure that resembled Giambologna's Mercury. It is described in detail in Anthony Beckles Willson's book *Mr Pope & Others*.

10.8. *A Prospect of the House of (sic) Twitenham, belonging to his Excellency the Earl of Strafford, Viscount Wentworth.* Unknown engraver, *c.*1711. (Orleans House Gallery, LDORL: 02041)

Strafford House (Mount Lebanon)

Immediately to the west of Orleans House stood Strafford House and gardens. Thomas Wentworth, Lord Raby and 1st Earl of Strafford (second creation), acquired the house in 1701 and set about its reconstruction. He was, however, absent for most of the time, either on diplomatic service abroad or at his principal seat of Wentworth Castle, South Yorkshire. In his place he installed his mother Lady Isabella Wentworth as the formidable chatelaine, expressing her forthright opinions in letters that exhibit the most idiosyncratic spelling. By 1709–10 work on the house was more or less complete, as an engraving shows (Fig. 10.8). There was some degree of competition with Secretary Johnston next door: Wentworth was no stranger to rivalry, as his northern mansion showed, a riposte to another branch of the family which had claimed what he regarded to be his ancestral seat, the neighbouring Wentworth Woodhouse. Wentworth was a Jacobite, which was indicated in some of the iconography at Wentworth Castle, but he would not have had time or opportunity to stir up local support for the cause in Twickenham, even though the architect Gibbs, who accompanied him north, was a covert Jacobite. It is thought, nonetheless, that he was responsible, albeit mostly from a distance, for the gardens, which were laid out in a formal style, as one would expect early in the eighteenth century. Thus there were parterres, a double arch and several gilded statues and vases, dismissed by John Macky for their 'glaring Appearance'. Some wooden urns near the house were painted to look like stone, which drew surprise that Wentworth could not seemingly afford real stone. He was cousin to Lord Bathurst at Cirencester Park, who doubtless advised him on the much larger landscaping at Wentworth Castle.

When Wentworth concentrated on his principal estate, he took with him Edward Reeves, as well as employing Gibbs. Reeves was a builder/joiner who worked for him first at Twickenham, his home, and then in Yorkshire from 1711. He stayed until 1734, being latterly assisted by his brother Thomas. The Reeves family had a number of branches, and it is likely that Edward and Thomas were part of the primarily bricklaying clan based at Cross Deep. Although the Reeves males were usually called Simon or William, there was a Thomas (b.1683), a bricklayer who contributed to the re-building of St Mary's Church, Twickenham, in 1714, who may be the same as Wentworth's Thomas.

Between them Wentworth and Johnston showed the possibilities and attractions of riverside gardens and villas. Both gardens were too early for the revolution that characterised the locality a little later, and both had walls, in contrast to, say, Marble Hill, but in neither case did the walls completely bar views of the gardens from the river or other public vantage points. The house was demolished in 1794, and a subsequent dwelling was known as Mount Lebanon by mid-nineteenth century on account of its cedars.

There was certainly a rivalry with Johnston over fruit as well as plantings. Under Lady Isabella the gardeners managed to produce grapes, peaches and nectarines in addition to the more prosaic apples and pears. In Batty Langley's *Pomona* of 1728 the 'Wentworth Plum' was singled out and illustrated as first planted in the garden and reckoned to be the 'very best Plumb in England for preserving'.

While we lack evidence of Wentworth's personal involvement in the kitchen garden and orchard elements at Strafford House, there is abundant proof of his close interest in the subject at Wentworth Castle, thanks to his correspondence with John Arnold, the head gardener there. The list of fruit encompasses many cultivars, e.g. six varieties of peach and of plum and five of apricot. Oranges and lemons were grown in the orangery and set outside in the summer. It is therefore more than likely, given Wentworth's fascination with fruit both native and exotic, that he gave advice on the subject for his Twickenham seat.

Ragman's Castle
The origin of this colourful name for a property squeezed into the very corner of Orleans Park next to Marble Hill is disputed – was it built by someone in the rag and bone trade, or did it replace the inn for beggars that was a favourite of the Marble Hill gardener Moody? The actress Hannah Pritchard moved in with her husband William in 1755 and was owner at the time of her death in 1768, although she had latterly rented it to Walpole for the use of his niece Maria and her daughters. The building stood 'behind three very fine lofty Trees, which fence it from the Sun and Wind, without intercepting the Prospect': one can see the house through those trees in the view by Heckel, to the right of Orleans House (Fig. 10.9). The garden was not especially worthy of note, nor would the property generally be, were it not for the principal room, designed as a Chinese pavilion. Mirrors were placed strategically in the room so that anyone could see, from whatever angle, the river traffic, particularly barges,

10.9. *Governor Pitt's House at Twickenham*. Engraving by James Mason after Augustin Heckel, 1749. (Orleans House Gallery, LDORL: 03204)

presenting 'the most beautiful moving Picture imaginable'. This calls to mind Pope bringing the passing river craft into his grotto by means of mirrors that could be turned so as to include or shut out the view. The most celebrated example of the use of mirrors to draw a waterscape in was at Dunkeld, Lanarkshire. Ragman's Castle stood opposite the walks of Ham House and also enjoyed a view of the wooded side of Richmond Hill.

Gordon House, Railshead
This property, perhaps chosen rather arbitrarily as the northernmost point of Twickenhamshire, is included here not so much for its gardens or its much-altered house as for the summer house, which stood close to the river and next to the boundary with the adjacent upstream property, Lacy House. Unfortunately there seems to be no record of its construction, but it appears in all views of the grounds from the river from 1750 and can be assigned accordingly to the ownership of Moses Hart, 1718–56. It was not demolished until *c*.1894. It was a domed open rotunda in classical style, of stone, with Corinthian columns, and was answered by the Gothic pavilion just the other side of the fence in Lacy's grounds, as shown in Fig. 1.11. This pairing strongly suggests that James Lacy, owner next door from 1749 to 1773, deliberately chose a different style as a riposte. It also neatly demonstrates the difference between the eras of Pope's classicism and Walpole's Gothicism. The configuration of the two summer houses resembles that between Cross Deep House and Radnor House, where garden buildings were similarly placed next to each other, separated only by a border between.

Lacy House, Railshead
James Lacy, Garrick's Drury Lane partner, moved in at around the same time as Garrick at Hampton, built a new house in the 1750s and created an appropriately theatrical garden.

10.10. *View of Rails Head formerly Mr Lacy's House at Isleworth, with a distant view of Richmond.* Engraving by S Sparrow after John Spyers, 1802 (originally published 1775). (Richmond Local Studies Collection, LCP 3497)

The summer house mentioned above (Fig. 10.10 gives the view from it) was placed on slightly higher ground than the Gordon House rotunda, and the innovative construction was a pointed statement of its modernity and implicit superiority. It was built from cast iron, very much a novelty, which dates it probably not before 1770. Willoughby Lacy, James's spendthrift son, inherited the place, but was forced to sell up to Walpole's brother, Sir Edward, a retiring man who often entertained Horace, who was enchanted by the prospects of the river, together with Richmond Hill and Richmond Gardens opposite, seen from the prominent bow window of the house. Sheridan later lived there as tenant for what Walpole regarded as insufficient rent, and gave equally lavish parties as Willoughby Lacy had, despite being similarly in debt: there is a story that the bailiffs entered in the middle of a party but such was Sheridan's Irish charm that shortly they were to be seen handing round the ices. The summer house contained busts of Garrick, Shakespeare and others, thus creating a manifest link with Garrick at Hampton. The plantings were rich and well-grown by the time of the 1793 print (see Fig. 1.11), and the garden was 'not large, but beautifully diversified. The Arches seen in the View in the distant Part of the Grounds, support a Bridge which is a Coach-way leading to the back of the House' (Angus's text opposite the 1793 print).

Figure 10.11. Interior of Grotto at Hampton Court House. Photograph by Michael Cousins

10.12. Exterior of Grotto at Hampton Court House. Photograph by Michael Cousins

AWAY FROM THE RIVER

There were a number of properties in the vicinity which stood inland, out of sight of the river, but nonetheless exhibit signs of garden design that fit in with the general ambience of Twickenhamshire and also confirm the sense of community and networking. One or two of these properties had gardens which play a prominent part in eighteenth-century garden history.

Hampton Court House

This garden is set apart from the others both physically and in terms of design, though it relates to some aspects of garden-making in the Walpole era. The 2nd Earl of Halifax was Keeper (later designated Ranger) of Bushy Park, opposite Hampton Court Palace, and took in three acres from the Crown land of Hampton Court Green (later a further five) in order to install his mistress there, the singer, actor and dancer Mrs Anna Maria Donaldson *c.*1757. The small garden followed some years later. It has sometimes been described as rococo, referring primarily to its size and the quirky architecture but also to a sense of playfulness. The creator of the garden is said to have been Thomas Wright, astronomer and mathematician who turned increasingly to garden design, planning buildings or layouts for more than thirty sites. He published two volumes entitled *Arbours and Grottos* in 1755 and 1758, demonstrating a particular interest in primitive and rustic structures.

In some ways Hampton Court House is a circuit garden in miniature. The pool at the centre is heart-shaped as a tribute from the Earl, and the circuit encompassing all the features of interest is close to the house. Maybe Garrick's Villa and the Strawberry Hill circuit, with its Shell Seat and Chapel in the Wood, furnished some inspiration. A short, straight terrace walk leads from the house to a small tiered exedra composed of burnt clinker and stone, materials also employed for the exterior of the grotto and icehouse. This produces a unifying effect, much as the application of external flintwork did for the buildings in Sir Francis Dashwood's park at West Wycombe. The exedra is now part of a later rockery that presumably masks what must have been a simple curved alcove. On one side of the pool stands the grotto; opposite are the remains of a rockwork fountain arch. The pool may have been derived from a pond on Hampton Court Green that figures in the background of Knyff's painting of the palace in 1702. Nearby is an octagonal Gothic building which presents something of a problem. Probably it was at first an icehouse, but the presence of a fireplace with shell decoration suggests that it may have been converted into a summer house at a later date.

The highlight of the garden, as with many of the time, was the grotto (Figs. 10.11 and 10.12). This is superb, a Wright masterpiece. It is built into an artificial mound, with ramps curving round the back. The two wings may be a later addition. The exterior is rustic and naturalistic, the brick core being faced with stone, burnt slag, spongestone ('tufa'), rock, shells and quartz. The large door, with rustic branchwork as in Wright's title illustration, is opened to reveal a stunning main chamber. Shells of all types, size and colour cover the walls, 40,000 having been obtained from Africa and the West Indies as well as Britain. The columns in the grotto have a coating of minerals, and that, combined with other resemblances, suggests that Wright, who had spent much time in Gloucestershire, knew Goldney, Bristol, similarly decorated with shells and minerals. The ceiling represents the heavens – stars and moon against a blue background, particularly apt as the work of an astronomer. The patterning of shells suggests flowers and trees, while two apsidal recesses contain light and dark shells as if to represent dawn and evening.

10.13. *A View of the House and part of the Garden of His Grace the Duke of Argyl at Whitton.* Drawn and engraved by William Woollett, 1757. (Orleans House Gallery, LDORL: 00036)

Whitton Park and Place

Whitton lies at the north-western point of the original Twickenham parish and considerably inland. What became Whitton Park was carved out of waste land on Hounslow Heath. It has one crucial importance in garden terms – not layout but plantings. This revolved round Archibald Campbell, Lord Islay and 3rd Duke of Argyll from 1743, who established the greatest private nursery of the day. He expanded his holdings from sixteen acres on purchase in 1722 to a considerable fifty-five acres by the time of his death in 1761 in order to accommodate his vast stock of plants. This included sixteen acres of pasture outside the estate and not included in the survey.

The garden, a mixture of nursery and arboretum, was not particularly notable for its design, which was decidedly out-of-date when the estate was offered for sale in 1765 (Mrs Pye dismissed it as 'in no very extraordinary Taste'). The principal garden scene was the 200' canal with a circular basin illustrated in William Woollett's engraving of 1757 (see Fig. 1.9). The canal is flanked by cedars and leads to a triangular Gothic Tower lifted up above an arch (and replacing an earlier rotunda). The triangular tower, normally a speciality of Henry Flitcroft, as at Virginia Water, Stourhead and Wentworth Woodhouse, is attributed to Gibbs or Roger Morris, both prominent Twickenhamians and both well known to Argyll. It was Gibbs who constructed the elaborate Green House from which the Woollett view is taken, i.e. set back from the near end of the canal. This was far more than a greenhouse, containing as it did three functional rooms above the plant hothouse. Woollett's view is from the north to the south. Whitton Park is unusual in that it was developed as a garden long before there was a proper house, which had to wait until 1737–8, probably designed by Morris (Fig. 10.13).

The estate in its mature form can be seen in a survey by James Dorret, Argyll's regular surveyor, whom he also brought in at Marble Hill. This was not the only link with Henrietta Howard: Argyll had helped to purchase the Marble Hill estate for her, as we have seen, and lent his gardener Daniel Craft (or other spelling), in addition probably advising her on plantings. The gardens were predominantly woodland, with winding walks, together with the canal and a parallel 'Orange Walk'. Across an intervening road lay the nursery, centred by a Chinese summer house amid a rabbit warren. The walled garden contained a curving wall heated by stoves which enabled citrus fruit and even an annona (paw-paw) to be grown: during the winter they were covered by glass.

The collection of trees included a wide range of conifers and a number of exotics grouped together, as listed by Mrs Pye – coffee tree, banana, chian pepper, palm, pistachio and torch thistle. Several trees were introductions: the Lombardy poplar, so ubiquitous subsequently, could well have been the first in England (*c*.1758) and the poplar-leaved birch (*Betula populifolia*) and the paper birch (*B. papyracea*) were introduced by Argyll in 1750. He had many sources throughout Europe and obtained North American species through the Bartram-Collinson scheme. A paper mulberry from China was raised from seed.

The confusion surrounding the names of Whitton Park and Whitton Place relates to the complicated history of the estate following Argyll's death. The lawyer George Gostling acquired the estate and split it into two, the western part being called Whitton Place, with the Green House serving as the mansion, and including the canal and tower. The eastern half, which included the original mansion, passed to William Chambers, who remodelled the house and incorporated a large number of classical ornaments in the grounds. This half was also called Whitton Place for a time, then became Whitton Park from 1809. The wealthy George Gostling the Second bought back the Chambers half in 1797, and brought in Humphry Repton to advise on the entire estate (named as Whitton Park).

For more information on Argyll's collection, see the article 'The Plantings at Whitton' (*Garden History* 14:2, 1986).

Kneller Hall
Known today as the home of the Royal Military School of Music, Kneller Hall owes its name to the founder of the property, Sir Godfrey Kneller, a famous artist of the early eighteenth century. In his time the gardens were formal and rather plain: an engraving by Johannes Kip portrays them in 1715. Rocque's plan of 1744–6 (see Fig. 1.4) appears to show that not much had changed, but it was a different matter in the second half of the century. Under the ownership of Sir Samuel Prime and Lady Prime, who had expert knowledge of growing fruit, but more especially under the industrious make-over by their son, Samuel Prime junior, the gardens were transformed in a way that slightly echoes Cambridge's operation at Twickenham Meadows inasmuch as the old walls round the house were demolished and a panoramic view was opened up. A narrow brook was expanded into a lengthy slim lake with an island lined by trees. A belt of trees was thrown round the edge of the park in the best Brownian manner. A wooden bridge spanned the lake. There was thus some landscaping, which lasted into the earlier nineteenth century.

For a full account of the history of Kneller Hall the reader is referred to Ed Harris's book.

Charles Jervas' House, Hampton

Jervas was a close friend of Pope's, and the poet often used to visit him in his London studio and to receive instruction in painting. Among his portraits the artist painted Henrietta Howard (see Fig. 9.1). It was highly likely that, when Jervas acquired a country seat in Hampton, Pope would help him plan his garden. The house was Elm Lodge, on the west side of High Street, Hampton, and survived until it was burnt down by suffragettes. Sadly, we do not know what the garden looked like, but a subsequent owner, the minor poet Edward Lovibond, who wrote about the gardens at Claremont, lived at Hampton from 1748 to 1775 and attracted a visit from Walpole. This was in 1770/71, and apart from listing some paintings in the house, one or two of which Walpole later bought, he announced that 'the garden seems to have been laid out by Pope after his own'. Not only would this have been no surprise, but Walpole gives the attribution credence since he, of all people, knew what Pope's garden looked like and of what manner.

TWICKENHAM GREEN AND COMMON

There were a number of houses built along the roads in the less crowded green spaces inland from the town centre that were well-known at the time, and had distinguished inhabitants, but for our purposes lacked sufficient garden interest. These included Fulwell Park, Colne Lodge (Paul Whitehead), Twickenham House (John Hawkins, author and Dr Johnson's first biographer) and Savile House (Lady Mary Wortley Montagu), the latter two along what is now Heath Road; and Gifford Lodge on the Green. The common led to Hounslow Heath on the west and was connected to Strawberry Hill by 'Drury Lane'. Worthy of attention is:

Isaac Swainson's Botanic Garden

This was positioned on the south side of the present Heath Road, and became known as Heath Lane Lodge or Heath Lodge. The house had been formerly owned by Countess Ferrers (see p.139), at the northern end of her large estate which featured the prominent summer house. Swainson established a botanic garden *c.*1789, arranging it in orderly fashion according to the Linnaean system, and it became one of the finest private collections anywhere in the land. It was laid out by a Mr Grimwood of Kensington, who was followed by Arthur Biggs, a future director of the Cambridge Botanic Garden. Part of the purpose seems to have been to produce 'popular vegetable medicines', thus fulfilling the role of the old physic gardens, but it expanded to contain what JC Loudon declared was 'every tree and shrub that could be procured at the time in British nurseries'. This makes it sound like a rival to Whitton Park, which was clearly an inspiration, albeit without Argyll's thirst for introductions. It included an herbarium, and a particular emphasis was on fruit, both forced and naturally growing, and Swainson was noted for cultivation of vines. This harks back to the era of Batty Langley and the fruit grown at Strafford House and Orleans House, which were perhaps at the back of Swainson's mind. He died in 1806, after which time the botanic garden became run down. Some attempt, however, was made to keep it partly going, through a little selling of plants and also exchange, while the herbarium and the botanic library were preserved.

Apart from the area covering the botanic garden, the grounds near the house were landscaped in a free, modern style (Fig. 10.14), with an open lawn, isolated trees and a shrubbery against the house.

10.14. *Mr Swainson's House, Twickenham.* Unknown engraver, *c.*1800. (Orleans House Gallery, LDORL: 02068)

Select Reading and Principal Sources

More detailed references are to be found in the books and articles listed below. Several publications are booklets produced by the Borough of Twickenham Local History Society, abbreviated to BOTLHS.

Mavis Batey, *Alexander Pope: The Poet and the Landscape*, Barn Elms, 1999

Mavis Batey et al., *Arcadian Thames: The River Landscape from Hampton to Kew*, Barn Elms, 1994

Morris Brownell, *Alexander Pope's Villa*, exhibition catalogue, GLC, 1980

Julius Bryant, *Marble Hill: The Design and Use of a Palladian Estate*, BOTLHS Paper no. 57, 1986

Maureen Bunch, *Cambridge Park, Twickenham, and its Owners 1616-1835*, BOTLHS Paper no. 63, 1989

Richard Owen Cambridge, *The Works of Richard Owen Cambridge, Esq.*, intro. George Owen Cambridge; T Cadell et al., 1803

Richard Cashmore, Donald Simpson and Alan Urwin, *Alexander Pope's Twickenham: 18th Century Views of his 'Classic Village'*, BOTLHS Occasional Paper no. 3, 1988

Anna Chalcraft and Judith Viscardi, *Strawberry Hill: Horace Walpole's Gothic Castle*, Frances Lincoln, 2007

Mike Cherry, *Radnor House, Twickenham: The Story of a Thames-side House*, BOTLHS Paper no. 101, 2018

Patricia Astley Cooper, *The History of Orleans House, Twickenham*, London Borough of Richmond upon Thames, 1984

Mark De Novellis (ed.), *Arcadian Vistas: Richmond's Landscape Gardens*, Orleans House Gallery, 1999 and 2013

Peter Foster and Donald Simpson, *Whitton Park and Whitton Place*, BOTLHS Paper no. 41, 1979

Brian Fothergill, *The Strawberry Hill Set*, Faber and Faber, 1983

Bamber Gascoigne and Jonathan Ditchburn, *Images of Twickenham with Hampton and Teddington*, Saint Helena Press, 1981

Marion Harney, *Place-making for the Imagination: Horace Walpole and Strawberry Hill*, Ashgate, 2013

Ed Harris, *Kneller Hall: Looking Backward, Looking Forward*, BOTLHS Paper no. 103, 2019

Eileen Harris, 'Villa for a mortal miss: Hampton Court House', *Country Life*, 5 August 1982

Gerald Heath, *Hampton Court House*, BOTLHS Paper no. 20, 1971

John Iddon, *Strawberry Hill and Horace Walpole: Essential Guide*, Scala, 2011

John R Inglis and Jill Sanders, *Panorama of the Thames: A Riverside View of Georgian London*, Thames & Hudson, 2015

Edward Ironside, *The history and antiquities of Twickenham*, J Nichols, 1797

Batty Langley, *New Principles of Gardening*, 1728

London Borough of Richmond upon Thames, *'Blest Retreats': A History of Private Gardens in Richmond upon Thames*, London Borough of Richmond upon Thames, 1984

Daniel Lysons, *Environs of London*, Vol. III, 1795

Maynard Mack, *Alexander Pope: A Life*, Yale University Press, 1985

John Macky, *A journey through England, in familiar letters*, 1714, 1722

Peter Martin, *Pursuing Innocent Pleasures: The Gardening World of Alexander Pope*, Archon, 1984

Orleans House: A History, Orleans House, n.d.

Emily Parker, '"The Taste of the Ancients": The Garden at Marble Hill', *Garden History* 46:2, 2018, 128-53

Brian Louis Pearce, *The Fashioned Reed: The Poets of Twickenham from St Margarets to Hampton Court from 1500*, BOTLHS Paper no. 67, 1992

[J Henrietta Pye], *A short view of the principal seats and gardens in and around Twickenham*, 1760 and later (various editions)

John Serle, *A Plan of Mr Pope's Garden, as it was left at his Death: with a plan and perspective view of the grotto*, R Dodsley, 1745

Donald Simpson, *Twickenham society in Queen Anne's reign from the letters of Isabella Wentworth*, BOTLHS Paper no. 35, 1976

Donald Simpson (ed.), *Twickenham 1600-1900: People and Places*, BOTLHS Paper no. 47, 1981

Michael Snodin (ed.), *Horace Walpole's Strawberry Hill*, Yale University Press, 2009

Joseph Spence, ed. JM Osborn, *Observations, Anecdotes and Characters of Books and Men*, Clarendon Press, 1966

Strawberry Hill: A History of the Neighbourhood, Strawberry Hill Residents' Association, 1991, 1995

Michael Symes, '"Twickenhamshire" rococo', *The English Rococo Garden*, Shire, 1991, 2011

Michael Symes, 'David Garrick and landscape gardening', *Journal of Garden History* 6:1, 1986, 34-49

Michael Symes, Alison Hodges and John Harvey, 'The Plantings at Whitton', *Garden History* 14:2, 1986, 138-72

Alan Urwin, *Railshead, Isleworth: The History of Gordon, Lacy and St Margaret's Houses*, The Hounslow and District History Society, 1974

Horace Walpole, *The History of the Modern Taste in Gardening* [orig. 1770], Ursus Press, 1995

Horace Walpole, *The Yale Edition of Horace Walpole's Correspondence* (edited by WS Lewis et al), 48 volumes from 1937

Anthony Beckles Willson, *Mr Pope & Others at Cross Deep, Twickenham, in the 18th Century*, author, 1996

Anthony Beckles Willson, *Alexander Pope's Twickenham 1719-1744: The major houses and people of Twickenham in the early 18th century*, Pope's Grotto Preservation Trust, 2007, 2018

Websites:

londongardensonline.org.uk (for London Gardens Trust's inventory)

twickenham-museum.org.uk

orleanshousegallery.org (for Richmond Borough art collection)

thames-landscape-strategy.org.uk

historicengland.org.uk (for national Register of parks and gardens); parksandgardens.org

popesgrotto.org.uk

strawberryhillhouse.org.uk

General reading:

John Dixon Hunt and Peter Willis (eds.), *The Genius of the Place: The English Landscape Garden 1620-1820*, Paul Elek, 1975 (and subsequent editions)

David Jacques, *Gardens of Court and Country: English Design, 1630-1730*, Yale University Press, 2017

Michael Symes, *The English Landscape Garden: A Survey*, Historic England, 2019

The Contributors

Mike Cherry has lived in Twickenham for over forty years and has a long-standing interest in local history. He is a committee member and past Chairman of the Borough of Twickenham Local History Society (BOTLHS), a volunteer and trustee of the Twickenham Museum, a trustee of the Pope's Grotto Preservation Trust and a volunteer at the Richmond Borough Local Studies Collection. He has contributed to a number of publications on local history including books in the Sutton Publishing series *Britain in Photographs* and the Amberly Publishing series *Through Time*. His book *Radnor House, Twickenham* was published by BOTLHS in 2018. He contributes regularly to the BOTLHS newsletter on a wide range of Twickenham-related subjects, has given talks on local history topics, and gives guided tours of Pope's grotto.

Suzannah Fleming is a garden historian and, since 1994, the founder member of The Temple Trust, a historic building preservation trust for England and Wales specialising in the rescue of derelict garden buildings and their settings. On behalf of the Trust she was closely involved with the 1998-2000 project to restore Garrick's Temple to Shakespeare at Hampton. She has published articles on various subjects in *The London Gardener* and elsewhere. Her most recent article is on the 3rd Earl of Shaftesbury entitled 'The Convenience of Husbandry in the adaptation of Lord Shaftesbury's garden and park at St Giles House in Dorset'.

Emily Parker is a Landscape Advisor at English Heritage. She specialises in garden history and designed landscape conservation. Her primary research interests are garden design in the eighteenth century, including the role of Pope, 'Capability' Brown and Humphry Repton. She has been researching the landscape at Marble Hill since 2014 and is currently involved in a project to restore the eighteenth-century garden which is supported by the National Lottery Heritage Fund. Emily has also researched and written interpretation content for numerous English Heritage sites including Belsay Hall, Marble Hill and Walmer Castle.

Chris Sumner was born in St Margarets and lives in Kew. He studied architecture at Hammersmith College of Art and Building and the conservation of historic parks and gardens at the Architectural Association. He worked in the Historic Buildings Division of the former Greater London Council until 1986, and from then until 2007 in the London Region of English Heritage. He is a founder member and one-time Chairman of the London Historic Parks and Gardens Trust (now simply the London Gardens Trust) and served on the officers' steering group of the Thames Landscape Strategy. Until recently he was a member of the gardens advisory group at Chiswick House and a trustee of Strawberry Hill House.

Michael Symes is an author, lecturer and garden historian. He specialises in eighteenth-century gardens in Britain and on the continent. As a number of key figures in garden history lived in Twickenhamshire, such as Pope and Walpole, he has always been interested in the area. He has been involved with The Gardens Trust and the London Gardens Trust for many years. Recent books include *The English Landscape Garden* and *The English Landscape Garden in Europe*, both published by Historic England.

List of Illustrations

Figure 1.1. *The House of the late Celebrated Mr. A. Pope fronting the River Thames at Twickenham.* Engraving by James Mason after Augustin Heckel, 1749. (Orleans House Gallery, LDORL: 03207)

Figure 1.2. *A View of the Countess of Suffolk's House near Twickenham* (Marble Hill). Engraving by James Mason after Augustin Heckel, 1749. (Orleans House Gallery, LDORL: 00040)

Figure 1.3. *A View of the Earl of Radnor's House at Twickenham.* Engraving by Anthony Walker after Augustin Heckel, 1750. (Orleans House Gallery, LDORL: 03206)

Figure 1.4. *An Exact Survey of the City of London, Westminster, the Borough of Southwark and the Country near ten miles round begun in 1741 and extended 1745 by John Rocque Land Surveyor & engraved by Richard Parr* (extract). (Chris Sumner collection)

Figure 1.5. Figure 1.4 annotated to indicate location of sites discussed in the text.

Figure 1.6. Panorama of Cross Deep from the Surrey bank, showing Radnor House, Pope's Villa, Countess Ferrers' Summer House, various dwellings, and St Mary's Church on the right. *The Prospect of the River Thames at Twickenham.* Painting by Peter Tillemans, *c.*1724-30. (Orleans House Gallery, LDORL: 00886)

Figure 1.7. View upstream from Richmond Hill, showing Orleans House, Marble Hill and Little Marble Hill. Painting by circle of Antonio Joli, *c.*1745. (Orleans House Gallery, LDORL: 00158)

Figure 1.8. View downstream from Richmond Hill, showing, on the Middlesex side, Twickenham Meadows, Twickenham Park, and the Railshead houses in the distance. Painting by Antonio Joli, *c.*1745. (Orleans House Gallery, LDORL: 00159)

Figure 1.9. *A View of the Canal and of the Gothick Tower in the Garden of his Grace the Duke of Argyl at Whitton.* Drawn and engraved by William Woollett, 1757. (Orleans House Gallery, LDORL: 00012)

Figure 1.10. *The Seat of Mrs Garrick at Hampton in Middlesex.* Drawn and engraved by William Watts, 1784. *Seats of the Nobility and Gentry*, Plate 68. (Private collection)

Figure 1.11. *Lacy House in Middlesex, the Seat of Richard Brindsley* [sic] *Sheridan Esq*. Drawn and engraved by William Angus, 1795. *Seats of the Nobility and Gentry*, Plate XXXVI. (Orleans House Gallery, LDORL: 01060)

Figure 1.12. Plan of Secretary Johnston's house (Orleans House) by Batty Langley. *New Principles of Gardening*, 1728. Plate IX (printed in reverse). (Private collection)

Figure 1.13. *Mr Hudson's gothic house opposite his own.* Watercolour by Johann Henry Müntz, 1757. (Richmond Local Studies Collection, LCP 3051)

Figure 1.14. *A Map of the Manor of Isleworth-Sion in the County of Middlesex belonging to his Grace the Duke of Northumberland* drawn by CJ Sauthier, 1786-87. (Extract showing southern portion). (Courtesy of the Archives of the Duke of Northumberland at Syon House, Sy:B.XIII.1e)

Figure 1.15. *The Prospect of Richmond in Surry.* Anonymous engraving, 1726, showing both sides of the river, Richmond to the left. (Richmond Local Studies Collection, LCP 2674)

Figure 2.1. Statue of Father Thames in Terrace Gardens, Richmond. Coade Stone, John Bacon, 1775. Undated photograph. (Richmond Local Studies Collection, LCF 21311)

Figure 2.2. *The First Bridge at Hampton Court.* Engraving after a pen drawing by Antonio Canaletto, 1760. (Orleans House Gallery, LDORL: 01951).

Figure 2.3. *A View from Richmond Hill up the River.* Engraving by Charles Grignion after Augustin Heckel, *c.*1752. (Orleans House Gallery, LDORL: 03205)

Figure 2.4. The view from Richmond Hill looking upstream over Petersham and Twickenham. Photograph by Chris Sumner, 2020.

Figure 2.5. The view from Richmond Hill looking upstream. Photograph by Chris Sumner, 2020.

Figure 2.6. The view downstream from Radnor Gardens towards Eel Pie Island and St Mary's Church, Twickenham. Photograph by Chris Sumner, 2018.

Figure 2.7. The summerhouse, formerly of Cross Deep House, in Radnor Gardens. Photograph by Chris Sumner, 2018.

Figure 2.8. Eel Pie Island from the riverside terrace at York House. Photograph by Chris Sumner, 2018.

Figure 3.1. *A View of the Seat of the late David Garrick Esq. at Hampton, with a prospect of the Temple of Shakespeare in the Garden.* Engraving for *The Modern Universal British Traveller*, 1779. (Suzannah Fleming collection)

Figure 3.2. Plan of Garrick's Villa (detail) showing 'The Lawn' and 'Temple Lawn'. Drawn by J Thompson, *c.*1770. Lithograph, from the sales particulars published 1822. (Orleans House Gallery, LDORL: 00368)

Figure 3.3. Interior of Garrick's Temple to Shakespeare showing the British Museum cast of the Roubiliac statue of Shakespeare. Photograph by Suzannah Fleming.

Figure 3.4. Garrick's Temple to Shakespeare from the Temple Lawn. Photograph by Suzannah Fleming.

Figure 3.5. *Mr and Mrs Garrick by the Shakespeare Temple at Hampton.* Painting by Johann Zoffany, 1762. (Reproduced by kind permission of The Garrick Club, London)

Figure 3.6. *A View in Hampton Garden with Mr and Mrs Garrick taking tea.* Painting by Johann Zoffany, 1762. (Reproduced by kind permission of The Garrick Club, London)

Figure 3.7. *David Garrick in the character of Lord Chalkstone in the farce Lethe; or Aesop in the Shades.* Engraving (detail), 1757. (Suzannah Fleming collection)

Figure 4.1. Portrait of Horace Walpole in his Library with the River Thames seen through the open window. Engraved by W Greatbatch after the *c.*1755 drawing by Johann Müntz. (Chris Sumner collection)

Figure 4.2. *Strawberry Hill chiefly taken in the year 1769 by Mr Sandby.* Watercolour by Paul Sandby, *c.*1769, showing the south and east fronts of the villa. (Lewis Walpole Library, lwlpr 31268)

Figure 4.3. *South Front of Strawberry Hill.* Watercolour by Paul Sandby, *c.*1769, looking past the south and east fronts downstream over the water meadows and river towards Twickenham. (Lewis Walpole Library, lwlpr 31267)

Figure 4.4. *Slight Sketch of the General Ground Plott of the Gothic Mansion and the Grounds adjacent at Strawberry Hill.* Engraving, *c.*1791. (Lewis Walpole Library, lwlpr 16005).

Figure 4.5. *Strawberry Hill from the West.* Aquatint by Joseph Charles Barrow or possibly William Pars, 1797. (Lewis Walpole Library, lwlpr 14835)

Figure 4.6. *View of the Prior's Garden at Strawberry Hill.* Engraving by Richard Bernard Godfrey after William Pars, *c.*1784. (Lewis Walpole Library, lwlpr 15093)

Figure 4.7. Watercolour drawing by Mark Laird showing his scheme for replanting The Shrubbery. (By kind permission of Mark Laird)

Figure 4.8. *The Shell Seat at Horace Walpole's Villa at Strawberry Hill*. Grey wash and watercolour. Unknown artist, *c*.1825. (Lewis Walpole Library, lwlpr 15053)

Figure 4.9. *View of the Offices at Strawberry Hill*. Ink and watercolour by Joseph Charles Barrow, 1791. (Lewis Walpole Library, lwlpr 16483)

Figure 4.10. *The Gothic Chapel which contains the Italian Shrine at Strawberry Hill*. Unknown artist, *c*.1822. (Lewis Walpole Library, lwlpr 15082)

Figure 5.1. Radnor House. Detail of painting by Peter Tillemans, *c*.1724-30 (Figure 1.6).

Figure 5.2. *A view of Mr Hindley's formerly Lord Radnor's at Twickenham*. Watercolour by Samuel Scott, 1758. (Lewis Walpole Library, Yale University lwlpr 16661)

Figure 5.3. 'A View of The Earl of Radnor's House at Twickenham'. Detail of engraving by Anthony Walker after Augustin Heckel, 1750 (Figure 1.3.).

Figure 5.4. Detail of Rocque Survey (Figure 1.4), showing the formal quadripartite layout of Lord Radnor's 'inland' garden contrasted with the more 'natural' layout of Pope's garden immediately to the north

Figure 5.5. *A View of Twickenham*. Engraving by J Green after Johann Müntz, 1756. (Orleans House Gallery, LDORL: 03222)

Figure 5.6. Cross Deep House. Detail of Figure 1.3.

Figure 5.7. Cross Deep Hall. Early twentieth-century photograph. (Mike Cherry collection)

Figure 5.8. Baroness Howe's House (*Pope's Villa*) (detail). Aquatint by C Bentley after William Westall, 1828. (Orleans House Gallery, LDORL: 00334)

Figure 5.9. Radnor House and War Memorial. Postcard, 1920s. (Mike Cherry collection)

Figure 6.1. *An Exact Draught and View of Mr Pope's House at Twickenham*. Engraving by Nathaniel Parr after Pieter Andreas Rysbrack, 1735. (Orleans House Gallery, LDORL: 00084)

Figure 6.2. *A Plan of Mr Pope's Garden*. Engraving after John Serle, 1745. (Richmond Local Studies Collection, LCP 3623)

Figure 6.3. *Plan of the Grotto of the late Alex*. *Pope Esq. at Twickenham*. Engraving after Samuel Lewis, 1785. (Orleans House Gallery, LDORL: 00345)

Figure 6.4. *A Perspective View of the Grotto*. Engraving after John Serle, 1745. (Richmond Local Studies Collection, LCP 3623)

Figure 6.5. *Pope's Villa*. Engraving by John Pye, 1811, after the painting *View of Pope's Villa at Twickenham During its Dilapidation, 1808* by JMW Turner. (Orleans House Gallery, LDORL: 00459)

Figure 6.6. Pope's Villa. Photograph by JS Catford, *c*.1897. (Chris Sumner collection).

Figure 6.7. Entrance to grotto following conservation. Photograph by Damian Griffiths. (Courtesy of Pope's Grotto Preservation Trust and Donald Insall Associates)

Figure 6.8. Interior of north chamber of grotto following conservation. Photograph by Damian Griffiths. (Courtesy of Pope's Grotto Preservation Trust and Donald Insall Associates)

Figure 6.9. Memorial garden to Alexander Pope. Photograph by Chris Sumner, 2018.

Figure 7.1. Lord Denbigh's House. Detail of painting by Peter Tillemans, c.1724-30 (Figure 1.6.)

Figure 7.2. *Dr Batty's House at Twickenham as Viewed from the opposite Shore of the River Thames*. Engraving, unknown artist, c.1770. The house to the left is Crossdeep shown without the wings added by James Gibbs.

Figure 7.3. *Poulett Lodge Twickenham* (Dr Punchard's). Early twentieth-century postcard. (Mike Cherry collection)

Figure 7.4. Interior of the Grotto. Photograph (Mike Cherry collection)

Figure 7.5. The Loggia. Photograph (Mike Cherry collection)

Figure 7.6. Arched opening to the Grotto. Photograph (Mike Cherry collection)

Figure 8.1. View downriver towards Glover's Island, Richmond Hill and Petersham Meadows from the Surrey bank opposite Marble Hill. Photograph by Chris Sumner, 2020.

Figure 8.2. Orleans House. Extract from sales plan, c.1925. (Orleans House Gallery, LDORL: 02697)

Figure 8.3. *The House of the Hon. James Johnston Esq. at Twittenham in the County of Middlesex 1710*. From *Vitruvius Britannicus, or The British Architect* by Colen Campbell, 1715. 'The Prospect to the Gardens' and plans of first floor and chamber floor. (Chris Sumner collection)

Figure 8.4. *The Octagon Room*. Plan, elevation and section. Engraving by E Kirkall after James Gibbs. Plate 71 from Gibbs's *A Book of Architecture*, 1728. (Orleans House Gallery, LDORL: 00857)

Figure 8.5. The Octagon Room. Photograph of exterior after 2018 restoration. (Orleans House Gallery, IMG 0065)

Figure 8.6. The Octagon Room. Photograph of interior after 2018 restoration. (Orleans House Gallery, Photography 179)

Figure 8.7. *Orleans House from across the River*. Watercolour by Auguste Garnerey c.1815. (Orleans House Gallery, LDORL: 00141)

Figure 9.1. *Henrietta Howard*. Painting by Charles Jervas, c.1724. English Heritage, Marble Hill. (Copyright Historic England Archive)

Figure 9.2. Plan of Marble Hill attributed to Alexander Pope, 1724. (Copyright Norfolk Record office, MC184/10/3 [rights reserved])

Figure 9.3. Plan of 'The House Garden and Inclosures at Marblehill 10 Miles West of London Belonging to the Right Honourable the Countess of Suffolk', c.1749. (Copyright Norfolk Record Office, MC184/10/2 [rights reserved])

Figure 9.4. Detail of Figure 9.3.

Figure 9.5. A page from the letter from Mary Lisles describing how to decorate a grotto. (The National Records of Scotland, GD/40/9/139/19)

Figure 9.6. Marble Hill (Earl of Buckingham). Watercolour, attributed to John Spyers, c.1780. (Orleans House Gallery, LDORL: 01001)

Figure 9.7. Visitors outside the stable block. Early twentieth-century postcard. (Richmond Local Studies Collection, LCF 13212)

Figure 9.8. Marble Hill House. (English Heritage photograph)

Figure 10.1. Extract from *The Prospect of Richmond in Surry,* 1726 (Figure 1.15).

Figure 10.2. *The Seat of R*^{d}*. Owen Cambridge Esq*^{r}*. at Twickenham Mid*^{x}*.* Engraving by Ravenhill, *European Magazine*, 1787. (Orleans House Gallery, LDORL: 02045)

Figure 10.3. *East Front of Twickenham Meadows and Richmond Bridge.* Engraving by J Landseer after J Webber, 1803. (Orleans House Gallery, LDORL: 01271)

Figure 10.4. *Twickenham Park House in Middlesex, the Seat of Lord Frederick Cavendish.* Engraving by William Angus, 1795. *Seats of the Nobility in Great Britain*, Plate XL. (Orleans House Gallery, LDORL: 01667)

Figure 10.5. *A View of Richmond, taken near Twickenham.* Engraving by Collert, 1753. (Orleans House Gallery, LDORL: 03174)

Figure 10.6. *Little Marble Hill* (wrongly captioned *Twickenham Meadows*). Engraving by S Middiman after William Watts, 1794. (Orleans House Gallery, LDORL: 02875)

Figure 10.7. *Cliveden near Strawberry Hill, Twickenham, formerly the Villa of Mrs Catherine Clive the Comedian, and now of Miss Mary and Miss Agnes Berry.* Watercolour by Joseph Charles Barrow, 1792, showing Little Strawberry Hill behind hedges and the fence that indicates the lane between the villa and the garden of another property in the foreground. (Lewis Walpole Library, lwlpr 16014)

Figure 10.8. *A Prospect of the House of (sic) Twitenham, belonging to his Excellency the Earl of Strafford, Viscount Wentworth.* Unknown engraver, c.1711. (Orleans House Gallery, LDORL: 02041)

Figure 10.9. *Governor Pitt's House at Twickenham.* Engraving by James Mason after Augustin Heckel, 1749. (Orleans House Gallery, LDORL: 03204)

Figure 10.10. *View of Rails Head formerly Mr Lacy's House at Isleworth, with a distant view of Richmond.* Engraving by S Sparrow after John Spyers, 1802 (originally published 1775). (Richmond Local Studies Collection, LCP 3497)

Figure 10.11. Interior of Grotto at Hampton Court House. Photograph by Michael Cousins.

Figure 10.12. Exterior of Grotto at Hampton Court House. Photograph by Michael Cousins.

Figure 10.13. *A View of the House and part of the Garden of His Grace the Duke of Argyl at Whitton.* Drawn and engraved by William Woollett, 1757. (Orleans House Gallery, LDORL: 00036)

Figure 10.14. *Mr Swainson's House at Twickenham.* Unknown engraver, *c.*1800. (Orleans House Gallery, LDORL: 02068)

Index

References in **bold** are to images. Minor and passing references are not included.

Adam, John 50, 51
Adam, Robert 27, 50, 51
Angus, William:
   Lacy House in Middlesex, the Seat of Richard Brindsley [sic] Sheridan Esqr. 22, **22**, 110, 136, 142, 143
   Twickenham Park House in Middlesex, the Seat of Lord Frederick Cavendish 135, **135**
Anne, Queen 75, 108
Anson, Admiral 130
Architectural Heritage Fund 61
Argyll, Duke of (Lord Islay) – see Campbell, Archibald 3rd Duke of Argyll (Lord Islay)
Argyll, John 2nd Duke of 21
Arnold, John 141
Artari, Giuseppe 113
Ashe, Thomas 30, 34, 60
Astley, John Dugdale 114
Audley, Bishop 72
Augusta, Princess of Wales 19, 26, 37

Bacon, Francis 16, 133, 136
Bacon, John
   Statue of Father Thames in Terrace Gardens, Richmond 35, **36**
Badminton 29
Bagutti, Giovanni 113
Banckes, Matthew 27
Barrow, Joseph Charles 69
   Cliveden near Strawberry Hill, Twickenham, formerly the Villa of Mrs Catherine Clive the Comedian, and now of Miss Mary and Miss Agnes Berry **138**, 139
   Strawberry Hill from the West **67**, 67
   View of the Offices at Strawberry Hill **72**, 72
Bateman, Richard 19, 62
Batey, Mavis 37, 39, 43, 64, 65, 68, 69, 89, 93
Bathurst, Lord 19, 24, 30, 129, 130, 141
Battie, Dr William (sometimes Batty) 100, 101
Beach, Mary 94
Beauclerk, Lady Diana (née Spencer) 29, 136
Bedford, Lucy Countess of 15, 133
Beechcroft 84, 85
Bentley, C
   Baroness Howe's House (Pope's Villa) **83**, 83
Bentley, Richard 22, 24, 33, 61, 68, 71, 79
Berry sisters, the 138
Berry, Mary 83, 95

Biggs, Arthur 148
Birkhead, Mary 100
Blount, Martha 21, 118
Bocconoc 30
Bodens, Colonel George 53, 54, 56
Borlase, Dr William 93
Boscawen, Lady Anne 76
Braham, Frances – see Waldegrave, Frances Countess
Bridgeman, Charles 14, 21, 24-26, 30, 32, 113, 114, 118-120
Briscoe, John 81
Briscoe, Stafford 80, 81
Bristol, Lady 117
Brooke, Henry 19
Brown, Lancelot 'Capability' 14, 18, 19, 25, 26, 29, 33, 44, 45, 50, 51, 53, 62, 114, 130, 131
Brown, Mortimer 85
Brunswick, Duchess of 130
Brydges, James 1st Duke of Chandos 57, 92
Buckinghamshire, Earl of 125
Bunch, Maureen 128
Burke, Edmund 29
Burlington, Lord (3rd Earl) 17, 21, 30, 49, 50, 53, 62, 88, 89, 119
Bushy Park 10, 28, 45, 145
Bute, Earl of – see Stuart, John 3rd Earl of Bute
Bute, Lord – see Stuart, John 3rd Earl of Bute
Buttery, Henrietta 43

Cambridge House 133
Cambridge Park – see Twickenham Meadows
Cambridge, George Owen 130, 133
Cambridge, Richard Owen 10, 12, 16, 23, 29, 33, 51, 128-131, **132**, 133, 136, 147
Campbell, Archibald 3rd Duke of Argyll (Lord Islay) 19, 21, 24, 26, 27, 30, 116, 117, 120, 146, 147
Campbell, Colen 57, 118
   The House of the Hon. James Johnston Esq. at Twittenham in the County of Middlesex 108, **109**
Canaletto, Antonio 76
   The First Bridge at Hampton Court **38**
Canons 57, 92
Caroline of Ansbach 19, 25, 30, 37, 54, 113, 114, 117
Caroline, Princess of Wales – see Caroline of Ansbach
Caroline, Queen – see Caroline of Ansbach
Castell, Robert 17, 89, 110
Catherine the Great 21, 57

158

INDEX

Cavendish, Lord Frederick 135
Chambers, Sir William 14, 19, 38, 147
Chandos, Duke of – see Brydges, James 1st Duke of Chandos
Chapel in the Wood – see Strawberry Hill
Charles II, King 108
Charles Jervas' House – see Jervas, Charles
Chatsworth 51
Chaucer, Geoffrey 64
Chauvigny, M (French Ambassador to Britain) 101
Chenevix, Mrs 59
China Room – see Marble Hill
Chiswick 14, 17, 21, 30, 49, 50, 62, 88, 89, 91, 135
   Chiswick Villa 89
   Ionic Temple 49
Chopped Straw Hall 59
Chute, John 22, 69, 72
Claremont 14, 25, 114, 148
Clive, Catherine 'Kitty' 21, 29, 138, 139
Closed Grove – see Strawberry Hill
Cobham, Lord 53, 118
Cole, Rev. William 68
Collert (possibly John Collet or Collett)
   A View of Richmond taken near Twickenham 136, **137**
Colne Lodge 29, 148
Conway, George 78
Conway, Henry 59, 62
Cooper, Susanna Ashley (née Noel) Countess of Shaftesbury (Lady Shaftesbury) 50
Countess Ferrers' Summer House 10, **15**, 27, 139, 148
Countryside Commission 43
Couse, Kenton 133
Coventry, Francis 131
Craft, Daniel (or Crafts, Craftes or Crofts) 25, 30, 120, 147
Cromwell, Oliver 108
Cross Deep 14, **15**, 16-18, 21, 26-28, 33, 75, 75, 78, 81, 83, 86, 89, 100-102, 105, 139, 141
   Cross Deep Hall 81-85, **82**
   Cross Deep House 10, 14, 33, 79, 80, **81**, 83-85, 142
Crossdeep 14, 102
Cumberland, Duke of (William Augustus) 114
Cunard, William 40, 114, 127
Curzon, (Sophia) Charlotte Baroness Howe – see Howe, Baroness of Langar

de Stern, Baron 60
du Quesne, Admiral Abraham 75
du Quesne, Gabriel 75, 76
du Quesne, Thomas 75
Damer, Anne Seymour 59, 83

Dashwood, Sir Francis 145
Delany, Mary 55
Devonshire, Duke of (of Chatsworth and Chiswick) 135
Dezallier d'Argenville, AJ 27, 109
Digby, Lord 21
Donaldson, Anna Maria 21, 145
Donne, John 16
Dorret, James 25, 120, 147

Earl Ferrers – see Shirley, Robert Sir 1st Earl Ferrers
Eel Pie Island 14, **41**, **42**, 43, 57
Elm Lodge 148
English Heritage 40, 43, 60, 61, 97, 116
English Landscape Garden 14, 32, 110
Erskine, John 11th Earl of Mar 100, 110, 116, 117
Esher Place 14
Essex, James 72
Exiles Club 114

Father Thames Trust, The 45
Ferrers estate 33
Ferrers, Countess 10, 27, 148
Ferrers, Earl – see Shirley, Sir Robert 1st Earl Ferrers
Fielding, Henry 19, 30
Flitcroft, Henry 146
Fox, Henry 130
Frascati 17
Frederick, Prince of Wales 19, 26, 37, 54, 114, 130
Frye, John 34

Garden Conference of 1719, The 30, 114
Garden History Society (now The Gardens Trust) 43, 64
Garnerey, Auguste
   Orleans House from across the River **113**, 114
Garrick Club, The 52
Garrick, David 9, 19, 21, 22, 25, 27, 29, 33, 46-55, **54**, 131, 142, 143
Garrick, Eva Maria (née Veigel) 46, 49, 51, 54
Garrick, George 46
Garrick, Peter 46
Garrick's Villa 12, 18, 46, **47**, 55, 134, 145
   Garrick's Walk 51
   Garrick's Temple and Lawn 45, **48**, **49**, **50**, **53**
   Temple to Shakespeare 33, **47**, **48**, 48, **49**, 49, **50**, 50, **52**, 52, 55, 56
Gay, John 19, 21
George I, King 57, 113
George II, King 19, 23, 37, 44, 54, 57, 113
George III, King 37, 83, 133
Gibbon, Edward 29

Gibbons, Grinling 69
Gibbs, James 25, 27, 86, 109, **111**, 111, 113, 139, 141, 146
Gifford Lodge 148
Gilpin, William 34, 64, 72, 130
Gladstone, William Ewart 60
Glasshouse Meadow 136
Glasshouse, The – see Little Marble Hill
Glover, Moses 40, 100, 106
Godfrey, Richard Bernard
   View of the Prior's Garden at Strawberry Hill **68**, 69
Goldney 145
Goldsmith, Oliver 29
Gordon House 12, 27, 136, 142, 143
Gostling, George 147
Gostling, George the Second 147
Grand Tour 17, 50, 57, 87, 88, 93
Gray, Thomas 22, 23, 57, 61, 64, 128
Green, J
   A View of Twickenham 79, **80**, 81, 139
Green House – see Marble Hill and Whitton
Grenville, George 130
Grignion, Charles
   A View from Richmond Hill up the River 38, **39**
Gunnersbury House 89

Hagley 99
Halifax, 2nd Earl of 28, 145
Ham House 21, 25, 35, 37, 38, 43, 45, 62, 106, 117, 142
Ham Lands 44
Hamilton, Duchess of 71
Hampton **20**, 21, 22, 27, 29, 37, 43, 46-48, 50-56, 134, 142, 143, 148
Hampton Court 9, 14, 26, 27, 29, 33, 36, 37, **38**, 45, 106
Hampton Court Home Park 45
Hampton Court House 10, 21, 29, 33, 103, **144**, 145
Hampton Court Palace 59, 145
Harcourt, George Granville Earl of Harcourt 60, 62, 64
Harcourt, Lord – see Harcourt, George Granville Earl of Harcourt
Harris, Ed 147
Hart, Moses 142
Haverfield, John 19, 21, 26
Haverfield, Thomas 26
Hawksmoor, Nicholas 109
Heath Lodge 139, 148, **149**
Heath Lane Lodge – see Heath Lodge
Heckel, Augustin 10, 11, 38, 39, 76, **77**, 79, 81, 111, 141, **142**, 142
   A View of the Countess of Suffolk's House near Twickenham **11**

A View from Richmond Hill up the River **39**
The House of the late Celebrated Mr. A. Pope **10**
Henri duc d'Aumale 114
Herbert, Lord Henry 9th Earl of Pembroke 28, 118
Heritage of London Trust 97
Hickey, Joseph 81, 83
Hindley, Frederick Atherton **77**, 82
Historic England 37, 97, 105
Hoare, Henry 82
Hobart, John 2nd Earl of Buckinghamshire 116
Hogarth, William 47, 48, 55
Hollar, Wenceslaus 69
Hotham, Henrietta 125
Houghton 57
Howard, Henrietta (later Countess of Suffolk) 21-26, 29, 30, 33, 116-121, **117**, 123, 125, 147, 148
Howe, Sophia Charlotte Baroness of Langar 83, 95, 96
Hudson, Thomas 21, 28, 81, 83, 139
Hudson's Gothic House **28**, 139
Hudson's Villa 27, 139

Iddon, John 62
Ilay, Duke of – see Campbell, Archibald 3rd Duke of Argyll (Lord Islay)
Ilay, Lord – see Campbell, Archibald 3rd Duke of Argyll (Lord Islay)
Inskip, Peter 61, 65
Ionides, Nellie 107, 114
Isaac Swainson's Botanic Garden – see Swainson, Isaac
Islay, Duke of – see Campbell, Archibald 3rd Duke of Argyll (Lord Islay)
Islay, Lord – see Campbell, Archibald 3rd Duke of Argyll (Lord Islay)

James I, King 89
James II, King 86
James, John 27, 108, 109, 111
James, Patrick 61
Jenkins, Peter 65
Jervas, Charles 21, 29, 148
   Henrietta Howard 116, **117**, 148
   House – see Charles Jervas' House
Johnson, Dr Samuel 29, 51, 64, 86, 87, 96, 148
Johnston, Archibald Lord Warriston 108
Johnston, James (also known as 'Secretary' Johnston) 21, **24**, 27, 108-111, **109**, 113, 114, 117, 140, 141
Joli, Antonio
   View downstream from Richmond Hill showing, on the Middlesex side, Twickenham Meadows, Twickenham Park, and the Railshead houses in the

distance 15, **16**, 128
View upstream from Richmond Hill showing Orleans House, Marble Hill and Little Marble Hill 15, **15**, 128, 136
Jones, Inigo 89

Kendall, Henry Junior 83, 96
Kensington Gardens 25
Kensington Palace 113
Kent, William 14, 21, 32, 37, 57, 62, 64-66, 89, 110, 113, 130, 134
Kenwood Gardens 19, 21, 26
Kew
   Kew Bridge 35
   Kew Gardens 14, 19, 21, 26, 33, 43-45, 113, 114, 131
   Kew Green 26
   Kew Palace 36, 59
   White House 37
Kew Gardens – see Kew, see also Richmond Gardens
Kilmorey, 2nd Earl 114
Kip, Johannes 147
Kirkall, E
   The Octagon Room 111, **111**
Kitty's Lodge 29
Kneller Hall 33, 81, 147
Kneller, Sir Godfrey 21, 147
Knyff, Leonard 37, 145

Lacy House 18, **22,** 22, 25, 27, 32, 33, 136, 142
   Gothic pavilion 136
Lacy, James 25, 27, 142
Lacy, Willoughby 27, 143
Lady Howe's Villa 95
Laird, Mark 61, 65, 69
   Watercolour drawing by Mark Laird showing his scheme for replanting The Shrubbery 69, **70**
Lambert, David 39, 43
Landscape Agency, the 65
Landseer, J
   East Front of Twickenham Meadows and Richmond Bridge 131, **132**
Langley, Batty 19, 21, 24, 27, 31, 32, 79, 110, 122, 123, 134, 135, 141, 148
   Plan of Secretary Johnston's House (Orleans House) **24**, 25, 110
Lee, James 21
Lewis, Samuel
   Plan of the Grotto of the late Alex. Pope Esq. at Twickenham 93, **93**
Lime Grove – see Strawberry Hill

Lisles, Mary 123
   A page from the letter from Mary Lisles explaining how to decorate a grotto 123, **124**
Little Marble Hill **15,** 21, 29, 38, 128, 136, **137,** 138
   Glass House 136
Little Strawberry Hill 21, 29, 95, **138,** 138
Lorrain, Claude 89
Loudon, John Claudius 148
Lovibond, Edward 19, 148
Lower Terrace Walk 67, 70

Mabland 62, 79
Macclary, John 65
Mack, Maynard 26
Macky, John 16, 17, 100, 110, 141
Maclew, Andrew 101, 102, 104
Mann, Horace 58, 61, 78, 94
Manor of Sion (earlier spelling of Syon) **31**, 106
Mar, Earl of – see Erskine, John 11th Earl of Mar
Marble Hill 10, 14, **15**, 17-19, 21-28, 30, 32, 33, 37, 38, 40, 43-45, 59, 90, 106, 115, 116-128, 136, 138, 141, 147
   China Room 116, 122
   Coach House 122
   Green House 116, 121, 122, 127
   Grotto 121, 122
   Marble Hill Cottage 136
   Marble Hill House **121**, **122**, **125**, **126**
   Stable Block **126**
Mary II, Queen 85, 86, 108
Mason, George 95
Mason, James
   A View of the Countess of Suffolk's House near Twickenham 10, **11**, 25
   Governor Pitt's House at Twickenham 111,141, **142**
   The House of the late Celebrated Mr. A. Pope **10**, 10
Mason, Rev. William 62, 64, 65
Meadowbank 133
Merlin's Cave, Richmond Gardens 113
Michelham, Lord 60
Middiman, Samuel
   Little Marble Hill 136, **137**, 138
Miller, Sanderson 129, 130
Milton, John 48, 88, 131
Montagu, George 69, 71
Montagu, Lady Mary Wortley 19, 26, 30, 100, 148
Monte Carlo Sports Club 105
Montpelier Row 10, 38
Montrose, Duchess of 135
More, Hannah 47
Morris, Roger 25, 27, 28, 81, 118, 121, 122, 139, 146

Morris, Valentine 130
Morris, William 39
Mount Edgcumbe 25, 30, 51
Mount Lebanon – see Strafford House
Mountrath, Earl of 135
Müntz, Johann Heinrich 57, **58**, 61, 69, 79-81, **80**, 139
   Mr Hudson's gothic house opposite his own 28, **28**, 139
   Portrait of Horace Walpole in his library with the River Thames seen through the open window **58**
Murray, Lady Margery 82
Murray, William 1st Earl of Mansfield 82

National Lottery Heritage Fund 61, 97, 115, 127
Newborough Club 105
Newcastle, Duchess of 135
Northumberland, Duke of 44
Nunez, Isaac Fernandez 80

Oatlands 14, 25, 36
Octagon Room, The – see Orleans House Gallery
Oliver, Dr 93
Orleans House **15**, 16, 17, 21, **24**, 25, 27, 32, 33, 37, 38, 40, **113**, 114, 117, 134, 140, 141, 148
Orleans House Gallery 37, 38, 45, 106-115, **108**, **109**
   Orleans Gardens 107
   Coach House Education Centre 115
   Octagon Room **111**, 111, **112**, 113-115
   Stables Gallery 115
Orleans House Trust 115
Orleans Park 122, 141
Orleans Park School 114

Paine, James 133
Painshill (Paine's Hill) 51, 75
Palladian 17, 21, 28, 30, 57, 81, 89, 116, 118, 119, 139
Palladianism 16, 17, 28, 30
Palladio, Andrea 17, 88, 89
Panini, Giovanni 115
Papworth, John Buonarotti 111, 114
Park Place 23
Parr, Nathaniel
   An Exact Draught and View of Mr Pope's House at Twickenham 86, **87**, 92
Parr, Richard
   An Exact Survey of the City of London, Westminster, the Borough of Southwark and the Country near ten miles round 12, **12**
Pars, William 62, **68**
Peel, Jonathan 116, 125
Peel, Lady 125

Peterborough of Bevis Mount, Lord – see Peterborough, Lord
Peterborough, Earl of – see Peterborough, Lord
Peterborough, Lord 19, 24, 118, 120
Petersham Common 106
Petersham Meadows 38, 39, 44, 106, **107**
Philippe, Louis duc d'Orleans (later King of France) 83, 106, 114
Pitt, George Morton (Governor Pitt) 114, **142**
Pitt, Thomas 1st Baron Camelford 22, 30
Pitt, William the Elder 30, 128, 130
Pliny the Younger 17, 89, 119
Pocock, Sir George 114
Pope, Alexander 9, **10**, 16-19, 21, 23, 24, 26, 28, 29, 30, 32, 33, 37, 46, 57, 59, 64, 75, 76, 78, 83, 86-101, 103, 110, 111, 114, 116-120, 123, 124, 129, 130, 134, 136, 139, 142, 148
   Plan of Marble Hill 118, **119**
   Pope's Garden 84, **90**
   Pope's Grotto 45, **93**, **94**, 97, 105
   Pope's Grotto Conservation Trust 97
   Pope's Villa **15**, 18, 27, 33, 44, **83**, **87**, 90, **95**, 95, **96**, 96, 134, 139
Pope Memorial Garden **98**, 98
Portmore Park 14, 33
Poulett Lodge 33, 100-105, **101**, **102**, **103**, **104**
Poulett, 5th Earl of 104
Poulett, Catherine 108
Poulett, Margaret dowager Countess 101
Poulett, Vere 3rd Earl of Poulett 101
Poussin, Nicholas 89
Powell, Sebastian Pugin 60
Prior's Garden – see Strawberry Hill
Priory of St Hubert 33, 121
Pritchard, Hannah 21, 141
Punchard, William Henry 102, 105
Pye, Henrietta 14, 23, 48, 79, 131, 133, 139, 146, 147
Pye, John
   Pope's Villa **95**, 96

Radnor Gardens **42**, 74-85, **78**, 80, 107
   Cold Bath 74, 76, 79, 83
Radnor House 10, **11**, **15**, 23, 33, 44, 74-85, **75**, **77**, **84**, 142
Radnor House School 96, 97
Radnor, Lord 62, 78, 82, 139
Ragman's Castle 141, **142**, 142
Railshead 12, **16**, 27, 142, **143**
Ravenhill
   The Seat of R^d. Owen Cambridge Esqr. at Twickenham, Mid^x. 131, **132**

Repton, Humphry 18, 29, 69, 138, 147
Reynolds, Sir Joshua 21, 29, 38
Richardson, Sir Albert 60, 69, 72
Richens, Paul 98
Richmond **32**, 36, 99, 106, 123, 131, 133, 136, **137**
   Richmond Bridge 37, 43, 133
   Richmond Ferry 37
   Richmond Gardens (see also Kew Gardens) 14, 19, 25, 26, 30**,** 44, 113, 143
   Richmond Hill 15, 37-40, 43, 57, 59, 61, 62, **107**, 133, 142, 143
   Richmond Lodge 19, 30, 37, 121
   Richmond Palace 14, 36, 59, 131
   Richmond Park 26, 29, 106
   White Lodge 27, 29
Richmond Petersham and Ham Open Spaces Act, The 39
River Deep 83-85
River Meadow 107
Riverside House 107
Robartes, Henry 3rd Earl of Radnor 76
Robartes, Honourable Francis 76, 82
Robartes, John 1st Earl of Radnor 76
Robartes, John 4th Earl of Radnor 29, 76, 79, 80, 82
Robartes, Letitia 76
Rocque, John 31, 36, 76, 79, 90, 106, 128, 135, 136, 147
   An Exact Survey of the City of London, Westminster, the Borough of Southwark and the Country near ten miles round **12**
   An Exact Survey (detail) **78**
Roehampton 14
Roubiliac, Louis François **49**, 49, 52, 55, 56, 87, 88
Rousham 65
Royal Botanic Gardens, Kew – see Kew Gardens
Royal Military School of Music 147
Rousseau, Jean-Jacques 62
Ryan House 83, 85, 95
Rysbrack, Pieter Andreas
   An Exact Draught and View of Mr Pope's House at Twickenham **87**, 92

Sandby, Paul
   South Front of Strawberry Hill 63, 64
   Strawberry Hill chiefly taken in the year 1769 by Mr Sandby **63**, 64
Sandycombe Lodge 37
Sauthier, CJ
   A Map of the Manor of Isleworth-Sion in the County of Middlesex belonging to his Grace the Duke of Northumberland **31**, 33, 135, 136
Scott, Samuel 21, 28, 76, 81, 82, 130

A view of Mr Hindley's formerly Lord Radnor's at Twickenham 28, 76, **77**
Secretary Johnston – see Johnston, James
Selkirk, Lord 118
Serle, John 90
   A Perspective View of the Grotto 93, **94**
   A Plan of Mr Pope's Garden 90, **90**
Serpentine Walk 47, 60, 62, 71, 72
Shakespeare Temple – see under Garrick's Villa
Shakespeare, William 27, 46, 48, 49, 50, 55, 79, 87, 143
Sharawaggi 61, 62
Sheen – see Richmond Palace
Shell Bench & Shell Seat – see Strawberry House
Sheridan, Richard Brinsley **22**, 27, 143
Shirley, Robert, Sir 1st Earl Ferrers 139
Shrubbery, The – see Strawberry Hill
Siberechts, Jan 38
Sloane, Sir Hans 93
Smythson, Robert 133
Solus Lodge – see Sandycombe Lodge
South Field 74, 80
South Sea Company 76
Southend House 38
Sparksmead Brook 74
Sparrow, S
   View of Rails Head formerly Mr Lacy's House at Isleworth, with a distant view of Richmond 143, **143**
Spence, Joseph 21, 92
Spencer Grove 136
Spenser, Edmund 36, 64, 65, 88
Spyers, John 19, 26, 136, **143**
   Marble Hill (Earl of Buckingham) 125, **125**
Spyers, Joshua 26, 27
St Catherine's Convent 96
St Catherine's School 97
St James's School – see Radnor House School
St Margarets House 16, 26
St Margarets Trust 133, 134
St Mary's Catholic Teacher Training College 60
St Mary's University, Twickenham 60, 69
St Mary's Church, Twickenham **15**, 16, 27, 28, **41**, 44, 57, 62, 71, 75, 94, **98**, 98, 109, 141
Stanhope, Sir William **80**, 94, 139
Stourhead 51, 82, 146
Stowe 30, 53
Strafford House 16, 19, 27, 28, 40, **140**, 140, 141, 148
Strawberry Hill 22, 29, 30, 33, 34, 44, 45, 47, 59-69, **63**, **66**, **67**, **72**, 75, 78, 82, 87, 145, 148
   Chapel in the Wood 33, 60, 62, 72, **73**, 145
   Closed Grove 71, 72

Friends of Strawberry Hill 60
Lime Grove 71
Prior's Garden 62, **68**, 68, 69
Shell Bench 61, 62, 66, **71**, 71, 145
Shell Seat – see Shell Bench
Shrubbery, The 62, 69, **70**, 70
Strawberry Hill Press 61
Strawberry Hill Trust 60
Stuart, John 3rd Earl of Bute 19, 21, 26, 27, 128
Suffolk, Countess of – see Howard, Henrietta
Summer House – see Countess Ferrers' Summer House
Swainson, Isaac 148, **149**
Swift, Jonathan 19, 21, 48, 121
Switzer, Stephen 24, 25, 110
Syon
   Syon House 14, 44, 106
   Syon Park 44, 45

Teddington, Abbot of (i.e. Horace Walpole) 14
Thames Eyot 105
Thames Landscape Strategy, The 9, 40, 43-45, 97
Thompson, J
   Plan of Garrick's Villa (detail) showing 'The Lawn' and 'Temple Lawn' 48, **48**
Tillemans, Peter 38, 105, 136
   The Prospect of the River Thames at Twickenham 14, **15**, 31, 44, 74, **75**, 92, 100, **101**
Tournefort, Joseph 134
Turner, Joseph Mallord William 21, 37, 95, 96
   View of Pope's Villa at Twickenham During its Dilapidation, 1808 **95**
Twickenham Bridge 14
Twickenham Green and Common 148
Twickenham House 148
Twickenham Meadows 14, **16**, 18, 23, 29, 33, 38, 44, **129**, 128, 131, **132**, 133, 136, 138,
Twickenham Park 14, **16**, 16, 25, 27, 32, 34, 131, 133, 134, **135**
Twickenham Local History Society 128
Twickenham village 14, 33
Twining, Thomas 9

Vale of Tempe 17
Van Nost, John 110
Vanbrugh, Sir John 25, 75
Veigel, Eva Maria (see Garrick, Eva Maria)
Vernon, Mrs 135
Vernon, Thomas 19, 26, 75, 86, 122, 128, 134
Victoria and Albert Museum 60, 62, 69
Victoria, Queen 114

Virginia Water 146
Voltaire, François-Marie Arouet 87
Vyne, The 22

Waldegrave, 7th Earl 59
Waldegrave, Frances Countess 59, 60, 62, 67, 70-72
Waldegrave, Lady – see Waldegrave, Frances Countess
Wales, Prince Albert Edward of (later Edward VII, King) 60
Wales, Prince of – see also Frederick, Prince of Wales
Walker, Anthony
   A View of the Earl of Radnor's House at Twickenham 10, **11**, 76, **77, 81**, 81
Walpole Oak 67, 71
Walpole, Horace 9, 14, 16-19, 21-26, 28-30, 32, 33, 47, 48, 51, 57-62, **58**, 64-72, 75, 78, 79, 82, 86, 87, 89, 91, 94, 95, 103, 114, 116, 121, 128, 131, 133-135, 138, 139, 141-143, 145, 148
Walpole, Sir Edward 22, 27, 143
Walpole, Sir Robert 57
Watts, William **137**, 138
   The Seat of Mrs Garrick at Hampton in Middlesex **20**, 21, 47
Webber, J
   East Front of Twickenham Meadows and Richmond Bridge **132**
Wells, J 138
Wentworth, Lady Isabella 27, 140, 141
Wentworth, Thomas Lord Raby then 1st Earl of Strafford (2nd creation) 19, 27, 140, 141
Wentworth Castle 140, 141
Westall, William
   Baroness Howe's House (Pope's Villa) **83**
Whately, Thomas 23
White House – see Kew
Whitehead, Paul 9, 19, 29, ,148
Whitminster 23, 129, 130, 133
Whitton 10, 19, **20**, 21, 25, 27, 29, 30, 81, 120, **146**, 146-148
   Green House 27, 146, 147
   Whitton Park 10, 27, 146-148
   Whitton Place 10, 146, 147
Wick House 38
Wilkie, Kim 39, 43, 45
William III, King 86, 108
Willson, Anthony Beckles 17, 34, 139
Wise, Henry 30
Woburn Farm 14, 33
Woollett, William
   A View of the Canal and of the Gothick Tower in the

Garden of his Grace the Duke of Argyl at Whitton 19, **20**, 25, 146
A View of the House and part of the Garden of His Grace the Duke of Argyl at Whitton 146, **146**
World Monuments Fund 60, 61
Wright, Thomas 19, 28, 33, 145
Wyatt, James 72

York House 34, 44, 59, 99, 115
Young, Arthur 130
Young, Thomas 96

Zoffany, Johann
Mr and Mrs Garrick by the Shakespeare Temple at Hampton 52, **52**, 55
A View in Hampton Garden with Mr and Mrs Garrick taking tea 52, **53**, 54, 55